THE
EXPANSION
OF
ECONOMICS

THE
EXPANSION
OF
ECONOMICS

Toward
A More Inclusive
Social Science

Shoshana Grossbard-Shechtman
and Christopher Clague
Editors

M.E. Sharpe
Armonk, New York
London, England

Library of Congress Cataloging-in-Publication Data

The expansion of economics: toward a more inclusive social science / Shoshana
Grossbard-Shechtman and Christopher Clague, editors.
    p. cm.
Includes bibliographical references and index.
ISBN 0-7656-0677-1 (alk. paper)
    1. Economics—History—20th century. 2. Social sciences—History—20th century. I.
Grossbard-Shechtman, Shoshana, 1948- II. Clague, Christopher K.

HB87 .E99 2002   2001040074
330′09′04—dc21   CIP

Printed in the United States of America

The paper used in this publication meets the minimum requirements of
American National Standard for Information Sciences
Permanence of Paper for Printed Library Materials,
ANSI Z 39.48-1984.

MV (c) 10   9   8   7   6   5   4   3   2   1

Contents

v

List of Tables and Figures

Tables

Figures

Foreword

The excellent introduction to this volume by Shoshana Grossbard-Shechtman and Christopher Clague distinguishes between the "expansion" and the "reorientation" of economics. We can think of the former as *economic imperialism* (see Radnitzky and Bernholz 1987; Radnitzky 1992). It reflects the contention—a well-supported contention, as demonstrated by several of the essays here—that the economic approach to human behavior is valid far beyond its traditional domain of market interactions, and in particular that the standard techniques and presumptions of economic analysis can tell us much that is useful and true about many other spheres of life, including politics, crime, religion, charity, family relations, and warfare. In contrast, emphasis upon the "reorientation" of economics more modestly suggests—again correctly, in my opinion—that economics has much to learn from, as well as much to teach, the other social disciplines.

Using a geopolitical metaphor, it is helpful to view the heartland of economics as an intellectual territory carved off by two narrowing conceptions: (1) "economic man"—*Homo economicus*—a rational self-interested decision-maker with fixed though arbitrary preferences, who (2) deals with other humans only via market exchange. But the power of its theoretical structure irresistibly drives economics beyond these boundaries. The self-interested goals and rational choice of means that characterize "economic man" are also operative, to a degree, in many domains apart from markets: for example, when political parties select candidates, when military commanders decide whether to advance or to retreat, when parents balance between helping one child versus another, when scientific researchers choose which line of investigation to pursue. True, in all those domains cultural, biological, ethical, and arguably "irrational" forces may also be involved—but such influences are present even for buying and selling in markets. In short, economics properly understood is not limited to the study of commerce, nor—even when dealing with commerce—should it be limited by the postulate of *Homo economicus*.

The expansion of economics was, to begin with, like a breath of fresh air: for example, when Anthony Downs (1957) revolutionized political science by boldly proposing that individuals seek political office solely for income, prestige, and power; or in the field of crime, when Gary Becker (1968) chose to set aside the possibly "deviant" personalities of criminals in order to deal with them as individuals rationally responding to opportunities in the form of punishment and reward. In law, Richard Posner (1981) proposed that judicial decisions and legislation should be grounded not upon abstract principles of justice, but strictly upon the costs and benefits of alternative legal roles. Political scientists, criminologists, and legal scholars now all recognize that economic reasoning has a large role to play in each of those disciplines. Nevertheless, time and further study have revealed puzzles resistant to standard economic analysis. In politics, it remains difficult to explain why people vote, why they are willing to provide public goods, why they fall victim to crazy ideologies. As to crime, faced with the same incentives, some people commit offenses while others do not. In law, perhaps it really is true that some actions are good or bad in themselves, apart from their cost-benefit implications.

These shortcomings have suggested to many researchers that standard economic analysis needs reorientation, as proposed in a number of ways in various chapters of this volume. The key to that reorientation, sometimes termed the "behavioral economics" program, consists of replacing *Homo economicus* with a more rounded image of how humans act.

I suppose that even the most aggressive of economic imperialists would not maintain that people always behave in accordance with the postulates that characterize economic man: self-interested goals, rational choice of means, and so forth. A judicious economic imperialist might claim only that these assumptions represent a surprisingly large part of the whole truth in all domains of life, and they constitute pretty much the whole truth in their traditional area of application—namely market interactions. Toward the other end of the spectrum, a very modest view might not only disclaim the relevance of *Homo economicus* outside the domain of markets, but argue that even market behavior itself cannot be understood without allowing for goals that take into account the needs of others, that allow for intangibles such as honor and prestige, that are socially constructed rather than arbitrary and fixed. Nor can behavior within or outside markets be fully explained without allowing for the fact that people make mistakes, act without proper thought, are subject to emotions, and otherwise violate the canons of rationality.

I will not attempt to preview here the various positions that the authors of the essays here profess with regard to the expansion or reorientation of economics, either in general or with specific application to fields such as national development, the household, social action, and religion. Instead, I will close with a few general thoughts. First, that in carrying out the program of this volume it is possible to err in either of two ways. We can be too aggressive in trumpeting the validity of the usual techniques and presumptions of economics, or alternatively be too modest in being over-ready to amend or even dismiss them. Second, to make an aggressive claim, what gives economics its imperialist invasive power is that its theoretical categories—scarcity, costs, preferences, competition, among others—are indeed truly universal. They apply not only to market behavior, but to every domain of life, among them politics, religion, persuasion, love, and war. Even more important is our analytic technique whereby these categories are structured into the distinct yet intertwined processes of *choice* on the individual decision level and, on a higher level of analysis, *principles of aggregation* leading to some form of social equilibrium—from which it follows that it is ultimately impossible to carve off a distinct territory for economics, bordering upon but separated from other social disciplines. Economics interpenetrates them all, and is reciprocally penetrated by them. There is only one social science, and economics provides a universal grammar for it.

Finally, only as we succeed in taking account of a more rounded picture of individual behavior will the promise of achieving a universal social science through the powerful techniques developed in economic analysis be fulfilled. Ultimately, good economics will also have to be good biology as well as good anthropology and sociology and political science and psychology.

Jack Hirshleifer

References

Becker, Gary. 1968. "Crime and Punishment: An Economic Approach." *Journal of Political Economy* 76: 169–217.

Downs, Anthony. 1957. *An Economic Theory of Democracy.* New York: Harper & Row.

Posner, Richard. 1981. *The Economics of Justice.* Cambridge, MA: Harvard University Press.

Radnitzky, Gerard. 1992. *Universal Economics: Assessing the Achievements of the Economic Approach.* New York: Paragon House.

Radnitzky, Gerard, and Peter Bernholz. 1987. *Economic Imperialism: The Economic Method Applied Outside the Field of Economics.* New York: Paragon House.

THE
EXPANSION
OF
ECONOMICS

1

The Expansion and Reorientation of Economics

Shoshana Grossbard-Shechtman and Christopher Clague

Academia can be thought of as a group of neighboring tribes, each occupying a particular territory, which it cultivates with tools that seem appropriate for that terrain and climate. Most of the time, members of tribes remain in their home areas, with amicable but not intimate relations with their neighbors. There is often some cultivation in border areas, with occasional collaboration across tribal lines. However, during some periods, perhaps because of technological developments, tribes invade one another's territories, and tribal members raised in one territory begin cultivation in another. Relationships may become hostile, but there may also be trade and cooperation. With apologies to Axel Leijonhufvud (1981), we will use this parable to discuss the relationships between economics and other social sciences. Our focus is on the expansion and reorientation of economics in the last forty years. However, to understand better these trends, we start with a brief overview of the first sixty years of the twentieth century. Even though we primarily review the evolution of economics in the United States, we mention some of the differences between social science in the United Kingdom and the United States (the Anglo-Saxon experience) and that of continental Europe.

After this historical overview we describe the expansion of economics into new subject areas, areas that had for many decades been considered the exclusive provinces of political science and sociology. The impact of this expansion on these disciplines is also sketched. Next, we describe what we call the "reorientation of economics": the modification of some of its basic

We thank Vernon Ruttan for helpful comments on this introduction.

Table 1.1

The Social Sciences for Most of the Twentieth Century

	Discipline		
	Economics	Political science	Sociology
Principal organization	Firm	Government	Family and voluntary associations
Principal tools of analysis	Market analysis Quantitative	Institutionalist Descriptive Qualitative	Institutionalist Descriptive Qualitative
Principal assumptions about individuals	Rational voluntary choice Selfish, nonaggressive, not altruistic Perfect information	Not necessarily rational Possibly aggressive Various cognitive assumptions Follow orders	Not necessarily rational Possibly altruistic Various cognitive assumptions Follows norms

assumptions and techniques of analysis. This reorientation may be related to the need to modify the neoclassical tools of economics, as the discipline is increasingly researching nonmarket interactions. Subsequently, we explain the organization of the text and present a brief description of each of the chapters. Concluding comments on the future of economics and its relationship to the other social sciences can be found at the end of this book.

Economics Before 1960

In Britain and the United States, social science entered the twentieth century as a tribal society, with various tribes or fiefdoms each taking claim over a separate territory. Table 1.1 provides a guide to the three major social sciences in the United States in the first half of the twentieth century. The disciplines were distinguished according to the subject matter on which they focused, their principal tools of analysis, and the principal assumptions they made about individuals. Each discipline was like a tribe responsible for the cultivation of a particular area of research. Research territory was defined primarily according to subject matter: economics studied the economy, defined as the production and consumption of marketed goods and services; political science studied the government and the legal system, and sociology and its sister disciplines (social anthropology and social psychology) studied families and voluntary associations such as religious bodies.

There was some overlap between the subject matters of the various disciplines. Economists studied government to the extent that government affects economic policy. Economics analyzed government actions, such as taxation, government expenditure, and monetary policy, with the goal of maximizing social welfare. Government agencies, like business firms, were treated as black boxes. Economics assumed that businesses knew how to maximize profits, and that government agencies could effectively implement the policies recommended by economists. There was also some overlap among sociology, political science, and economics, leading to the subfields of political sociology and economic sociology. In these subfields, sociologists mostly studied those aspects of the economy and the polity that were not addressed by economics and political science.

In addition to the fields listed in Table 1.1, researchers in business schools studied business organizations and those in schools of public administration studied government agencies. Some of these organizational specialists were trained in psychology and sociology. Psychology, apart from social psychology and the study of organizations, is a discipline focused primarily on understanding individual thinking, emotions, and behavior, rather than social organizations, and in this sense it is not really a social science.

The various social sciences were also clearly distinguished by the tools they applied to the cultivation of their territory, economics standing out from other social sciences in its more mathematical and quantitative tools and its more restrictive assumptions about human behavior. The principal tools underlying economic theory were "rational choice analysis" and "market analysis." Most economic models assumed that individual households and firms act rationally, voluntarily, and not from coercion. Implicitly or explicitly, economists generally assumed that individuals are selfish, not aggressive, and not altruistic. At the level of cognition, it was assumed that economic agents had no difficulty receiving, processing, and storing information.

As is also summarized in Table 1.1, other social sciences have tended to be less quantitative and less abstract, thus requiring fewer mathematical skills. Relative to economics, the comparative advantage of sociology and political science has been in the identification of factors relevant to their subject matter, in the description of such factors, and in the development of ideas connecting various aspects of human behavior and institutions.

The subject matter of the different disciplines was influenced by the emergence of academic departments in universities and colleges. Political science and economics had no difficulty establishing themselves as separate departments, as each field had a long history of serious inquiry and a well-defined subject matter. In continental Europe, sociology was not clearly distinguished from economics in university studies. Thanks to figures such as Max Weber, Werner Sombart, Emile Durkheim, and Vilfredo Pareto—who simultaneously studied the economy, the state, religion, and culture—economics and sociology remained linked not only to each other but also to political science and law. In Germany, Weber, his brother, and many others had training in economics and taught in schools of public policy, welcoming all the disciplines that could possibly help policymakers in the design of better laws and policies (see Backhaus 2001). It is in one of the best known of these schools, the University of Heidelberg, that prominent American sociologist Talcott Parsons got his doctorate in economics in the 1920s. Pareto, whose name appears on every economist's lips, was a sociologist in addition to being an economist. He inspired American sociologist George Homans, an important contributor to social exchange theories in the mid-twentieth century (see chapter 9).[1]

In the United States, however, sociology was not considered part of economics, and sociologists had to struggle for acceptance in the universities. Most American universities did not have sociology departments until relatively recently. Not wanting to perform research about forms of exchanges and social relations that lay outside their concept of the economy, economists made room for sociology, social psychology, and social anthropology (in short, sociology). For instance, Harvard did not have a sociology department until 1931. Partly to gain acceptance in American universities, sociology left the study of the economy to economics and confined itself to subject areas that economics did not aspire to handle (Swedberg 1990, 10–14). The study of production handled by households and not by firms was relegated to home economics departments (see Yi 1996; Beller and Kiss 1999). Home economics often also included consumer studies, an area also mostly a function of decision making within households. This lack of interest on the part of economists is one of the reasons that in the early twentieth century many American universities created home economics departments.

In the first six decades of the twentieth century, economics, especially in the Anglo-Saxon countries, devoted most of its energies to refining its techniques of analysis of the production and market exchange of material goods and services. During this period economic theory became increasingly formalized. (Institutional economics, which was prominently represented in American universities before World War II, took a broader view of economics' subject matter and vigorously resisted the formalism and methodological individualism of the mainstream, but it lost influence after the war; [Hodgson 1994, 1998].) The resulting edifice of economic theory was an impressive intellectual accomplishment, in comparison with what the other social sciences had to offer. Among the achievements were neoclassical microeconomic theory (or "price theory," as it was then called), classical monetary theory (Keynesian macroeconomic theory), the Heckscher-Ohlin theory of international trade, and the theory of externalities and public goods. These theories offered many insights about how the economy functioned and about the effects of government policies on the economy.

The Expansion of Economics After 1960

After the rise of Adolf Hitler and World War II, continental universities lost their prominence. Since World War II, most new developments in economics and many innovations in other social sciences occurred primarily in the United States. Starting approximately in the 1960s, American economists began to invade other social sciences, especially political science and sociology. Political science witnessed the penetration of economists Anthony Downs (1957), James Buchanan and Gordon Tullock (1962), and Mancur Olson (1965), who applied economic models to politics and launched the new field of "public choice." Buchanan eventually received the Nobel Prize, largely in recognition for this line of work. Economists who received the Nobel Prize in part for their contributions to the economic analysis of politics and law include Ronald Coase, who wrote on property rights (Coase 1960), Douglass North, who wrote on property and contract rights (e.g., North and Thomas 1973; see also Harold Demsetz 1964, 1967), Gary Becker, who wrote on democracy,[2] discrimination (1957), and crime deterrents (1968), and George Stigler (1971), who contributed an economic theory of regulation.[3]

Together with Jacob Mincer, his colleague at Columbia University in the 1960s, Becker was also at the forefront of economics' penetration into some of the territory traditionally cultivated by sociology. Becker (1960) contributed to the earlier literature on economics of fertility (see chapter 9 of this volume). A breaking point was the onset of the *New Home Economics*, which originated when Mincer (1962, 1963; reproduced in Mincer 1993) and Becker (1965) placed companies and households on an equal footing as far as the applicability of economic analysis is concerned (see Grossbard-Shechtman forthcoming). They thereby erased borders that previous generations of American economists had erected among economics, sociology, and home economics. This return of economics into the territory of home economics and family production was strengthened after Becker published his theory of marriage and divorce (Becker 1973, 1974) and his *Treatise on the Family* (Becker 1981). More recently, economists have started researching other voluntary organizations such as churches and social movements. Most prominent in that area is the work of Laurence Iannaccone, who was a student of Becker at Chicago (see chapter 10 of this book).

The invasion of economics since the 1960s benefited from the marginalist revolution that gained momentum in the United Kingdom in the latter part of the nineteenth century[4] and early part of the twentieth century, and from the mathematical revolution that originated in the United States after World War II and which owes much to the influence of Paul Samuelson. As a result, economists had become very effective at the use of economic analysis defined as the use of rational choice and market analysis. In a broader perspective, taking account of the history of the social sciences, economists' recent invasions into fields traditionally tended by sociologists can be seen as a return to an earlier academic structure from which sociology was virtually absent. The expansion of economics after 1960 can be understood as a correction for the narrowing of the scope of economics that took place in the United Kingdom and the United States in earlier decades of the twentieth century. In contrast, during most of this time, some continental European economists took a broader view of the subject matter of economics (see Swedberg 1990; Backhaus 2001).

These forays of economists into neighboring territories disturbed the established order there and generated two kinds of reactions. One reaction was to deny the applicability of the economists' framework and to try to push back the invaders by either attacking them verbally or by producing alternative research replacing economic analyses. Examples of sociologists going after economists verbally include Judith Blake's (1968) attack on the economics of fertility, Remi Clignet and Joyce Sween's (1977) critique of an economic analysis of polygamy (Grossbard 1976), and Stephen Bruce's (1993) attack on economic theories of religion such as Laurence Iannaccone's (see chapter 10 of this book). Home economists have not shown much resistance to the invasion from economics, which is in part the result of the gradual cutbacks of home economics departments in U.S. academia.

Another reaction from other social sciences was to take the new ideas seriously and to incorporate them into their research. Business researchers, who have always been familiar with economics, have continued to follow the new developments in the field, especially the dramatic innovations in industrial organization. Although initially a lot of resistance existed within political science to the rational-choice approach, some political scientists (e.g., Riker 1962) were among the pioneers in the new field that has come to be called "political economy" (Ordeshook 1990). The Public Choice Society, founded in the 1960s, has always enlisted substantial numbers from both political science and economics. A buzzword in political science today is "institutionalism," which comes in three forms: historical, rational choice, and sociological (Hall and Taylor 1998). These grow out of different intellectual traditions, but they do communicate with each other and with economics. In his survey of the impact of economics on political science, Gary Miller observed:

The rediscovery of institutions is an intellectual accomplishment of economists and political scientists together—and it is potentially the most important way that the confrontation of economic tools with political reality can change economics itself. In the near future, the channeling of preference and information flows through institutional channels will be the growth field in political science. (1927, 1200)

Economics appears to have had less impact on sociology than on political science. However, given the wide subject matter of sociology, and economics' separate impact on many of the unrelated topics studied by sociologists, it is possible that the total contribution of economics to sociology over the last forty years has been substantial. What follows are some of the separate contributions of economics to sociology of which we are aware:

- The field of rational-choice sociology (Hechter 1987; Coleman 1990, 1994) was clearly influenced by economics. Many, including Coleman, have explicitly recognized that influence.
- More specifically, sociologists have applied rational-choice analysis and other techniques developed in economics to study marriage and the family (see chapter 8).
- Sociologists have also applied insights from economics to the study of religion (see chapter 10).
- Economic sociology was influenced by ideas from information economics. In particular, Harrison White, one of the founders of modern economic sociology, drew on Michael Spence's (1974) concept of signaling in his own work (see Swedberg 1990, 83).

The Reorientation of Economics After 1960

In the 1960s and 1970s, as economics was invading other fields using the traditional tool kit of the discipline, the tool kit itself was being modified, even in the home area of economics. We call this the "reorientation of economics." As mentioned above, prior to 1960 neoclassical economic models were principally populated by selfish, rational individuals who had access to abundant information and had the ability to process it. In the late 1960s, the relaxation of the traditional assumptions of economic models had become a widespread phenomenon. One modification was the recognition that information is costly and that self-interested individuals will use it to their own advantage. This modification was quite readily accepted in the discipline, for two reasons: It was very consistent with economists' conception of people as self-interested utility maximizers, and the new field of information economics yielded important insights into such topics as adverse selection and moral hazard (Akerlof 1970), screening and discrimination (Schelling 1971; Spence 1974), sharecropping (Cheung 1969; Stiglitz 1974), and principal-agent theory (Jensen and Meckling 1976).

Prior to 1970, economists did little to enrich their conceptions of human motivation; psychology remained for them a largely unvisited territory. Already in the 1950s and 1960s, Herbert Simon and others at Carnegie University (Simon 1957; March and Simon 1958; Cyert and March 1963) had developed the concept of "bounded rationality" and the "behavioral theory of the firm" (see also Leibenstein 1960, 1966), but these did not have much impact on standard economic analysis. However, in the 1970s, Oliver Williamson, addressing a long-neglected question originally posed by Ronald Coase (1937), incorporated bounded rationality into his analysis of the relative strengths of markets and hierarchies (Williamson 1975). He and other researchers opened the black box of the firm and revolutionized industrial organization. Williamson was unusual in that his assumptions included not only bounded rationality and opportunism, but also the capacity of people to develop bonds of trust and loyalty.

In the 1980s, economists and political scientists were studying economic institutions, using the new tools of information economics and game theory. By the mid-1980s the term "New Institutional Economics" was being applied to the literature in economic history on property rights and contract enforcement (North 1981) and to Williamson's transaction-cost economics (Williamson 1985). The term "new" was added to distinguish the school from the "old" institutional economics, which was regarded as descriptive and not theoretical (but see Hodgson 1998 for a critique). Economists also began studying social norms (Elster 1989). In studying these nonmarket interactions, some economists began to incorporate a richer psychology of human motivation (e.g., compare North 1990 with North 1981; see also Clague 1993 for an example of how institutions mold preferences).

Over the last couple of decades, psychologists and economists have accumulated experimental evidence that people's behavior does not conform to the neoclassical economics' model of self-oriented expected utility maximization (e.g., Thaler 1996). Some of the experimental evidence comes from the new field of experimental economics, which has provided an opportunity to test the new theories of cooperation and market behavior developed by game theorists (Camerer 1995; Ledyard 1995). Economists had, of course, long been aware that their model of human motivation was not realistic in all situations, but the profession had resisted psychological enrichment on the grounds that no alternative model was suitable for economic analysis.[5] This resistance is diminishing, as can be seen from recent prominent review articles on psychology and economics (Rabin 1998; Conlisk 1996), emotions and economic theory (Elster 1998), and endogenous preferences (Bowles 1998).

In the last forty years both an expansion and a reorientation of economics have taken place, resulting in much crossing and recrossing of disciplinary borders. Quite a bit of trade has occurred. The expansion of economics brought economists into sociology and political science. In turn, once they got there, economists learned from other disciplines and started importing ideas into economics. Gary Becker, for instance, has recognized his debt to sociologists. As a result of his extensive research in the domain of sociology, in 1983 Becker became a professor of sociology in addition to being a professor of economics. His frequent interactions with sociologists, especially with Chicago colleague James Coleman, led him to abandon the assumption of "stable preferences" (forcefully espoused in Becker 1976), replacing it with that of "endogenous preferences" (see Becker and Murphy 2000).

Some border areas that were previously left barren or that were sparsely populated are now jointly colonized by members of neighboring tribes. Some of this movement is peaceful. The growth of psychological economics, economic psychology, and the subfield of networks and markets are examples of successful joint colonization of border areas. As mentioned earlier, there have also been invasions and counterattacks.

This volume intends to help readers decide what in their opinion should be the relation between economics and other disciplines. We present various chapters that connect to either the reorientation of economics, or the expansion of economics. These chapters deal with various subject matters and various disciplines. In every instance, the authors are familiar not only with the economic approach to their topic, but also with much of the literature in other disciplines.

Organization of the Text

The present volume is divided into five parts. The first part contains comparisons between economics and two other disciplines defined around the analytical skills that they provide: statistics and system dynamics. The first of these (chapter 2) is by Clive Granger, an eminent econometrician. All econometricians operate at the border between economics and statistics, and Granger is no exception. He draws on his immense experience with the two disciplines to derive a number of points that distinguish economists from their colleagues in statistics. At times, reading Granger's contribution makes one proud to be an economist. It is nice to know that we approach data with a better sense of what to look for. But Granger also warns us against some undesirable traits often fostered by economics departments: a tendency to believe that there is an absolute truth out there, a conviction that one theory is clearly superior to any other, and then a proclivity to milk the data until they corroborate this truth. Statisticians may not have a good enough idea of what they are looking for in the data, but at least they respect the data and have less of a tendency to overlook features that do not suit them.

Chapter 3, by Shlomo Maital, is a manifesto for *System Dynamics* (SD) and a plea for economists to collaborate with SD instead of ignoring it, as they have been doing for the last thirty years. System Dynamics is a method of modeling complex systems through computer simulation. The chapter sketches several examples of SD modeling by pioneer Jay Forrester, including *Industrial Dynamics* (a model of markets and industries), *Urban Dynamics* (a model of the city of Boston, showing how public housing exacerbated, rather than solved, the basic problem of inner cities), and *The Limits to Growth* (a model of the world economy containing dire predictions of the future). In contrast to economics, SD focuses not on equilibrium outcomes, but on the dynamics of disequilibrium processes. Maital believes that SD is potentially very useful for understanding phenomena such as the global financial crisis of 1997 and 1998 and R&D-driven cyclicality in technology industries.

The rest of the book is organized by subject matter: Parts II through V compare economics with at least one discipline that deals with similar subject matter. Part II contains two chapters on aspects of economic development. Vernon Ruttan, the author of chapter 4, is a well-known specialist in development economics and agricultural economics. Ruttan draws on his extensive experience with technical change in agriculture, especially with the "green revolution," which produced tremendous gains in rice yields in Asia in the 1970s. Over his long career, he has interacted with many specialists trained in other disciplines and has read related work by noneconomists. His chapter presents interesting comparisons among economics, anthropology, sociology, and political science. It is a compelling testimony to the importance of cooperation among the disciplines. While participating in the research that led to the green revolution, he learned that the goal of making a practical difference—in this case raising rice yields—overrides any partisan interests. Questions such as "who is a better scientist" or "which discipline is the better one" matter little when the goal is to eradicate hunger and reduce mortality. That experience transformed Ruttan, who has maintained a remarkably cooperative perspective toward other disciplines. There are some outstanding lessons that we can learn from what Ruttan distilled from extensive readings in some of our sister disciplines. These lessons should not only be of interest to economists, but also to anthropologists, sociologists, and political scientists. For instance, Ruttan encourages us to pay more attention to the sociology of science and technology, and to wonder why underdevelopment theories developed by economists attract so many more followers among sociologists than among economists.

In chapter 5, Christopher Clague examines the recent wave of economic liberalization in less-developed countries and examines the explanations for this phenomenon offered by economists and political scientists. After reviewing some thirty examples of economic liberalization, he discusses three approaches to understanding them: the comparative politics approach, economic models based on economic interests, and approaches based on information and learning. The discussion illustrates both the rapprochement of economics and political science that has occurred in the last few decades, and their continuing differences in styles of research. As mentioned earlier, the two disciplines have jointly developed the fields of public choice, political economy, and the New Institutional Economics, and they share a common vocabulary of discourse. Nevertheless, economists tend to be more interested in abstract models, whereas political scientists tend to build up generalizations from careful study of cases. With regard to the explanation of the wave of liberalizations, Clague gives higher marks to studies in the comparative politics tradition than to a prominent stream of economics articles based on a very simplistic model of the political process, and on assumptions clearly inconsistent with what we know about human behavior. He argues in favor of a view of these liberalizations that emphasizes the role of ignorance, uncertainty, and changed perceptions of how the world works.

Part III consists of two chapters dealing with firms and their workers. Chapter 6, by Michael Gibbs and Alec Levenson, considers how the economic approach to organizations and personnel management can benefit from closer collaboration with the behavioral approach. They describe one type of behavioral research, which is to take a systems view of the business organization. In brief, in the systems view the firm's strategy and environment strongly influence the organizational design, which consists of job design, internal labor markets, performance evaluation, and implicit contracting. The organizational design leads to the intermediate outcomes: skills of recruits; the firm's human capital; organizational culture; matching of skills, tasks, and decision rights; and worker involvement. These intermediate outcomes then lead to business outcomes: profit, market share, growth, product quality, service quality, innovation, and adaptability. Finally, these business outcomes feed back to the firm's strategy. A number of topics are treated extensively in the behavioral literature and largely ignored by economists; some of these, the authors argue, lend themselves to productive theorizing and empirical investigation by economists. For the most part, economic theories of organizations do not specify the type of products the firm is producing, nor the type of work that employees actually do. The systems view suggests that organizational design and personnel practices should correspond in various ways to the firm's business strategy and external environment (this is called "external fit"), and the different components of organizational design should complement one another (this is called "internal fit"). The authors suggest that economic theorists might provide a deeper understanding of external and internal fit, but only if they are more specific about what is being produced and what the productive tasks are. A potentially fascinating area largely neglected by economists is job design. Which tasks should be bundled together? How can jobs be designed to be interesting and fulfilling, so as to elicit intrinsic motivation? Ever since Adam Smith, economists have extolled specialization and the division of labor, while behavioral researchers have called for job enrichment, in order to elicit intrinsic motivation. Gibbs and Levenson suggest a way of modeling intrinsic motivation, by relating the worker's human capital to the challenge of the job; in their formulation, it may be optimal to assign workers to tasks they have not fully mastered, and to rotate workers through jobs so as to make the work more interesting. Chapter 6 offers many other suggestions of how economics could illuminate organizational design and personnel practices.

In chapter 7, Richard Audas and John Treble contrast research by psychologists and economists on absenteeism and present the outlines of a new model of absenteeism. Psychologists naturally take the work environment as exogenous to their analysis of absenteeism and they focus on characteristics of individual workers. Much of the early psychological research was based on the conception that absenteeism was one manifestation of a more general phenomenon of worker withdrawal from the workplace. In the 1970s, two psychologists, Steers and Rhodes, presented a rather comprehensive model that included the job situation, employee values and expectations, personal characteristics, job satisfaction, pressure to attend, attendance motivation, and ability to attend. This model denies the previous conception that absence, lateness, and turnover are all manifestations of the single phenomenon of withdrawal. The Steers-Rhodes model, and its descendants, are quite interesting for their comprehensive view of the phenomenon, taking into account both the job situation and worker characteristics, but economics can bring a different perspective: There is an employment market in which employers offer job packages, including rewards and penalties associated with attendance and absenteeism, and workers sort themselves among the available jobs. Employers' offers are conditioned by technological and organizational requirements, and workers' choices are conditioned by, among other things, the demands of household production functions.

Part IV deals with applications of economics to some traditional topics in sociology: marriage, fertility, and religion. These are topics related to institutions that until recently economists preferred not to study: voluntary associations. Two chapters explore marriage and the family, and one chapter deals with religious institutions. In chapter 8, Shoshana Grossbard-Shechtman examines the evolution of economic analyses of marriage pioneered by Gary Becker. The chapter then makes some comparisons between the economics of marriage and the economics of fertility, and between the economics and sociology of marriage. Particular differences between a sociological and economic approach to marriage are emphasized via the example of two theories of division of labor within marriage: the dependency model developed by sociologists and an economic model of Work-in-Marriage markets that is in the New Home Economics tradition. The chapter also examines reactions of sociologists to economic models of marriage. Overall, the study of marriage remains overwhelmingly under the control of sociologists, and that is one reason why economic models—including models based on demand and supply—are not very commonly used in the study of marriage formation and decision making within marriages. Another reason is that marriage is not considered to be an issue of major policy importance, and interdisciplinary cooperation tends to develop first on topics considered sufficiently important to justify the extra effort of looking into the work of scholars trained outside one's discipline.

The policy importance of fertility was at the origin of the Population Association of America (PAA), the professional organization that brings together demographers trained in various disciplines. In her interview with sociologist/demographer David Heer (chapter 9), Grossbard-Shechtman inquires into the history of demography. According to Heer, many of the demographers who founded the PAA in the early 1930s were sympathetic to eugenics, and they were interested in studying fertility owing to their preference for slower global population growth. Some other early demographers were interested in promoting birth control in the United States. To avoid potential conflict among demographers with different policy goals, it was agreed to minimize political discussions at PAA meetings. Given that scholars trained in different disciplines often tend to differ in their political preferences, this strategy helped promote understanding among scholars trained in various disciplines including economics, sociology, and biology. Heer has other interesting insights into the history of demography, including his analysis of the effect of World War II on the nature of demography as an academic discipline. Chapter 9 also deals with the relationship between economics and sociology. Heer studied at Harvard not long after Harvard started its sociology department. He studied with George Homans and Talcott Parsons, crucial contributors to sociology who both had extensive training in economics. The second part of this interview reveals very interesting and little-known insights on the connection between the two social sciences.

Laurence Iannaccone in chapter 10 makes a compelling case for the application of economic theory to the study of religion. It is quite remarkable that economists had neglected the systematic study of religious behavior until the 1970s, for, as chapter 10 demonstrates, an enormous amount of low-lying fruit was waiting to be gathered by a member of the economist tribe. Prior to this invasion, leading sociologists acknowledged that the field of religious studies was very descriptive and lacked unifying concepts around which focused debate could take place. The theory of "utility maximization" offers a conceptual framework that explains a wide variety of phenomena at the level of individual behavior, such as patterns of intermarriage and divorce, church attendance, conversion ages, and financial contributions to religious entities. The theory of "market competition" similarly provides many insights into the structure, doctrines, and proselytizing strategies of religious organizations. Not surprisingly, the economics invasion has drawn severe criticism from sociologists, and Iannaccone considers their objections and finds them largely unconvincing. Chapter 10 provides a beautiful illustration of a Becker-type economics invasion into a new territory, by the most prominent pioneer in the field.

Finally, Part V consists of two chapters addressing topics in the psychology of individual and collective behavior. Louis Lévy-Garboua and Serge Blondel in chapter 11 present a brief exposition of a theory of decision making that reconciles cognitive dissonance with rationality. In the proposed theory, the individual does not know her true preferences, but has temporary preferences that depend on the information perceived at each moment. As she ponders different aspects of the choices, her temporary preferences change as her cognitions change. These cognitions each represent a random draw from a stable distribution. This conception of the decision-making process as sequential process draws on recent neuroscience research, which shows activity occurring over time at different points in the brain. Past decisions contain information about the distribution of cognitions, and thus they can influence perceived information and current preferences. The authors use their model to show how Kahneman and Tversky's "certainty effect," which is an example of behavior inconsistent with a strong conception of rationality, can be reconciled with their concept of cognitive consistency, and they draw further implications for the behavior of a person displaying the certainty effect. Their chapter offers a framework for integrating cognitive dissonance and a type of rationality that they call "cognitive consistency."

In chapter 12, Dipak Gupta examines the inability of standard economic theory to explain the phenomenon of collective action. As Mancur Olson argued back in 1965, under ordinary conditions rational, self-interested members of a large group will not act to achieve their common group interests. This argument was a startling revelation to the field of political science, which devoted substantial effort to examining it. By and large, Olson's argument has received a great deal of empirical confirmation, and it illuminates a wide variety of political behavior, but there remains much behavior that contradicts Olson's conclusion (Ostrom 2000). Gupta scrutinizes the attempts of political scientists and economists to reconcile the phenomenon of collective action with their theories of individual behavior, and he finds that all these attempts come up short. Gupta then describes some research in social psychology on the formation of group identity, the role of authority figures, and framing effects. Drawing on this research, he proposes a generalized framework in which the individual maximizes utility by consuming optimal amounts of private goods and collective goods. This parsimonious framework readily admits some commonly observed characteristics of collective action, such as its volatility and its manipulability by political entrepreneurs. This chapter provides an excellent example of the advantages of incorporating social psychology into an expanded economics.

We hope that the juxtaposition of all these materials will be thought-provoking and helpful for readers wondering about the definition of economics in the twenty-first century. Some of our own thoughts on this issue can be found in this book's conclusion (chapter 13).

Notes

1. Homans's theory is part of the rational-choice tradition that later became popularized by James Coleman after he moved to the University of Chicago. Coleman was a student of Homans.

2. Becker reports that his 1958 article was ignored at the time of publication (see interview with Becker in Swedberg 1990).

3. Other Nobel Prize winners around this time applied economics to topics that had been treated by other disciplines: Theodore Schultz on education (Schultz 1963) and Robert Fogel on slavery (Fogel and Engerman 1974).

4. It has been argued, for example, by Mark Blaug (2001), that the marginalist theories originated in France and Germany in the mid-nineteenth century. However, these theories did not gain influence until they were adopted and spread by English economists.

5. For an amusing description of this resistance, see the introduction to Thaler (1996).

References

Akerlof, George A. 1970. "The Market for Lemons: Quality Uncertainty and the Market Mechanism." *Quarterly Journal of Economics* 84: 488–500.

Backhaus, Jurgen G. 2001. "Fiscal Sociology: What For?" Public lecture presented at the University of Maastricht, the Netherlands, January 19.

Becker, Gary S. 1957. *The Economics of Discrimination*. Chicago: University of Chicago Press.

———. 1960. "An Economic Analysis of Fertility." In A. Coale et al., eds., *Demographic and Economic Change in Developed Countries*, 209–231. Princeton, NJ: Princeton University Press.

———. 1965. "A Theory of the Allocation of Time." *Economic Journal* 75: 493–515.

———. 1968. "Crime and Punishment: An Economic Approach." *Journal of Political Economy* 78: 189–217.

———. 1973. "A Theory of Marriage: Part I." *Journal of Political Economy* 81(4): 813–846.

———. 1974. "A Theory of Marriage: Part II." *Journal of Political Economy* 81(2, Part 2): S11–S26.

———.1976. *The Economic Approach to Human Behavior*. Chicago: University of Chicago Press.

———. 1981. *A Treatise on the Family*. Cambridge, MA: Harvard University Press.

Becker, Gary S., and Kevin M. Murphy. 2000. *Social Markets*. Cambridge, MA: Harvard University Press.

Beller, Andrea H., and D. Elizabeth Kiss. 1999. "On the Contribution of Hazel Kyrk to Family Economics." Paper presented at the meetings of the Society for the Advancement of Behavioral Economics, San Diego, June.

Blake, Judith. 1968. "Are Babies Consumer Durables? A Critique of the Economic Theory of Reproduction Motivation." *Population Studies* 22: 5–25.

Blaug, Mark. 2001. "No History of Ideas, Please, We're Economists." *Journal of Economic Perspectives* 15(1): 145–164.

Bowles, Samuel. 1998. "Endogenous Preferences: The Cultural Consequences of Markets and Other Economic Institutions." *Journal of Economic Literature* 361: 75–111.

Bruce, Stephen. 1993. "Religion and Rational Choice: A Critique of Economic Explanations of Religious Behavior." *Sociology of Religion* 54(2): 193–205.

Buchanan, James M., and Gordon Tullock. 1962. *The Calculus of Consent: Logical Foundations of Constitutional Democracy*. Ann Arbor: University of Michigan Press.

Camerer, Colin. 1995. "Individual Decision Making." In John H. Kagel and Alvin E. Roth, eds. *Handbook of Experimental Economics*, 587–703. Princeton, NJ: Princeton University Press.

Cheung, Steven N. 1969. *The Theory of Share Tenancy*. Chicago: University of Chicago Press.

Clague, Christopher K. 1993. "Rule Obedience, Organizational Loyalty, and Economic Development." *Journal of Institutional and Theoretical Economics* 149: 393–414.

Clignet, Remi, and Joyce Sween. 1977. "On Grossbard's Economic Analysis of Polygyny in Maiduguri." *Current Anthropology* 18: 100–2.

Coase, Ronald. 1937. "The Nature of the Firm." *Economica* 4: 386–405.

———. 1960. "The Problem of Social Cost." *Journal of Law and Economics* 3: 1–44.

Coleman, James S. 1990. *Foundations of Social Theory*. Cambridge, MA: Harvard University Press.

———. 1994. "A Rational Choice Perspective in Economic Sociology." In Neil J.

Smelser and Richard Swedberg, eds., *Handbook of Economic Sociology*, 166–180. Princeton, NJ: Princeton University Press for the Russell Sage Foundation.

Conlisk, John. 1996. "Why Bounded Rationality?" *Journal of Economic Literature* 34(2): 669–700.

Cyert, Richard M., and James G. March. 1963. *A Behavioral Theory of the Firm.* Englewood Cliffs, NJ: Prentice-Hall.

Demsetz, Harold. 1964. "The Exchange and Enforcement of Property Rights." *Journal of Law and Economics* 3: 1–44.

———. 1967. "Toward a Theory of Property Rights." *American Economic Review Papers and Proceedings* 57: 347–359.

Downs, Anthony. 1957. *An Economic Theory of Democracy.* New York: Harper & Row.

Elster, Jon. 1989. "Social Norms and Economic Theory." *Journal of Economic Perspectives* 3(4): 99–119.

———. 1998. "Emotions and Economic Theory." *Journal of Economic Literature* 361: 47–76.

Fogel, Robert W., and Stanley L. Engerman. 1974. *Time on the Cross: The Economics of American Negro Slavery.* Boston: Little, Brown.

Grossbard, Amyra. 1976. "An Economic Analysis of Polygamy: The Case of Maiduguri." *Current Anthropology* 17: 701–707.

Grossbard-Shechtman, Shoshana. Forthcoming. "The New Home Economics at Columbia and Chicago." *Feminist Economics.*

Hall, Peter A., and Rosemary C. R. Taylor. 1998. "Political Science and the Three New Institutionalisms." In Karol Soltan, Eric M. Uslaner, and Virginia Haufler, eds., *Institutions and Social Order*, 15–44. Ann Arbor: University of Michigan Press.

Hechter, Michael. 1987. *Principles of Group Solidarity.* Berkeley: University of California Press.

Hodgson, Geoffrey M. 1994. "The Return of Institutional Economics." In Neil J. Smelser and Richard Swedberg, eds., *Handbook of Economic Sociology*, 58–76. Princeton, NJ: Princeton University Press.

———. 1998. "The Approach of Institutional Economics." *Journal of Economic Literature* 361: 166–192.

Jensen, Michael, and William H. Meckling. 1976. "The Theory of the Firm: Managerial Behavior, Agency Costs and Ownership Structure." *Journal of Financial Economics* 3: 305–360.

Ledyard, John O. 1995. "Public Goods: A Survey of Experimental Research." In John H. Kagel and Alvin E. Roth, eds. *A Handbook of Experimental Economics*, 111–194. Princeton, NJ: Princeton University Press.

Leibenstein, Harvey. 1960. *Economic Theory and Organizational Analysis.* New York: Harper & Row.

———. 1966. "Allocative Efficiency Versus X-Efficiency." *American Economic Review* 56(3): 392–415.

Leijonhufvud, Axel. 1981. "Life Among the Econ." In A. Leijonhufvud, ed., *Information and Coordination*, 347–360. New York: Oxford University Press.

March, James G., and Herbert A. Simon. 1958. *Organizations.* New York: Wiley.

Miller, Gary J. 1997. "The Impact of Economics on Political Science." *Journal of Economic Literature* 35(3): 1173–1204

Mincer, Jacob. 1962. "Labor Force Participation of Married Women: A Study of Labor Supply." In H. Gregg Lewis, ed., *Aspects of Labor Economics*, 63–97. Princeton, NJ: Princeton University Press.

———. 1963. "Market Prices, Opportunity Costs, and Income Effects." In C. Christ, ed., *Measurement in Economics*, 67–82. Stanford, CA: Stanford University Press.

———. 1993. *Studies in Labor Supply, Collected Essays of Jacob Mincer*, Vol. 2. Aldershot, UK: Edward Elgar.

North, Douglass C. 1981. *Structure and Change in Economic History*. New York: Norton.

———. 1990. *Institutions, Institutional Change, and Economic Performance*. Cambridge: Cambridge University Press.

North, Douglass C., and Robert Thomas. 1973. *The Rise of the Western World*. Cambridge: Cambridge University Press.

Olson, Mancur. 1965. *The Logic of Collective Action: Public Goods and the Theory of Groups*. Cambridge, MA: Harvard University Press.

Ordeshook, Peter C. 1990. "The Emerging Discipline of Political Economy." In James E. Alt and Kenneth A. Shepsle, eds., *Perspectives on Positive Political Economy*, 9–30. Cambridge: Cambridge University Press.

Ostrom, Elinor. 2000. "Collective Action and the Evolution of Social Norms." *Journal of Economic Perspectives* 14(3): 137–158.

Rabin, Matthew. 1998. "Psychology and Economics." *Journal of Economic Literature* 36: 11–46.

Riker, William. 1962. *The Theory of Political Coalitions*. New Haven, CT: Yale University Press.

Schelling, Thomas C. 1971. "Dynamic Models of Segregation." *Journal of Mathematical Sociology* 1: 143–186.

Schultz, Theodore W. 1963. *The Economic Value of Education*. New York: Columbia University Press.

Simon, Herbert. 1957. *Models of Man*. New York: Wiley.

Spence, A. Michael. 1974. *Market Signaling: Information Transfer in Hiring and Selected Screening Processes*. Cambridge, MA: Harvard University Press.

Stigler, George. 1971. "The Theory of Economic Regulatrion." *Bell Journal of Economic and Management Science* 2: 3–21.

Stiglitz, Joseph E. 1974. "Incentives and Risk-Sharing in Sharecropping." *Review of Economic Studies* 41: 219–255.

Swedberg, Richard. 1990. *Economics and Sociology, Redefining Their Boundaries: Conversations with Economists and Sociologists*. Princeton, NJ: Princeton University Press.

Thaler, Richard H. 1996. *Quasi-Rational Economics*. New York: Russell Sage Foundation.

Williamson, Oliver. 1975. *Markets and Hierarchies Analysis and Anti-Trust Implications*. New York: Free Press.

———. 1985. *The Economic Institutions of Capitalism: Firms, Markets, Relational Contracting*. New York: Free Press.

Yi, Yun-Ae. 1996. "Margaret G. Reid: Life and Achievements." *Feminist Economics* 2: 17–36.

Part I

Comparing Research Methods

2

Comparing the Methodologies Used by Statisticians and Economists for Research and Modeling

Clive W.J. Granger

Introduction

I have always thought that a major reason for visiting another country is to better understand the strengths and weaknesses of the country in which one usually lives by observing how other people tackle problems similar to those faced at home. I have been asked to compare the methodologies of statisticians and economists for the same kind of reason.

I should explain my personal background and thus my perspective. My doctorate was in statistics from an English mathematics department. I eventually became a professor of Applied Statistics and Econometrics in England, but I have spent most of my forty-four years as a university teacher in economics departments. This was for entirely pragmatic reasons. I believed that economists dealt with more interesting questions—and they were also paid more than statisticians. I have been chairman of two economics departments, one in England and one in California, and thus I proved that one need not understand very much economics to do that.

In what follows, I shall want to make some generalization of the form "economists do this, but statisticians do that." Such statements will be inherently untrue; there are very few things or topics on which all economists agree, and there is only a little more agreement among statisticians. Naturally, I understand that, but I do believe there are beliefs or methodologies that are used by many economists. If I generalize about economists I hope that your reaction will not be simply "but I do not do that" but rather consider whether or not a majority of your colleagues in fact do fall into such a category.

There are many important subdivisions between both groups being considered. I will use just a simple division, which I will take as not requiring careful definitions even though it is not easy to place actual individuals into them.

Economists

(a) Theorists, using nonempirical constructs
(b) Applied, possibly building empirical models

Statisticians

(a) Theorists, mathematical statisticians, probability theorists
(b) Applied, analyzing data

I view econometricians as statisticians who concentrate on economic data, which may have properties rather different from data found in other disciplines.[1]

Rather than trying to adapt a sequential argument, I will initially present just a sequence of disjointed comparisons before eventually attempting an overview and conclusion.

Variety of Comparisons

1. At the start of a project a statistician or an econometrician will be aware of the type of data available and that at some stage, they believe, will have to be analyzed. They will know whether the data is a vector of a time series, a panel, or a cross section. They will have some idea of the number of variables available, the amount of data (i.e., the sample size), and possibly have some idea about the data quality; that is, if there are missing sections, if changes of definitions have occurred, and so forth. This type of knowledge is likely to influence greatly the approach taken to the project; certain aspects may be dropped from consideration if there is no relevant data available, for example. A pure economic approach would start the project with a theory that is constructed with no attention to data form, properties, or availability. Only later in the project, when a model based on the theory is estimated, will data problems be considered. The eventual empirical model achieved by the two approaches may be similar but will be achieved by different routes.

2. In a somewhat related comparison, statisticians are inclined to believe that all the available information about the problem being considered is in the data. The economist starts with the belief that the fundamental truths

about the problem will be revealed from the use of economic theory, using basic ideas about behavior of rational, optimizing, economic agents. The theory and institutional knowledge will provide constraints on the specification of any empirical model that is to be constructed. If asked, a statistician would be happy to accept the institutional constraints, as he or she would intuitively believe that they are likely to be correct. They are much less likely to accept the theory-driven constraints as they are less obviously true, given that there may be alternative theories. The statistician will believe that if the theory-derived constraints are correct, then they will be found by data analysis unless the amount of the data or its quality is insufficient.

3. A very basic belief of a statistician is that the economy—in fact, most of the observable world, is stochastic. This is in direct contrast to much of the methodology, at least at the (nonquantum) macrolevel, used by physicists and engineers. The latter consider the basic mechanism to be deterministic, so that classical geometry, calculus, and algebra from pure mathematics can be applied. Many specifications used in economic theory are essentially deterministic: Equilibrium relationships hold perfectly without error, and economic agents have perfect foresight, for example. Only when the equilibrium relationship is fitted to data and the fit is not exact is a "measurement error" added so that the problem is with the data rather than with the theory. Of course, that is *one* possible explanation, but not the only one. From the statisticians' viewpoint the appropriate mathematics involves probability theory and stochastic processes. Relationships are determined within joint and conditional distributions.

4. I believe a substantial difference exists in the deep aims of many statisticians and economists. A general belief among economists is that they are searching for the "truth" about some aspect of the economy, whereas I do not see statisticians having such an aim. A statistician will want to try to understand "data-generating processes," or DGP, that produce the data available to explain the economy. There are two important aspects of this last sentence. A statistician expects the DGP to be complicated and the data to be insufficient in many ways so that only an approximation to the DGP can be achieved. As better data and newer methods of analysis become available, sequences of improving approximations will be achieved. Further, the basic data generated by the agents in the microeconomy, the individual consumers, traders, investors, and so forth, are not usually observed. It is the DGP of these data that might be considered the truth that the economist is actually seeking. In practice, this raw data is aggregated in various ways, using both temporal and cross-sectional aggregation, and then manipulated in various ways by government statistical offices—indices are formed, the series are seasonally adjusted, and so forth. After all this processing, the summary data

are issued and, as a first-order generalization, this is the data available to search for its DGP. Of course, changes are happening, with higher-frequency data and comprehensive panels becoming available, so that both the analysis and the situation are becoming more complicated. Nevertheless, the ultimate aims of economists and statisticians appear to be quite different.

5. Different methodologies are used in considering a basic model against alternatives. The standard procedure in economics has been to consider a single theory, build an empirical model based on it, and consider just a few varieties by adding extra variables. Then the interpretation of what appears to have been discovered from the empirical analysis is considered. Statisticians are more inclined to identify a bare model as the null hypothesis, embed it in a much wider alternative hypothesis, and test between them. The procedure usually chosen by econometricians using parametric models is to start with a model involving many parameters (the "general" form) and then test parameter values and reduce down to the "simplified form." The general form will include the theory specification, but the simplified form may not. This reduction is not completely lacking in controversy.

6. There used to be a lively debate in economics on "empty boxes"; see, for example, the article on this topic in the *New Palgrave* (1987) dictionary. That discussion has ended, but the need for it has not. It considered a body of work, quite possibly of high quality, about some topic or problem that does not occur in the actual economy. The whole area becomes completely an "academic exercise" in the worse sense of this term. Theoretical statisticians fall into a similar situation on occasions, basing a huge amount of impressive research on a type of process for which there is very little evidence of its occurrence in economics. An example seems to be the long-memory processes known as "fractionally integrated" for which there are several hundred papers but little evidence that they occur in practice.

7. The basic training for virtually all statisticians will include lectures on the design and analysis of experiments. Those statisticians that are still near to their roots might consider undertaking experiments either to obtain basic data and estimates, or to discover relationships. These experiments are likely to be "real-world," involving real consumers, traders, or decision-makers in actual situations rather than laboratories where all aspects are under control. An economist is very unlikely to consider using an experiment to gather relevant data, virtually never outside the laboratory.[2] This is in complete contrast to our cousins who work in the area of marketing and who regularly organize and analyze the results from experiments on the actual economy, at the individual consumer and shop level.[3]

8. A "natural experiment" occurs when some situation changes in a way that a designer of an experiment would have chosen to investigate a possible

relationship. For example, say a law changes about minimum wages but it affects some locations but not others, so that the impact of a minimum wage can be investigated—possibly—by comparing regions. Although such experiments can occur in the macroeconomy, such as when a major natural disaster occurs or when several countries are invited to join an economic union but not others, they are most useful in various microeconomic and applied areas, particularly labor economics. There are two controversial aspects of the use of natural experiments. The first is that they compare unfavorably with standard experiments for which the organizer has full control of all aspects, whereas in natural experiments virtually nothing is under control, so that the experimental design is far from optimal for the investigation.

The second problem is that the timing and form of the natural experiment may be endogenous rather than exogenous, so that the natural experiment may occur because of the state of the economy, making the analysis of data generated by it particularly difficult. Because at least some economists realize this, they will provide a sounder analysis of data from a natural experiment than will a statistician, who is likely to view all natural experiments as being similar to those due to natural events, such as a flood or an earthquake. This discussion leads to the question of how economists and statisticians differ in their handling of the concept of causality. My viewpoint here is largely determined by a strong prior belief that the cause has to occur temporally prior to the effect, but that there is no need for spatial proximity. Those parts of economics and econometrics that concentrate on time series will use causality tests that make use of temporal priority. Usually, classical statistics does not worry about time, and it uses causality concepts based on simple correlations and partial correlations between variables. In my opinion, economists are sounder in their handling of causality than are statisticians, largely because the economists are more focused on pragmatic, real-world problems. Similarly, for the same reason, you will find that lawyers' opinions about causality are more sensible, and understandable, than those found in the writings of philosophers. In the thinking of economists, the concepts of endogeneity and exogeneity are linked with causality, although precise definitions are not always available. Similar ideas are not central to statistical analysis.

9. At the extremes, there are two quite different types of statisticians: the Bayesians and the classical, or non-Bayesians. Although sizable groups exist at both extremes, the majority of statisticians fall in between. The crux of the distinction is whether one should rely just on the data for the analysis or if one's personal beliefs should enter formally into the estimation of parameters, inference, or interpretation of the results of an analysis. It is virtually inevitable that some aspect of one's own beliefs enters into how an empirical

problem is approached; for example, not everyone has sufficiently firm beliefs to state them in terms of a prior distribution on the value of some parameter to be determined. One difficulty with prior beliefs is knowing how to convince someone else of their usefulness. It is clear that if one is good at being a Bayesian, one's prior beliefs will help guide the estimated value toward the correct value, and thus effectively expand the data set. However, a bad prior belief pushes one away from the correct value and thus corrupts the data set.

I would place many economic theorists together with very strong Bayesians, as they are inclined to believe the correctness of their theory very firmly and do not want to know about data that may disrupt these beliefs. Most economists would be classified as a type of Bayesian in that they will use a mixture of beliefs—that is, the theory and then data, although the actual methodology used is quite different as no specific prior distributions are involved.

10. If I am shown a fully specified and estimated empirical economic model, would I necessarily know whether it was constructed by an economist or by a statistician? I believe that the answer is "possibly not." As we are seeing only the final stage of the modeling process it is quite likely that a competent member of either group would reach a similar form. It is possible that a model obtained by a statistician would be unacceptable by an economist. It might appear to be "irrational" in some economic sense; it might contradict some well-established economic law or some institutional "fact" not known to the statistician. Similarly, the model found by the economist may have dynamic properties that look strange to the statistician, such as generating an explosive process in some subtle way.

My experience with statisticians is that when they first enter a new field they produce models that are strong statistically, naturally, but may be weak in specification. This is because of a lack of background knowledge or too strong an emphasis on just a few stylized facts. However, after working in the field for a year or two, they become experts in how to produce superior model specifications. They have a strong learning curve. For economists, they believe that their theory provides a close approximation to a very good specification, and their learning is about statistical or econometric techniques used to study this specification or somewhat extend it if it appears to be inadequate.

I am not sure that either group consistently uses a general to simple methodology (starting with a complicated model and moving to a simple one by dropping insignificant terms) or a simple to general (starting with a simple model and testing its adequacy against nearly more general models) as in Box and Jenkins (1970). As data sets get larger and models more complicated a clearer methodology is going to be required.

11. An important component of many statistical analyses is the evaluation phase, asking whether the statistical model achieved its desired purpose. This is best developed in the area of forecasting, but even here, where the purpose may seem to be clear, there is still debate about how evaluation should be carried out. In one part of economics, evaluation gets a great deal of attention, particularly finance, where again the purpose is usually clear. For other parts of economics, there is not a stated, clear purpose, and so evaluation is not possible. I would classify much of economic theory that way: so that like pure mathematics, it is an intermediate good rather than a final good. At most it can be judged both on intellectual grounds and on how much the results are eventually used in solving realistic problems. Some facets of economics have unclear purposes such as "explaining" or "helping understand" some question in an aspect of economics. Unfortunately, one never knows whether these objectives have been achieved; the fact that an explanation has been provided or that someone believes they understand something better needs further proof and elaboration. I am taking the position that economics is a decision science, so that discussing the decisions made by consumers, investors, traders, families, policymakers, employers, and so forth, suggests a way to judge a model, by asking if the model produces better decisions. This is fairly easy to do in forecasting and finance, at least conceptually, but not so easy elsewhere. It is particularly difficult with cross-sectional models because there is inevitably a time interval between the model producing an outcome and the quality of a decision-maker's rulings being evaluated.

For parts of economics, evaluation is conducted casually, if at all. Real business-cycle models appear to be mostly concerned with the question of how well the model calibrates with some given set of empirical facts and ignores other parts of the available information in the data. General equilibrium models are often "evaluated" by using simulations, and with little or no use of data from the actual economy. All such methods would not be acceptable for evaluation by a statistician.

12. I consider economists as being more imaginative than statisticians, achieving impressive results on a wide range of topics within a single field. They behave like social scientists with mathematical knowledge, whereas statisticians are nearer to being just mathematicians. However, the tools developed by statisticians have been applied successfully in many areas, from demography and politics to medicine and biology, and to meteorology and oceanography. The experiences learned in psychometrics or biometrics, say, can certainly be used by a statistician with some knowledge in these fields to other areas. This potentially gives a statistician a wider perspective than an econometrician. A statistician is likely to bring a successful model from another area and apply it by analogy to economic questions. Sometimes the

idea might be interesting and innovative; on other occasions it will be just bad economics ignoring the behavior of a rational agent.

13. I believe there are major differences in attitude toward research between different subsections of economics. If one compared the research of labor economists with those working in finance, I would say that the first group, concerned with labor, are more explorative, interested in discovering and explaining properties and relationships. Conversely, financial economists are more concerned with direct actions resulting from their work, such as obtaining sufficient capital for a project, managing various forms of risk, and obtaining satisfactory levels of returns while keeping risk low through sound diversification. Financial economists are aware of competition from others, particularly in the current hectic and innovative markets, and so are very interested in new techniques. Promising methods from other areas are considered and applied, such as *chaos*, *neural networks*, *catastrophe theory*, and *extreme value theory*. Some methods will be kept and others discarded. In other parts of economics, the introduction of new procedures proceeds at a more considered, careful pace, such as the use of nonlinear time series models in empirical macroeconomics.

14. I believe statisticians' views toward introducing new procedures are similar to those of financial economists rather than to the majority of economists. The attitude of statisticians is not to use these new methods and to evaluate their success on data, but rather the theoretical properties of the technique are explored and simulations of its use conducted. Only then, if it still seems promising, is it applied to data.

15. A major topic in the writings of economists is policy or control, and many academic papers, both entirely theoretical and those involving empirical models, end with policy prescriptions. Although statisticians certainly realize that their models might be used for policy purposes, this will not generally influence the way the modeling process proceeds. I do not believe that a statistician would consider building a different model depending on the purpose, whereas econometricians certainly traditionally discussed building different models depending on whether they wanted to test a hypothesis or make a forecast or consider a policy. Different models for different uses or a single overall "best" model represents dramatically different methodological approaches.

16. In this section I will compare the activities of two groups with similar training, namely econometricians and statisticians, rather than the two groups so far considered, namely economists and statisticians, whose backgrounds and training are quite different. The main reason for the existence of a subgroup of statisticians with the designation of *econometricians* is that economic data has properties not obviously found elsewhere. Particularly:

a. very high noise/signal ratios, so the quality of the "explanation" can be rather low, even when using a complicated model;

b. high levels of simultaneity in systems. The residuals from a vector autoregression are likely to have high cross-correlations, for example. This suggests that a lot is happening in the economy at short time intervals that is not captured in a reduced form. This may represent a data collection or measurement problem. It is a classical controversy as to whether variables are related strictly simultaneously.

c. Many economic time series are persistent, containing deterministic trends and unit root components, and possibly other so-called long-memory processes. Because of these properties many classical techniques cannot be used, and it has been necessary to develop new methods, based on novel mathematics. Some of these ideas, such as "cointegration," can be linked with basic economic concepts such as some forms of equilibrium. A number of methods developed for economic data have been used successfully in other areas, such as political science and sociology.

All the activities of econometricians rest on basic statistical foundations that have been developed in particular directions to account for the properties of economic data.

Conclusions

I have often found it advantageous to have been trained as a statistician rather than as an economist, as I will come to a problem from a viewpoint different from that of my colleagues. I believe that it is better to have several specifications of a model available to compare and evaluate rather than just one. Team members having different backgrounds are likely to produce such alternative specifications.

The biggest differences this survey has found between economists and statisticians are in the attitudes toward data, toward the correctness of theory, the importance of policy and control, the use of correct evaluation, and the use of realistic experiments. I hope that the two groups will continue to intermingle and learn from each other, like citizens of different countries facing similar problems.

Notes

1. This definition does not correspond to members of the Econometric Society, who can be only mathematically sophisticated economic theorists.

2. There is an encouraging increase in experimental work by economists within laboratories, although unlike marketing researchers, they often do not tackle practical questions. Rather, they concentrate on questions of how to measure utilities, uncertainty puzzles, and game theory.

3. In an earlier life, when I was a professor in England, I was involved in the design and implementation of several experiments using local supermarkets. We changed prices of branded goods by up to 20 percent and observed how sales of that brand changed.

References

Box, G.E.P., and C.M. Jenkins. 1970. *Time Series Analysis, Forecasting and Control.* San Francisco: Holden Day.

Newman, Peter, Murray Milgate, and John Eatwell, eds.

Weatwell, John, Murray Milgate, and Peter Newman, eds. 1987. *The New Palgrave. A Dictionary of Economics.* London: Macmillan.

3

Modeling Economic Behavior with System Dynamics: Theory and Practice

Shlomo Maital

Introduction

For over forty years, a discipline known as *System Dynamics* (SD) has offered a powerful complementary tool for economics. Whereas economics emphasizes the concept of equilibrium, SD stresses almost exclusively the concept of disequilibrium and ways to model it. It has been largely ignored by economics, except for brief periods when economists enlisted to attack the bleak models predicting scenarios of global environmental collapse that SD experts produced (see Meadows et al. 1972)—scenarios that in part appear to be coming true.

Economics and SD should be allies, yet they are foes. The purpose of this chapter is to seek to understand why and to examine how best to remedy this destructive feud.

The structure of the chapter is as follows. First, a brief exposition of the nature and history of SD methodology is presented. Next, this methodology is compared and contrasted with that of economics. Two practical examples are then provided, outlining the diverse approaches of SD and economics to modeling "contagion" and "cascades." These examples include: the global

This chapter was written while the author was visiting professor at the MIT–Sloan School of Management and MIT–Center for Advanced Educational Services. I wish to thank, and absolve, Professor Jim Hines and doctoral candidate Laura Black for their excellent hands-on course on business process modeling. Research for this chapter was supported in part by a grant from the Technion VP Research Fund.

financial crisis (macro); and cyclicality in an R&D-intensive company (micro). Finally, conclusions are drawn regarding how economics and SD can become intellectual allies in the search for a better understanding about how people and organizations behave.

System Dynamics: A Vest-Pocket Description and History

Intellect plays a key role in scientific inquiry, but so does serendipity. When they are joined by standards of rigor and discipline, great ideas often emerge. System Dynamics is an example.

Jay Forrester, inventor of SD, pursued an illustrious career as an MIT electrical engineer and researcher. He holds the basic patent for random-access matrix memory, a key breakthrough for computers, and he designed the computer system for the SAGE early-warning system. When Alfred P. Sloan gave MIT a $10 million grant to fund an "experiment"—launching a business school within an engineering university—Forrester was persuaded to move over to the new Sloan School of Management from the School of Engineering. Forrester, a computer visionary, felt he could not contribute substantively to the business uses of computers, but he did see computing as a powerful tool for understanding complex organizations. His seminal 1958 Harvard Business Review article (Forrester 1958) first described "industrial dynamics," the computer modeling of markets and industries. (See annotated bibliography.)

In the 1960s, the former mayor of Boston, John Collins, chose to spend a sabbatical year at MIT and found himself in a ground-floor office next to Forrester. The two discussed the severe urban problems afflicting Boston and other major metropolises. They decided to try to model the City of Boston, much in the same way that electrical engineers model complex systems, as a kind of wiring diagram—literally, a series of feedback loops. Weekly, key Boston officials visited MIT–Sloan and recounted what they did, how they did it, and how they believed that affected the city and its residents. Forrester and his colleague gradually built a model of Boston, as a series of interlocking feedback loops that grew in complexity. This model grew *not* out of theory or hypotheses, but out of key officials explaining how *they* believed the city worked, and by building step-by-step a simulation model based on the mental constructs of those with hundreds of years in aggregate experience. The project took a year. It resulted in a controversial book, *Urban Dynamics* (Forrester 1969), in which Forrester used his feedback-loop model to reach a conclusion that infuriated liberals: that building public housing in inner cities is the CAUSE of the problem, not the solution. By attracting more low-income people there, without generating sources of employment, poverty is increased and perpetuated, as businesses flee the inner city.

In this model, a kind of "death-spiral" feedback loop emerged, in which growing amounts of public housing generated rising poverty, driving away businesses, and necessitating even more public housing for the growing army of the poor—a process of inherent disequilibrium. Forrester went on to study complex organizations as kinds of wiring diagrams, now gaining adherents and becoming known as *System Dynamics*, applying the technique to the study of companies, in *Industrial Dynamics* (Forrester 1961) and later with his students, to the entire world in *The Limits to Growth* (Meadows et al. 1972). Forrester's long friendship with a former Lincoln Labs engineer named Ken Olson, who left to found the Digital (DEC) Corp., led to a prolonged term as board of directors member for DEC. Forrester used SD to model the cyclical processes confronting Digital's managers in a highly cyclical industry; his model helped him guide Digital and Olson in its formative years. Like other academic disciplines, SD has a scholarly society, a journal, and a doctoral program (principally at MIT).

As its name suggests, SD focuses on the interrelation of parts of a system, and on the dynamic and ever-changing process that links those parts. Although equilibrium is *possible*—in so-called balancing loops—it is not assumed from the outset nor is it the *sine qua non* of theorizing. Most SD models contain a melange of balancing loops and reinforcing loops that embody exponential growth, cyclical sinusoidal fluctuations, and declining negative-exponential growth (death spirals). The focus is on characterizing the *dynamic* behavior of systems that are ever-changing, rather than the distant and usually never-attained equilibrium position.

System Dynamics has proved itself a powerful tool in consulting. In a technique known as "business process modeling" or "group modeling," consultants work with clients to characterize the dynamic behavior of organizations, or parts of them. Together, they build a SD model, first conceptually, then in a form that can be simulated. Sensitivity analysis is conducted to examine the response of the model to changes in key parameters. Key policy variables are identified. As Jay Forrester has often noted, even the simplest of organizations behaves like a 32nd-order differential equation—and who among us is able to comprehend the solution to such an equation mentally? Simulation is essential.

The SD models nearly always reveal surprising insights about organizations and the variables that drive them—including policies that we think work in one direction, but in fact turn out to drive the organization in the precisely opposite direction (not unlike the public-housing policy Forrester studied). I believe that SD is a special case of what Harvard Business School

Professor Robert Kaplan (1998) has called "innovation action learning": a process through which theoretical models are field-tested in companies, modified and improved, written up as $N = 1$ case studies, then tested again, and finally, after at least three such iterations, presented to fellow scholars as articles and books, and to management as useful decision-making tools. The iteration and calibration processes are a key part of SD modeling. Only when an SD model can, for example, closely track the historical evolution of the price of crude oil, is it usable for building future policies and strategies.

Economic Methodology

"Teach me the entire Torah [body of Jewish knowledge] while I stand here on one foot!"

The Talmud, in a famous incident, tells of an impudent individual who approached the two greatest rabbis of the time, Shammai and Hillel, with the same question. Shammai, known to interpret Jewish Law severely, sent him away abruptly. But Hillel, blessed with the quality of mercy and patience, agreed to try.

"Love others like yourself. All the rest of the Torah is commentary," Hillel said.

I sometimes relate this episode to my students, replacing "Torah" with "the entire body of microeconomic theory," and the Golden Rule (love others like yourself), with "Supply equals Demand." From the simplest models to the most complex, from classical to neoclassical to general equilibrium, from micro to macro, economic theory almost universally models the buying and selling sides of markets, then characterizes the conditions under which each of the two sides is happy, and presumes that this indeed will be the ultimate result. The supply-demand cross has been economics' Golden Rule for two centuries. I believe this is true even for models that integrate unconventional, behavioral elements.

Here is University of Michigan Professor (emeritus) Daniel Fusfeld's thumbnail sketch of modern economic theory:

> High theory in economics represents a utopian vision of the market economy of modern capitalism. . . . All markets, including labor markets, are in an equilibrium at which supply equals demand at the market price. New neoclassical macroeconomics defines the level of economic activity at which unemployment is consistent with a stable rate of inflation. The theory of real business cycles shows that the level of economic activity can rise or fall in response to shocks of various kinds without disturbing the general economic equilibrium, as long as market prices are flexible. Equilibrium

growth theory can be added to this picture, defining the rate of growth in terms of population growth and increases in productivity generated by savings and investment. Schumpeter's entrepreneur creates new products, new technologies and new forms of organization. . . . (1999, 222–223)

In short, while economists seek to model *equilibrium* as their prime focus, and at times attempt to pin down the characteristics of that equilibrium (stability, uniqueness, optimality), adherents of SD focus on modeling systemic processes that are largely in disequilibrium by nature, examining the nature of the dynamics and seeking high-leverage policies that would alter them in the desired direction.[1] From this, it is clear how complementary the two disciplines are and how powerful a combined economics-SD tool could be—a subject to which this chapter returns later.

How Economics and System Dynamics Model Systems: Two Examples

In this section, two very different systemic problems are presented, and the approaches of SD and economics to modeling them are compared and contrasted. Those problems are (a) the global financial crisis, which began on July 2, 1997, with Thailand's devaluation, and which continued with Russia's debt default on August 17–18, 1998; and (b) an attempt to model R&D-driven cyclicality at an aerospace firm.

The Global Financial Crisis

The Economic Approach

Consider, for instance, Kuran and Sunstein's (1999) interesting paper on *availability cascades*. An availability cascade is a "self-reinforcing process of collective belief formation by which an expressed perception triggers a chain reaction that gives the perception increasing plausibility through its rising availability in public discourse." Although seemingly implying a disequilibrium process—the very name "cascade" suggests an avalanche, or steamrolling, bandwagon process. In fact, it is a model of multiple equilibria, where groups move from equilibrium A to equilibrium B, often to society's detriment. The Love Canal episode, for instance, moved society from "unconcern with waste dumps" to "extreme concern with waste dumps and toxic waste disposal"—while more serious health risks remained relatively ignored. Demand for Superfund investment rises here, triggering media attention and inducing supply of resources, at the new equilibrium. This is an example of

Figure 3.1   **Multiple Equilibrium: The Global Financial Crisis, 1997–1998**

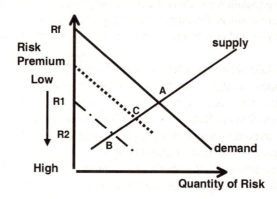

"multiple equilibrium"—a term former treasury secretary Larry Summers used to describe the 1997–1998 global financial crisis (see below).

Or, take Allen and Gale's (1998) model of *financial contagion.* The authors state explicitly that "financial contagion is modeled as an equlibrium phenomenon" and find that in the presence of aggregate uncertainty (translation: financial panic and excessive fear), "the first-best [equilibrium] is not attainable . . ." (p. 4). Basically, the "supply" of risk rises after a bank crisis, and demand for holding such risk responds only after interest-rate premiums soar.

Both the above processes are complex phenomena, with expectations, emotions, and in general psychology underlying them. In a sense, the models describing them are a part of "behavioral economics." Yet I believe the papers describing "cascades" and "contagion"—while brilliantly written and well argued—are unsatisfactory. By accepting the conventional economics straitjacket of demand-supply equilibrium, they fail to focus on the most fascinating element of cascades and contagion: the *disequilibrium* process that creates and sustains them. By focusing on the characterization of equilibrium, scholars are not unlike a small child who buys a pistachio ice cream cone, then discards the ice cream and munches on the waffle cone.

In a May 5, 1999 address at MIT, then-Secretary of the Treasury Larry Summers referred to the global financial crisis, which began with Thailand's devaluation of the baht, from about 25 to the dollar to about 58, beginning in July 1997, and progressed through Russia's default of part of official government debt on August 18, 1998. He specifically called it an instance of "multiple equilibrium." Summers praised the role of basic economic theory, stressed how "economics works," and used the IS-LM model, an equilibrium model, to explain Japan's liquidity trap.

Figure 3.2   **System Dynamics: 'Feedback Loop' Model
of Global Financial Crisis**

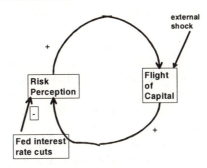

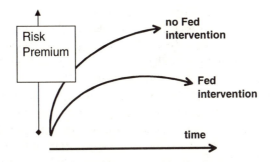

A rudimentary "multiple equilibrium" model of the financial crisis might look as follows: Consider the demand for, and supply of, risk. Let the price of risk (the risk premium: the addition to the risk-free interest rate necessary to persuade investors to hold risky assets, or the addition to the interest-free rate that suppliers of risk are willing to pay) be expressed as an annual percentage (see Fig. 3.1).

The y-axis is inverted, because the higher the risk premium, other things being equal, the greater the demand for risk, and the lower the supply.

The situation in June 1997 and later might be described as follows. Equilibrium is reached at point A. In July 1997, global investors are surprised by Thailand's devaluation, which causes large capital losses to those holding capital in emerging markets, as the effects spread to other parts of Asia. The demand for risk shifts sharply downward, and the risk premium rises from Rf R1 to Rf R2. A new equilibrium is reached, at point B. As market panic calms, during 1999, the demand for risk increases, but the risk premium remains above its level in June 1997, at point C. This is a case of "multiple equilibrium."

The System Dynamics Approach

Now, consider the System Dynamics (SD) approach to modeling the crisis (see Fig. 3.2).

A flight of capital from emerging markets (perhaps generated by an external shock, such as the Thai devaluation and later, Russian default, both of which events signaled their impending arrival long in advance, but nonetheless seemed to surprise global capital markets) increases the perceived riskiness of investing in foreign countries—which in turn leads to a further flight of capital. This is a reinforcing feedback loop, or "death spiral," which leads to continuing and persisting increases in the risk premium. Far from approaching equilibrium, this simple loop has global markets headed toward collapse. Recognizing this, Federal Reserve Chairman Alan Greenspan acts decisively in September 1998, and on three separate occasions, through November, lowers Fed interest rates by a total of ¾ of 1 percent, even though the U.S. economy does not seem to require such a reduction, as a response to global capital-market jitters. This policy stabilizes the perception of risk, and it is later reinforced by a parallel, though much belated, decline in interest rates in Europe, by the new European Central Bank.

Far from modeling the process as a series of leaps from one equilibrium to another, SD (as its name implies) struggles to capture the dynamic disequilibrium process and to model and simulate the time-path followed by complex systems—whether explosive growth, constant decline, cyclical growth, cyclical decline, or persistent constant-amplitude cycles. For instance, an SD model of the global financial crisis might show the continual increase in the risk premium, without Fed intervention, compared to an initial rise, and then decline in the risk premium (bottom panel, Fig. 3.2). In terms often used by Jay Forrester, inventor of SD, the global financial crisis is *a complex dynamic system that probably reflects an underlying 32nd-order differential equation*. Modeling that ever-changing system as a series of comparative statics misses the key point: It is not the fact that the global system stumbles from one crisis to another that is relevant and interesting—but how it gets there from here. The dynamic modeling is essential, because few if any mortals are capable of grasping the complexities of a 32nd-order differential equation mentally, without simulating it numerically.

Cyclicality in R&D-Intensive Firms

> Most new [R&D-intensive] firms fail. Some grow for a while but then stagnate. Still fewer manage to grow but experience periodic crises, often inducing turnover of top management. Only a very small number seem able to grow rapidly and steadily for extended periods of time." (Sterman 2000, 605)

Economic approaches to innovation generally model supply-demand *equilibrium*, and they attempt to pin down the characteristics of that equilibrium (stability, uniqueness, optimality). Among the few exceptions that tend to prove the rule is the model by Bass (1969) and Bass, Krishnan, and Jain (1994) of innovation diffusion, widely used for thirty years, and based on a single differential equation. Few such attempts exist to explicitly model the dynamics of other key parts of the innovation process in ways that generate calibrated, quantitative models susceptible of simulation.

System Dynamics focuses on modeling systemic processes that are largely disequilibrium in nature, examining the nature of the dynamics and seeking high-leverage policies that would alter them in the desired direction (Sterman 2000). If, as Joseph Schumpeter and others argued, the innovation process is inherently "disequilibrium" in nature, economic supply-demand models may be inappropriate, failing to capture the key dynamic nature of innovation (see Grupp 1998).

A version of SD exists that has proved especially valuable in modeling and analyzing innovation dynamics. Known as Business Process Modeling (BPM), it is the application of SD to specific key processes within organizations, and is implemented jointly by a team comprising senior managers internal to the organization and external experts (Roberts 1978; Hines 1987; Sterman, Repenning, and Kofman 1997). In BPM, outside experts elicit the knowledge of internal experts, and together they build, calibrate, and apply dynamic SD models to solve operational problems. The BPM culminates in a computable model driven by a set of time-dependent differential equations, and hence is uniquely suited to capture the subtleties of dynamic change. For example, Keen, Richter, and Rosberg (1998) use SD and BPM to tackle recurring boom-bust cycles at an aerospace firm, with the following characteristics:

1. Delays in production and orders lead to oscillations in demand;
2. Improving operating cost increases demand;
3. Differences in delays and fuel-price shocks lead to mismatches between supply and demand for innovations;
4. Similar cyclicality occurs in manufacturing costs;
5. Depending on oil prices, R&D priority shifts from improvements in manufacturing cost to improvements in operating costs for aircraft;
6. Reducing manufacturing cost may increase operating cost and vice versa.

This cycle greatly impairs the firm's profitability and ability to grow, and is a source of great concern among the firm's senior managers.

Figure 3.3 shows the complex feedback loop diagram used to characterize

Figure 3.3   **System Dynamics and Business Process Modeling: Feedback Loop Diagram for Aerospace Firm Showing How Markets and R&D Interact**

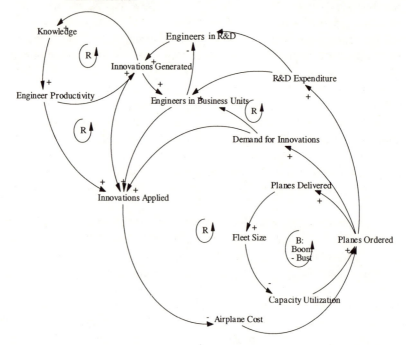

the dynamics of this boom-bust cycle. A boom-bust cycle exists among airlines, when fleets grow excessively and capacity exceeds demand (boom), then shrink as airlines wait for demand to catch up. Layered on this cycle is another cyclical effect: The aerospace firm must allocate R&D resources between cost-saving innovations that reduce aircraft operating costs, and innovations that produce more comfortable, safer, and larger planes. In this decision, engineers are allocated between business units and R&D departments. This allocation must anticipate the preferences of aircraft purchasers, whether primarily for cost-efficiency or comfort, driven in part by the prices of jet fuel, in turn feeding off cyclicality in the global crude-oil market. In the BPM scenario, the model is constructed by building the feedback-loop diagram in a step-by-step fashion together with experienced senior managers, who have lived through the cycles and have a deep intuitive understanding of it. The ultimate degree of complexity is determined by seeking the least complex model capable of capturing the key phenomena that managers describe.

This model can be simulated with a software package known as Vensim (1998), calibrated (fitted to the firm's past history), then used to examine alternate management strategies. The net present value (NPV) graph (Fig. 3.4)

Figure 3.4   **System Dynamics Simulation of Alternate R&D Policies**

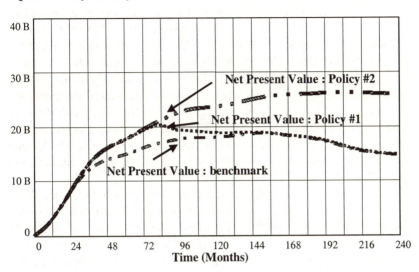

shows how revised R&D policies could help stabilize the firm's NPV over time, while existing strategies lead to an eventual decline in NPV. In today's capital markets, where failure to meet earnings estimates is met by an often drastic decline in stock prices, finding strategies that stabilize earnings has become exceedingly important. Only by harnessing tools like SD to understand the complex dynamics that drive cyclicality can senior management minimize fluctuations in earnings despite the inherently cyclical nature of the industry.

Economics and System Dynamics as Collaborators

How can economics and SD join forces? I believe that Clive Granger (chapter 2, this volume) provides a crucial insight. Economists are searching for the "truth," Granger notes, whereas statisticians "want to try to understand 'data generating processes.'" The statistical methodologies of economics are constrained by economic theories. No such constraints exist in statistics, or in fact in SD.

Thus, SD has been accused of being "measurement without theory." A large part of the economics literature is prone to the charge of "empty theorizing without measurement." Each discipline can provide a partial solution to the lacunae inherent in the other.

System Dynamics is, I believe, ideally suited as a tool for behavioral economics research. As can be seen in our model of the private school, in systems models there is almost always rich, complex interaction among economic, social, and psychological forces. These forces interact in a dynamic fashion. The resulting pattern of changes over time in the organization is modeled by SD, and the impact on this dynamic behavior of changes in key policy variables can be studied. Thus, far from searching for static equilibrium, this approach seeks to characterize dynamic behavior and to find ways it can be altered in desired directions. System Dynamics' skill at simulating dynamic processes provides a valuable "calibration" tool that could allow economics to model how organizations (whether firms, industries, or countries) change and evolve over time. At the same time, economics' skill at theory-building, and the useful basic organizing principle of supply-demand analysis, can provide valuable theoretical balance to the strong measurement bias of SD.

Perhaps more than any other topic, the so-called Kondratieff Long Wave (a 45–60 year cycle in global economic activity) has been identified with SD (Forrester 1971; Sterman 1986). Economics, for the most part, doubts its existence, as the long wave lacks theoretical underpinnings. In his original long-wave paper published in 1926, Kondratieff himself simply noted a statistical observation he had made by analyzing time series, and he made no claim to offer a theoretical explanation (Maital and Maital 1984). The SD models show the existence of a long wave, but the underlying theory—the human tendency toward greed and hence excessive investment—is rather weak. I believe that combining the theoretical insights of, say, the large "endogenous growth" literature with the dynamic-modeling skills of SD could greatly enrich our understanding of our planet's future and how to improve it.

Stalin's denigration of the Pope—how many divisions does he have?—could be applied to SD, which has relatively few "divisions," and to my knowledge only one leading university has a full-fledged academic graduate degree–granting department in SD. Economics has a great many divisions. And it has largely rejected SD. So, let us ask: Where can we find common ground, on which economics and SD can meet creatively?

Perhaps, when a third element is introduced—the social science disciplines, sociology, anthropology, and psychology, which focus on behavior—a powerful triangle is born. The theory of economics can then be combined with behavioral elements to build underpinnings of SD; and SD can be used to enhance and elucidate the dynamic behavior of economic models (Richardson 1991). Just as behavioral economics seeks to integrate economics with other social and behavioral sciences—psychology, sociology, anthropology—so should it now seek to embrace the tool of SD that mainstream economics has rejected. The result—dynamic behavioral economics—will greatly deepen and enrich our understanding of how people, in small and large groups, behave.

Notes

1. Ruttan (chapter 4, this volume) is an exception. By "endogenizing" technical change and in particular, institutional innovation, he and Hayami created a "feedback loop," on both the supply and demand sides, in which technical change was induced rather than imposed exogenously. This exposition of the dynamics of technical change was especially valuable, but it took Economics many years before "endogenous growth" became a serious subdiscipline embraced by growth theorists, replacing the "exogenous growth" theory.

References

Allen, Franklin, and Douglas Gale. 1998. "Financial Contagion." Working paper. CV Starr Center for Applied Economics, RR#98–33, October.
Bass, F. 1969. "A New Product Growth Model for Consumer Durables." *Management Science* 15: 215–227.
Bass, F., T. Krishnan, and D. Jain. 1994. "Why the Bass Model Fits Without Decision Variables." *Marketing Science* 13(3): 203–223.
Forrester, Jay. 1958. "Industrial Dynamics—A Major Breakthrough for Decision Makers." *Harvard Business Review* 36 (4): 37–66.
———. 1961. *Industrial Dynamics*. Cambridge, MA: MIT Press.
———. 1969. *Urban Dynamics*. Portland, OR: Productivity Press.
———. 1971. *World Dynamics*. Portland, OR: Productivity Press.
Fusfeld, Daniel. 1999. *The Age of the Economist*, 8th ed. Reading, MA: Addison-Wesley.
Grupp, Hariolf. 1998. *Foundations of the Economics of Innovation*. Cheltenham, UK: Edward Elgar.
Hines, James. 1987. "Essays in Behavioral Economic Modeling." Unpublished doctoral dissertation, MIT–Sloan School of Management, Cambridge, MA.
Kaplan, Robert. 1998. "Innovation Action Research: Creating New Management Theory and Practice." *Journal of Management Accounting Research* 10: 89–118.
Keen, Shuja U., Karl Richter, and James Rosberg. 1998. "R&D in a Boom-Bust Industry." Unpublished presentation, MIT–Sloan School of Management, Cambridge, MA.
Kuran, Timur, and Cass R. Sunstein. 1999. "Availability Cascades and Risk Regulation." *Stanford Law Review* 51 (4): 683–769.
Maital, Shlomo, and Sharone L. Maital. 1984. *Economic Games People Play*. New York: Basic Books.
Meadows, Donella H., Dennis L. Meadows, Jorgen Randers, and William Behrens III. 1972. *The Limits to Growth*. New York: Universe Books.
Richardson, George. 1991. *Feedback Thought in Social Science and Systems Theory*. Philadelphia: University of Pennsylvania Press.
Roberts, Edward, ed. 1978. *Managerial Applications of System Dynamics*. Portland, OR: Productivity Press.
Sterman, John, 1986. "The Economic Long Wave: Theory and Evidence." *System Dynamics Review* 2(2): 87–125.
———. 2000. *Business Dynamics: Systems Thinking and Modeling for a Complex World*. New York: McGraw-Hill.
Sterman, John, Nelson Repenning, and Fred Kofman. 1997. "Unanticipated Side Ef-

fects of Successful Quality Programs: Exploring a Paradox of Organizational Improvement." *Management Science* 43(4): 501–521.

Vensim PLE (Personal Learning Edition). 1998. *User's Guide Version 3.0.* ©1988–97 Ventana Systems. See: http://www.vensim.com.

Annotated Bibliography

Jay Forrester. 1958. "Industrial Dynamics—A Major Breakthrough for Decision Makers." *Harvard Business Review* 36(4): 37–66. A seminal article on using SD to model companies, industries, and markets.

———. 1961. *Industrial Dynamics.* Cambridge, MA: MIT Press. The first systematic book-length treatment of markets and industries through the SD approach.

———. 1969. *Urban Dynamics.* Portland, OR: Productivity Press. An SD model of cities, showing how public housing exacerbated, rather than solved, the basic problems of inner cities.

———. 1971. *World Dynamics.* Portland, OR: Productivity Press. An ambitious attempt to model the global economy, showing how failure to deal with any of the fundamental economic problems—pollution, excess population growth, underinvestment—can lead to collapse.

———. 1979. "An Alternative Approach to Economic Policy: Macrobehavior from Microstructure." In N.M. Kamrany, and R.H. Day, eds. *Economic Issues of the Day.* Baltimore: Johns Hopkins University Press. An early discussion of—and SD solution for—economics' chronic failure to link macroeconomic systems with underlying microeconomic behavior.

J.B. Homer. 1993. "A System Dynamics Model of National Cocaine Prevalence." *System Dynamics Review* 9(1): 49–78. A behavioral model of addiction.

Donella H. Meadows, Dennis L. Meadows, Jorgen Randers, and William W. Behrens III. 1972. *The Limits to Growth.* New York: Potomac Associates. A follow-up on *World Dynamics,* with bleak prognosis for the world. Arising out of the so-called Club of Rome project; highly controversial.

Alexander Pugh. 1961. *DYNAMO User's Manual.* Cambridge, MA: MIT Press. The original software that Pugh constructed to model systems. Pugh was cofounder of a leading consulting firm, Pugh-Roberts, that used SD as a consulting tool.

George Richardson. 1991. *Feedback Thought in Social Science and Systems Theory.* Philadelphia: University of Pennsylvania Press. By the leading practitioner of SD in social theory.

Edward Roberts, ed. 1978. *Managerial Applications of System Dynamics.* Portland, OR: Productivity Press. An early collection of articles on using system dynamics for corporate decision making.

Peter Senge. 1990. *The Fifth Discipline: The Art and Practice of the Learning Organization.* New York: Doubleday. The bible of systems thinking.

John Sterman. 1986. "The Economic Long Wave: Theory and Evidence." *System Dynamics Review* 2(2): 87–125. Models of SD tend to corroborate Kondratieff's discovery of a 60-year "long wave" business cycle.

Vensim PLE (Personal Learning Edition). User's Guide Version 3.0. ©1988–97 Ventana Systems Inc. The best SD software available. See: http://www.vensim.com.

Eric F. Wolstenholme. 1990. *Systems Enquiry: A System Dynamics Approach.* New York: Wiley. A useful resource, with many real-world examples.

Part II

Comparing Ideas on Economic Development

4

Imperialism and Competition in Anthropology, Sociology, Political Science, and Economics: A Perspective from Development Economics

Vernon W. Ruttan

My interest in the subject emerged out of an interest in the sources of technical change. In research initiated in the early 1970s, Yujiro Hayami and I extended the theory of induced technical change and tested it against the history of agricultural development in the United States and Japan (Hayami and Ruttan [1971] 1985; Binswanger et al. 1978).

Our demonstration that technical change could be treated as largely endogenous does not imply that either agricultural or industrial technology can be left to an "invisible hand" that drives technology along an efficient trajectory determined by differential rates of growth in demand or changes in relative resource endowments. Scientific and technical progress is also driven by an internal logic. But the capacity to advance knowledge in science and technology is itself a product of institutional innovation—"the great invention of the nineteenth century was the invention of the method of invention" (Whitehead 1925, 96).

In work published in the mid-1980s Hayami and I elaborated a theory of institutional innovation in which institutional change is induced, on the demand side, by changes in relative resource endowments and by technical

This chapter is a revision of a paper presented at the annual meeting of the Society for the Advancement of Behavioral Economics, San Diego, California, June 12–14, 1999. The author is indebted to Robet E. Holt and Shoshana Grossbard-Shechtman for comments on an earlier draft of the paper.

Figure 4.1   **Interrelationship Among Changes in Resource Endowments, Cultural Endowments, Technology, and Institutions**

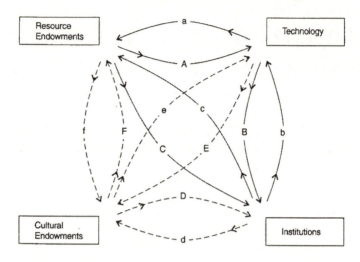

Source: Daniel R. Fusfeld, "The Conceptual Framework of Modern Economics." *Journal of Economic Issues* 14 (March 1980): 1–52.

change and, on the supply side, by changes in cultural endowments and advances in social science knowledge (Ruttan and Hayami 1984; Hayami and Ruttan 1985, 94–110). Beginning in the mid-1980s I initiated a program of research and writing designed to explore in greater depth what development economists should learn from scholars in other nomothetic social sciences—anthropology, sociology, and political science—working in the field of development (Ruttan 1988, 1991, 1992, 1995, 1998). I am now in the process of assembling this and related work in a book tentatively titled *Social Science Knowledge and Economic Development* (Ruttan, Forthcoming).

The elements of a pattern model that maps the relationships among changes in resource endowments, cultural endowments, technology, and institutions is shown in Figure 4.1. The model goes beyond the conventional general equilibrium model in which resource endowments, cultural endowments, institutions and, until recently, technology are treated as exogenous. In the study of long-term economic and social development, however, the relationships among the several variables must be treated as at least partially endogenous.

An advantage of the pattern model is that it helps to identify areas of ignorance. Our capacity to model and test the relationships between changes in resource endowments and technical change is relatively strong. But our capacity to model and test the relationships between change in cultural endowments and either technical or institutional change is relatively weak.

A second advantage of the model is its usefulness in locating the contributions of economists and other social scientists to account for the role of the several sources of change in resource and cultural endowments and of technical and institutional change (Hayami and Ruttan 1985, 110–114).

Let me refer to a few examples. Historians working within the Marxian tradition have tended to view technical change as dominating both institutional and cultural change. In his book *Oriental Despotism* (1957), Karl Wittfogel (mistakenly) viewed the irrigation technology used in wet rice cultivation in East Asia as determining political organization. His primary emphasis was on the impact of resources and technology on institutions—on lines (B) and (C) in Figure 4.1. Douglas North and Robert P. Thomas attempted to explain the growth of Western Europe primarily in terms of changes in property institutions. Population decline in the fourteenth and fifteenth centuries was viewed as a primary factor leading to the demise of feudalism and the rise of the national state—line (C) in Figure 4.1. Mancur Olson has emphasized the proliferation of distributional coalitions as a burden on the diffusion of technology—line (B)—and on the reallocation of resources—line (C)—in Figure 4.1.

The relationships in the lower left-hand corner of Figure 4.1. have received relatively little attention from economists. An important exception is an analysis by Avner Greif (1994, 912–950) of how the differential impact of collectivist cultural endowments of Maghribi traders and the individualistic cultural endowments of Genoese traders—line (D)—influenced the development of commercial institutions in the Mediterranean region in the eleventh and twelfth centuries. In a celebrated article, *"De Gustibus Non Est Disputandum"* Stigler and Becker (1977) insisted that tastes, which I include under the rubric of culture, "neither change capriciously nor differ importantly between people" (1996, 24). More recently Becker (1996) has significantly modified this position. In *Accounting for Tastes* he introduces differences and changes in culture as arguments in a utility function that includes the stock of personal and social capital (1996, 5).

In this chapter I attempt to respond to the question: Will advances in social science knowledge occur more rapidly through multidisciplinary (or interdisciplinary) cooperation or through disciplinary imperialism?

The first post–World War II generation of development economists attached considerable importance, at least at the rhetorical level, to the role of cultural endowments, social structure, and political organization in the process of economic development. But professional opinion did not deal kindly to the reputations of development economists, who made a serious effort to incorporate knowledge from the other social science disciplines into development theory or into the analysis of the development process. The names of Irma Adelman, Peter Bauer, Everett Hagen, Albert Hirschman, Bert Hoselitz, and Gunnar Myrdal come to mind. Their work typically received favorable reviews—and then was promptly ignored.

Anthropology

The economist who attempts to "read anthropology" is confronted by many anthropologies (Marcus and Fischer 1986, 16). In my review (Ruttan 1988) I focused primarily on the "materialist" and "interpretive" schools of anthropology. I drew particularly on the work of Marvin Harris (1968, 1980) as representative of the *materialist school* and Marshall Sahlins (1976) as representative of the *interpretive school.* The polemical style employed in their work has helped sharpen the distinctions that are of interest to development economists.

Materialist Perspectives

Scholars who approach anthropology from a materialist perspective interpret differences in social life and behavior as arising out of universal psychological, economic, and political concerns. Their approach seems, at first instance, congenial to economists. Objectively measurable behavioral elements encompass (a) an infrastructure that includes the ecosystem and the modes of production and reproduction, (b) a structure that includes elements of the domestic and international political economy, and (c) a superstructure that includes both universal (etic) and culturally specific (emic) approaches to interpretation.

This congeniality is illustrated in the exploration, by Marvin Harris, of the differing regional cow demographics in India (Harris 1980, 56). In the southwestern Indian state of Kerala the mortality rate of male calves is much higher than that of female calves. In the northern state of Uttar Pradesh the mortality rate of female calves is much higher than that of male calves. In both areas farmers indicated a strong personal commitment to Hindu prohibitions against the slaughter of domestic cattle. They insisted that they would never kill or starve one of their cattle. Yet economic factors were, in both provinces, powerful indicators of cattle sex ratios. In Kerala, cattle were valued primarily for milk rather than traction. In Uttar Pradesh, cattle were valued primarily for traction rather than for milk. The differences in mortality rates were precisely those that would have been predicted from the analysis based on the neoclassical theory of the firm. Harris's interpretation would have carried more conviction, at least among economists, had he employed the more formal tools of microeconomic analysis and a conventional statistical test of his hypothesis.

Interpretive Perspectives

During the 1960s and 1970s efforts emerged, drawing on a wide range of philosophical perspectives, social science theory, and ethnographic research, to direct anthropology away from the older "cultural anthropology " and "social anthropology" schools and to redirect anthropological theory and ethnographic research "to elucidate how different cultural constructions of reality affect social action." These interpretive approaches involved an explicit rejection of materialist approaches. In Sahlins' words, "anthropology can no longer be content with the idea that custom is merely fetishized utility" (Sahlins 1976, 76). He suggested, somewhat more pungently, that materialist theory assumes that "manure is thicker than blood" (1976, 25).

In a more positive tone, Sahlins argued: "The real issue posed for anthropology . . . is the existence of culture. The utility theories have gone through many changes . . . but always play out the same denouement: the elimination of culture as a distinct object of the discipline. One sees through the variety of these theories two main types: one is naturalist or ecological while the second is utilitarian involving the familiar means-ends calculus of the rational human subject" (1976, 101). He goes on to insist that neither the rationalist nor utilitarian theories have been able to explain fully the anthropological discovery that the creation of meaning is the distinguishing quality of humans.

Implications

I now return to the question that motivated my interest in anthropology: What help can the development economist obtain from anthropology? My response must be ambiguous. The results of the materialist research program are generally consistent with the research by economists. But materialist anthropology has avoided, almost as thoroughly as economics, attempts to understand the sources of change in cultural endowments and the impact of cultural endowments on economic development (Kuran 1995, 328).

Interpretive anthropology, despite its tendency to slip into idealism and romanticism, places the impact of cultural differences and the sources of cultural change at the center of its research agenda. In the long run the results of this focus are likely to become more helpful to development economists than research carried out within the materialist agenda.[1] It is important that interpretive anthropology, if it can recover from its flirtation with deconstruction and avoid the temptation to abandon its commitment to social science, continues to pursue an agenda that will generate a more adequate understanding of the sources and impacts of cultural change. It may not be completely unreasonable to view interpretive anthropology as an attempt to protect the discipline of anthropology from the imperialistic ambitions of economics and sociobiology. Nevertheless, if the interpretive research agenda is successful it will substantially facilitate the ability of economists to collaborate with anthropologists in incorporating the role of cultural endowments into economic development analysis and to utilize that knowledge in institutional design and reform.

Sociology

There are two possible motivations for interest by development economists in research by sociologists. One is the potential use of sociological knowledge by economists who are involved in development planning or policy. Knowledge of the implications of different social structures for response to policy initiatives could improve the effectiveness of project or policy design. A second reason development economists have been interested in sociology is because of a concern about the social impacts of the changes associated with economic growth. Are changes in technology, for example, so disruptive of communal values that they generate resistance to the economic development "project"?

My own answer to the question of "why sociology?" is similar to that of James S. Coleman, the leading social theorist of the last generation: "A major question that a theory of institutions should answer is how, and under what conditions, formal institutional structures come into being?" (Coleman 1990, 337). In my review of the sociological literature on development I gave special attention to modernization theory and dependency theory.

Modernization

When economists began, after World War II, to extend their analysis of economic development they carried with them the economic accounting system that had been developed by pioneers such as Simon Kuznets and Richard Stone, along with the neoclassical microeconomics of Marshall and Hicks and a macroeconomics recently erected by Keynes and his followers. When sociologists entered the same territory they did not bring with them a clear metric of social development. What they did bring was a set of empirical generalizations from classical nineteenth century sociology that characterized the differences between "traditional" and "modern" societies. They also brought with them a "structural-functionalist" or "social systems" theory of organization and action that had been elaborated by Talcott Parsons during the 1930s.

As social research led to a deepening of knowledge about traditional societies Parsons introduced an evolutionary orientation into the structuralist-functionalist model (Parsons 1964, 339–357). In this model even the simplest social system includes four evolutionary essentials: Culture, in the form of religion; communication through language; social organization based on kinship; and technology embodied in artifacts and knowledge. Societies that advance beyond the "primitive" stage of evolution are characterized by development along four evolutionary universals: (1) social stratification and cultural legitimization; (2) bureaucratic organization, money and markets; (3) generalized universalistic norms; and (4) demographic association.

Parsons' evolutionary model provided an attempt to answer this question: What grows in the process of social development? Looking back at the Parsonian system from a late 1990s perspective it appears that Parsons was searching for what economists would term a "general equilibrium model." A basis was established for the pursuit of a more rigorous and productive social development research agenda. Further advances along this line would have required a level of formalization in sociological analysis comparable to that in economics. Sociology as a discipline was not prepared to move to the level of abstraction and formalization implied by such an agenda.

Dependency and Underdevelopment

By the end of the 1960s both the theme of modernization and the evolutionary version of the structuralist-functionalist model had largely been abandoned as guides to research by sociologists concerned with Third World development. Research on the sociology of development became fragmented, as in anthropology, among a plethora of antipositivist, subjectivist, interpretive, and constructionist perspectives. The search for an alternative perspective was the product of profound disillusionment among many social scientists with the impact of Western cultural, political, and military penetration into non-Western societies (Horowitz 1972, 1982).

One response to these concerns was to embrace a new radical macrosociology that owed more to economists and historians, working within a neo-Marxist paradigm, than to work by sociologists. The speed with which this new perspective, variously labeled "underdevelopment theory" or "world systems theory," was embraced by sociologists was surprising, even to many radical critics of modernization theory (Horowitz 1972, 509). To an economist it was particularly surprising how a school of economics, radical political economy, largely ignored or viewed as "bad economics" by mainstream economists, so rapidly established a bridgehead and then set an agenda for theory and policy research in the sociology of development.[2]

The central theme of underdevelopment theory, popularized by the vigorous rhetoric of André Gunder Frank, was that it was world capitalism that created and maintained the conditions of underdevelopment in the Third World—that simultaneously generated both economic development at the center and underdevelopment on the periphery (Frank 1967, 1969). By the mid-1980s commitment to the "development of underdevelopment" perspective had largely eroded. It has, however, continued to retain greater currency in the developed world, even as it had lost much of its intellectual appeal in the developing world, particularly in Latin America, where it had initially exerted its greatest impact on development policy.

Implications

Let me now return to the issue of what development economists can, or should, learn from sociology. My response at this stage is to abandon, for the time being, the search for assistance from metatheory in sociology. I find greater value in research in several areas, which Robert Merton referred as "middle range" research agendas (Merton 1948; Hedström and Swedberg 1998). These include (a) the sociology of science and technology, (b) the sociology of work and production, and (c) the sociology of project design and implementation.

A "new economic sociology" has emerged as a direct challenge to the economic understanding of work, production, and market organization. The pioneering research in this tradition include the studies by Harrison White on labor mobility within organizations, the studies by Mark Granovetter of how labor market participants obtain information, and the research by William Friedland and associates on the organization of agricultural production (White 1970; White and Eccles 1987; Granovetter 1985, 481–451; Swedberg 1990, 78–114). The potential significance of the new economic sociology for development economics is related to the rapid transition from a rural to an urban-industrial labor force in most developing countries. As developing countries make the transition from societies in which the majority of the population live in rural areas to societies in which upwards of 80 percent or more will live in urban areas the issues that are beginning to be addressed by the economic sociologists will become increasingly important.

Political Science

The subject matter of economic development and political development intersect over a broad front. Economic policy is made by incumbent politicians in the context of political institutions. The analysis of the economic impact of alternative policies is the stock in trade of the economist. But there is a deep fault line that divides scholarship in the two fields. Each field tends to treat the knowledge it draws from the other as implicit rather than explicit. Important advances have, however, been made by political scientists and economists, loosely grouped within the collective-choice field of political economy, in advancing our understanding of the processes by which economic resources are translated into political resources and political resources are translated into economic resources. But similar convergence has not yet been achieved among students of political and economic development.

Political Systems

The 1960s was a period of intense intellectual ferment in the field of political science. Insights based on advances in understanding of individual and group behavior, drawing on psychology, sociology, and economics, were incorporated into the theoretical domain of politics. The concept of political system was elaborated and distinguished from changes in the environment in which political activity takes place. New quantitative methods from statistics and econometrics were adapted to explore the relationship between the political system and its environment. The emergence of new states turned the attention of political scientists to applying these advances in theory and method to the problem of mobilizing political resources for nation building and economic development.

By the mid-1970s, however, scholarship in political development found itself facing a series of methodological, empirical, and ideological challenges. The methodological foundation of the major research effort in political development sponsored by the Social Science Research Council Committee on Comparative Politics was characterized as "persuasive discourse"—lacking in an analytic-deductive approach to theory construction and empirical analysis (Holt and Turner 1975). The empirical challenge centered around the continued relevance of the Anglo-American linear model of political development—in which the political development of a country could be measured by its linear distance from the attributes of English and American liberal constitutional democracy. No society could be properly modern in the absence of autonomous individualism, a democratic polity, and market capitalism. And Huntington (1968), in particular, argued that political development should be measured in terms of the strength or capacity of government institutions—as whatever strengthens government institutions.

The ideological challenge was posed by a number of younger political scientists who, like many younger sociologists, were attracted to the dependency or underdevelopment perspective (Duvall 1978).

Political Development

It is difficult to escape a conclusion that the scholars who had been engaged in advancing knowledge in the field of political development have been reluctant to confront the central question of political development—what is it that grows in the process of political development? I have argued in my paper on political development that the most obvious candidate for what grows in political development is power! In the 1950s power was viewed as the central phenomenon to be explained by political science. But the traditional concept of power was as an instrument or resource to alter the behavior of agents. This "limited good" or "zero sum" definition of power was challenged in an insightful, and largely neglected, paper by Talcott Parsons (1963). In Parsons' view, the political system or polity of a society is composed of ways in which the relevant components of the total system are organized to achieve action—that is the "power to" achieve individual and collective goals rather than by the zero sum concept of "power over."

In my paper on political development (Ruttan 1991) I argue that, conceptualized as the "power to," growth in political development can be measured in terms of both its concentration and its distribution. By conceptualizing power in terms of both growth and distribution it is possible to advance two important theoretical propositions about its growth: (1) power that is closely held, or highly concentrated, faces severe constraints on its growth and effective utilization; and (2) power that is loosely held—that is, equally or widely distributed—also faces severe constraints on its growth. In both cases the growth of power, primarily along a single dimension, runs into diminishing returns.

If one accepts these two propositions, then it is possible to maintain that political development has advanced (a) if the amount of power available to a society grows with no worsening of the distribution of power, or (b) as the distribution of power becomes more equal with no decline in the amount of power available to society. By these criteria it seems apparent that political development has decayed in the former Soviet Union and has grown in China over the last several decades.

Imperialism or Cooperation

Several inferences might be drawn from this review of the literature on social science knowledge and economic development. One is that economists should continue to search for the sources of economic development—measured in terms of the growth and distribution of income—without much help from or collaboration with the other social sciences. Processes are underway, however, that are leading toward a synthesis of social science knowledge. Sociobiologist E.O. Wilson has argued that science has embarked on a voyage that will lead to a unification of all knowledge. But he is skeptical that the social science disciplines will willingly venture on such a voyage. "The social sciences will continue the split, . . . already rancorously begun, with one part folding into or becoming continuous with biology and the other fusing with the humanities" (Wilson 1998, 12). My own vision is similar to that articulated by Hirshleifer: "Good economics will also have to be good anthropology and sociology and political science and psychology" (1985, 53). The reciprocal of this view is that good anthropology, good sociology, good political science, and good psychology will have to become good economics. But how can the unification or integration of social science knowledge occur?

There are two options. One is imperialism. A second is cooperation. I will argue that both have different roles to play in the voyage toward unification. Let me first present the argument for imperialism.

Imperialism

The most ambitious colonization effort has been directed, since the mid-1950s, by Gary Becker (Coleman 1993, 169–173; Fuchs 1994, 183–192). Becker has insisted, with great vigor, that the economic approach (Becker 1976, 4) provides a unified framework for understanding all human behavior. He has applied this vision to areas of human behavior as diverse as discrimination against minorities, the analysis of crime and punishment, investment in human capital, and family behavior—including marriage, divorce, and fertility, and the relations between husbands, wives, parents, and children (Becker 1981, 1993). Coleman notes that Becker's work, by focusing on areas viewed by sociologists as strongly insulated from market forces, has contributed to the transformation of entire subfields of sociology by "the introduction into sociological theory and research of the paradigm of rational choice as developed and used in neoclassical economics" (Coleman 1993, 169).

Becker's work on the family represents his most extended and comprehensive exercise into a field previously regarded as almost the exclusive domain of sociology (Becker [1981] 1991). It is also the work that has had the most pervasive impact on how sociology is done. In his research on the family he examines marriage markets, the specialization and division of labor within the household, and the trade-off between the demand for quantity and quality in the nurture and education of children. He also touches on related issues such as the determinants of fertility, intergenerational mobility, the effects of imperfect information on divorce, and altruism within the family.

In each of these areas he has combined rigorous theoretical reasoning with a wide-ranging dialogue between theory and data. A consequence of Becker's research on the family is that it is not possible to conduct serious work in the field of family sociology or, as it is sometimes termed, "the new home economics," without reference to Becker's contributions (Coleman 1993; Grossbard-Shechtman 1993, 7–16).[3]

There are, however, limits to economic imperialism. Hirshleifer has noted that the invasions of neighboring disciplines by economists—whether in sociology, political science, or anthropology—have failed to achieve a complete conquest and have at times been followed by strategic retreat. The initial phase of easy successes has often yielded quick results. But this has often been followed by a second phase. "In the partially conquered new territories, behavior persists that remains difficult to square with the postulate of rational self-interested behavior. Rational self-interested interpretations of intra- and extra-family altruism, the act of voting, and the willingness to provide public goods have been less than fully convincing" (Hirshleifer 1985, 53). After conquering the border regions and collecting the "low hanging fruit" the leader of an invasion often finds it difficult to keep the troops on the frontier rather than to retreat to native territory.

If sociology is conceived as the science of society, all social behavior falls within its domain. Similarly, anthropology, conceived as the science of culture, includes the norms that govern economic relationships. It is somewhat surprising that both disciplines have largely abandoned substantial territory to which they have legitimate claims to economics—which has traditionally laid claim to the limited territory governed by rational choice. If imperialism is to succeed in creating a unified body of social science knowledge it is important that the related disciplines also mount a vigorous campaign to regain lost territory. Among economists, George Akerlof has been particularly aggressive in attempting to import concepts from sociology into economics (Akerlof 1970, 1984). But I would like to see a much more aggressive effort on the part of other social sciences to export concepts to economics. If they are to succeed they must actively begin to occupy the ports of entry into economics. I applaud the perspective expressed by Mark Granovetter, in an interview with Richard Swedberg. "The reason that I concentrate my own efforts on the more hard-core economic matters of production of goods and services is partly polemical, since it seems to me that if one can show that this imperialistic project of economics is not even appropriate within its own domain, then it is of course clear that it would have more difficulty outside of that domain, in the more traditional sociological areas" (Swedberg 1990, 105).

My own sense is that there are a number of entry points where economics is vulnerable. Advances in our understanding of sources and implications of transition from the traditional to the modern family type, in which the family abandons much of its household production activities and specializes in more affective relationships and joint consumption, represent one such point (Ben-Porath 1982, 61; Grossbard-Shechtman and Neuman 1998). A better understanding of decision making by couples, including decisions about labor supply can also benefit from a broader perspective (see, e.g., Grossbard-Shechtman and Neuman 1998). Although political science, as noted earlier, was successfully colonized by the economic theory of public choice, a vigorous reverse colonization has been initiated (Freeman 1989).

Similarly, the sociology of work has begun to occupy territory previously held by economists. And economic anthropology, by linking its commitment to ethnography with the formal tools of microeconomics, could very well reclaim considerable territory that has fallen by default to economics. In my own fields, namely agricultural and development economics, I would like to see anthropology reoccupy the analysis of household-firm behavior in peasant agricultural systems. I see little evidence, however, that anthropologists are inclined to do battle with economists even in an area where their traditional capacities would give them considerable advantage. In contrast, substantial imperialistic energy is being expended by anthropologists in pushing the margin between anthropological and humanistic approaches in the area of "cultural studies" (Clifford 1997, 61).

Cooperation

Let me now turn to conditions under which interdisciplinary or multidisciplinary collaboration or cooperation between economists and other disciplines can be more productive than imperialism—where such collaboration is essential for success. I briefly touch on three examples, ranging from the design of rural development projects in Africa, to the impact of the fundamentalist revival in the world's religions, to my personal experience in the research effort that led to the "seed-fertilizer" or "green revolution" in Asian agriculture.

Integrated Rural Development

In a retrospective assessment of assistance to rural development Lele (1991) found that 75 percent of World Bank–supported rural development projects in East Africa that were initiated between 1974 and 1979 failed. The failures were due to a substantial degree to "a lack of understanding among expatriate personnel of the complex farming systems evolved by African farmers, inadequate knowledge of producer preferences, and an inadequate awareness of the risk-averting responses of subsistence farmers " (Lodewijks 1994, 85). It is hard to avoid a conclusion, given the wealth of sociological and ethnographic literature on East African agriculture, that the incorporation of knowledgeable economic anthropologists and rural sociologists into the project planning teams could not have resulted in at least a modest improvement in project performance.[4]

The Fundamentalism Project

The second example is the Fundamentalism Project carried out over a five-year period (1988 to 1993) under the direction of Martin E. Marty of the University of Chicago Divinity School. The project employed a comparative approach in an attempt to analyze the reasons for the rise and the social and political significance of fundamentalist (and fundamentalist-like) movements in the world's major religions during the late twentieth century.[5]

A common feature of all of the several fundamentalisms is that they arose as a reaction to modern, secular, pluralistic societies in which the cultural constraints and the traditional support networks of rural and preindustrial societies where severely disrupted. Almost all fundamentalisms are grounded in an absolute truth, generally but not always enshrined in a particular holy scripture that is independent of historical change. But they are not simply traditionalist. They tend to be vigorous critics of what they regard as the corruption of traditional religious institutions. Although most set themselves apart from the rest of societies, they also share a common missionary goal to reform and convert society to their way of life. In perusing this objective they have tended to politicize intimate and private issues such as sexuality, family life, and education.

The success of the Fundamentalism Project depended on several factors. The first was concern about the social and political implication of resurgent fundamentalism in the 1970s and 1980s. The emergence during the late twentieth century of religious movements that were "intense, impassioned, separatist, absolutist, authoritarian and militant" was difficult to comprehend by a world that viewed itself as becoming modern, or even "postmodern" (Marty 1996, 24). A second factor in the success of the Fundamentalism Project was the commitment to the project by scholars from a wide range of humanistic and social science disciplines. This commitment was precipitated by the charismatic intellectual entrepreneurship of Martin Marty.

Inventing the Green Revolution

The third example draws on my personal experience as a member of the staff of the International Rice Research Institute (IRRI) in the mid-1960s. The high-yielding rice varieties developed at IRRI, and at cooperating research centers throughout Asia, became the source of the "seed-fertilizer" or "green revolution" in rice production in Asia in the 1970s. At the time I joined IRRI in June 1963 I was the only economist among the eighteen senior scientists on the IRRI staff.

Seminars, attended by senior scientific staff, research scholars, and assistants, were held every Saturday morning. At a seminar held a short time after my arrival, the IRRI director, Robert Chandler, responded to a question about research priorities by pounding on the table and announcing: "The purpose of this institute is not to do good science!" After a shocked silence he continued: "The purpose of this institute is to raise rice yields in Asia!" Then after a pause he added: "And raising rice yields in Asia may require that you do good science!"

My initial reaction was disbelief. The objective struck me as extremely audacious. In retrospect, however, the objective that Chandler set before the IRRI staff was responsible for establishing an IRRI culture (ideology? dogma?) that was largely responsible for the successful development of modern high-yielding rice varieties. The objective of raising rice yields in Asia, when internalized, overrode personal disciplinary loyalties. It helped create an environment in which cooperation across disciplines became routine rather than exceptional.

The lesson that I draw from this and related experiences is that where multiple sources of knowledge must be drawn on to advance knowledge or technology, or for institutional design, both multidisciplinary collaboration and cooperation are important—and possible. Disciplinary imperialism would be destructive of the necessary cooperation. For such cooperation to be effective there must be commitment to an objective that is broader than the subject matter of an individual discipline or a personal research agenda. This commitment does not come easily. The objectives must be regarded as of such overriding importance that the participants will "buy into" the objective of the program.

Notes

1. One of the problems with materialist anthropology is that economists have been able to bring more formal tools to bear on essentially the same problems. See, for example, the Laguna village studies by Hayami and Kikuchi (1982), the North India village studies by Bliss and Stern (1982), and the study of marriage markets by Grossbard (1976, 1978)

2. As an example, in his widely adopted text, *The Sociology of Modernization and Development*, David Harrison (1988) devotes more pages to underdevelopment and world systems theory than to modernization theory. Few of his references are to works by sociologists.

3. Other invasions by Becker into neighboring territory have captured less ground. I have in mind, for example, his early research on the economics of discrimination ([1957] 1971). The essential point of this work is that discrimination occurs when economic agents reveal a willingness to pay for not entering into contracts with other agents, for example, who possess a different religion, skin color, or ethnic origin. This willingness is described by an exogenously given discrimination coefficient. Becker's analysis focused primarily on the economic consequences of discrimination, but he provided little insight into the sociological or cultural factors that determine the magnitude of the discrimination coefficients.

4. For a comprehensive assessment of the consequences of the neglect of sociological knowledge in the design of agricultural development projects, see Cernea (1991).

5. The project involved nearly 200 scholars from the fields of history, political science, sociology, economics, and theology. The product, reported in five volumes, is one of the major scholarly accomplishments of its time (Marty and Appleby 1991; 1993a, 1993b, 1994, 1995).

References

Akerlof, George. 1970. "The Market for 'Lemons': Quality Uncertainty and the Market Mechanism." *Quarterly Journal of Economics* 84: 488–500.

———. 1984. *An Economic Theorist's Book of Tales: Essays That Entertain the Consequences of New Assumptions in Economic Theory.* Cambridge: Cambridge University Press.

Becker, Gary. [1957] (1971). *The Economics of Discrimination.* Chicago: University of Chicago Press.

———. 1976. *The Economic Approach to Human Behavior.* Chicago: University of Chicago Press.

———. [1981] (1991). *A Treatise on the Family.* Cambridge, MA: Harvard University Press.

———. 1993. "The Economic Way of Looking at Behavior." *Journal of Political Economy* 101: 385–409.

———. 1996. *Accounting for Tastes.* Cambridge: Harvard University Press.

Ben-Porath, Yoram 1982. "Economics and the Family-Match or Mismatch? A Review of Becker's 'A Treatise on the Family.'" *Journal of Economic Literature* 20: 52–64.

Binswanger, Hans, et al. 1978. *Induced Innovation: Technology, Institutions and Development.* Baltimore: Johns Hopkins University Press.

Bliss, Christopher, and Nicholas Stern. 1982. *Palanpur: The Economy of an Indian Village.* Oxford: Clarendon Press.

Cernea, Michael. 1991. *Putting People First: Sociological Variables in Rural Development.* 2d ed. New York: Oxford University Press.

Clifford, James. 1997. *Routes: Travel and Translation in the Late Twentieth Century.* Cambridge: MA: Harvard University Press.

Coleman, James. 1990. *Foundations of Social Theory.* Cambridge, MA: Harvard University Press.

———. 1993. "The Impact of Gary Becker's Work on Sociology," *Acta Sociologica* 36: 169–178.

Duvall, Raymond D. 1978. "Dependence and Dependency Theory: Notes Toward

Precision of Concept and Argument." *International Organization* 32: 52–78.

Frank, André. 1967. *Capitalism and Underdevelopment in Latin America*. New York: Monthly Review Press.

———. 1969. *Latin America: Underdevelopment or Revolution: Essays on the Development of Underdevelopment and the Immediate Enemy*. New York: Monthly Review Press.

Freeman, John. 1989. *Democracy and Markets: The Politics of Mixed Economics*. Ithaca, NY: Cornell University Press.

Fuchs, Victor. 1994. "Gary S. Becker: Ideas About Facts." *Journal of Economic Perspectives* 8: 183–192.

Granovetter, Mark. 1985. "Economic Action and Social Structure: A Theory of Embeddedness." *American Journal of Sociology* 91: 481–510.

Greif, Avner. 1994. "Cultural Beliefs and the Organization of Society: A Historical and Theoretical Reflection on Collectivist and Individualist Societies." *Journal of Political Economy* 102: 912–950.

Grossbard, Amyra. 1976. "An Economic Analysis of Polygyny: The Case of Maiduguri." *Current Anthropology* 17: 701–707.

———. 1978. "Toward a Marriage Between Economics and Anthropology and a General Theory of Marriage." *American Economics Review* 68: 33–37.

Grossbard-Shechtman, Shoshana. 1993. *On the Economics of Marriage: A Theory of Marriage, Labor and Divorce*. Boulder, CO: Westview Press.

Grossbard-Shechtman, Shoshana, and Shoshana Neuman. 1998. "The Extra Burden of Moslem Wives: Clues from Israeli Labor Supply." *Economic Development and Cultural Change* 46: 491–517.

Harris, Marvin. 1968. *The Rise of Anthropological Theory: A History of the Theory of Culture*. New York: Thomas Y. Crowell.

———. 1980. *Cultural Materialism: The Struggle for a Science of Culture*. Chicago: University of Chicago Press.

Harrison, David. 1988. *The Sociology of Modernization and Development*. London: Unwin Hyman.

Hedström, Peter, and Richard Swedberg. 1998. "Social Mechanisms: An Introductory Essay." In *Social Mechanisms: An Analytical Approach to Social Theory*, eds. Peter Hedström and Richard Swedberg, 1–31. Cambridge: Cambridge University Press.

Hayami, Yujiro, and Masao Kikuchi. 1982. *Asian Village Economy at the Crossroads: An Economic Approach to Institutional Change*. Baltimore: Johns Hopkins University Press.

Hayami, Yujiro, and Vernon W. Ruttan. [1971] (1985). *Agricultural Development: An International Perspective*. Baltimore: Johns Hopkins University Press.

Hirshleifer, Jack. 1985. "The Expanding Domain of Economics." *American Economic Review* 755: 53–68.

Holt, Robert T., and John E. Turner. 1975. "Crisis and Sequences in Collective Theory Development." *American Political Science Review* 69: 979–994.

Horowitz, Irving. 1972. *Three Worlds of Development: The Theory and Practice of Stratification*. New York: Oxford University Press.

———. 1968. *Political Order in Changing Societies*. New Haven, CT: Yale University Press.

Kuran, Timar. 1995. *Private Truths, Public Lies: The Social Consequences of Preference Falsification*. Cambridge, MA: Harvard University Press.

Lele, Uma, ed. 1991. *Aid to African Agriculture: Lessons from Two Decades of Donors' Experience.* Baltimore: Johns Hopkins University Press.

Lodewijks, John. 1994. "Anthropologists and Economists: Conflict or Cooperation?" *Journal of Economic Methodology* 1: 81–104.

Marcus, George, and Michael Fischer. 1986. *Anthropology as Cultural Critique: An Experimental Moment in the Human Sciences.* Chicago: University of Chicago Press.

Marty, Martin. 1996. "Too Bad We're So Relevant: The Fundamentalism Project Projected." *Bulletin of the American Academy of Arts and Sciences* 59: 22–37.

Marty, Martin, and R. Scott Appleby, eds. 1991. *Fundamentalisms Observed.* Chicago: University of Chicago Press.

———. 1993a. *Fundamentalism and Society: Reclaiming the Sciences, the Family and Education.* Chicago: University of Chicago Press.

———. 1993b. *Fundamentalism and the State: Remaking Politics, Economics and Militance.* Chicago: University of Chicago Press.

———. 1995. *Fundamentalisms Comprehended.* Chicago: University of Chicago Press.

Merton, Robert. 1948. "Discussion [of Talcott Parsons, 'The Position of Sociological Theory']." *American Sociological Review* 13(1): 164–168.

Parsons, Talcott. 1963. "On the Concept of Political Power." *Proceedings of the American Philosophical Society* 3: 232–262.

———. 1964. "Evolutionary Universals in Society." *American Sociological Review* 29: 339–357.

Ruttan, Vernon W., and Yujiro Hayami. 1984. "Toward a Theory of Induced Institutional Innovation." *Journal of Development Studies* 20: 203–222.

———. 1988. "Cultural Endowments and Economic Development: What Can We Learn from Anthropology?" *Economic Development and Cultural Change* 36: S247–S271.

———. 1991. "What Happened to Political Development?" *Economic Development and Cultural Change* 39: 265–291.

———. 1992. "The Sociology of Development and Underdevelopment: Are There Lessons for Economics?" *The International Journal of Sociology of Agriculture and Food/Revista Internacional de Sociologia sobre Agricultura y Alimentos* 2: 17–38.

———. 1995. "Cultural Endowments and Economic Development: Implication for the Chinese Economies." *China Economic Review* 6: 91–104.

———. 1998. "The New Growth Theory and Development Economics: A Survey." *The Journal of Development Studies* 35: 1–26.

———. Forthcoming. *Social Science Knowledge and Economic Development.* Ann Arbor: University of Michigan Press.

Sahlins, Marshall. 1976. *Culture and Practical Reason.* Chicago : University of Chicago Press.

Stigler, George J., and Gary S. Becker. 1977. "De Gustibus Non Est Disputandem." *American Economic Review* 67(2): 76–90.

Swedberg, Richard. 1990. *Economics and Sociology, Redefining Their Boundaries: Conversations with Economists and Sociologists.* Princeton, NJ: Princeton University Press.

White, Harrison. 1970. *Chains of Opportunity: System Models of Mobility in Organizations.* Cambridge, MA: Harvard University Press.

White, Harrison, and R. C. Eccles. 1987. "Producers' Markets." In *The New Palgrave: A Dictionary of Economic Theory and Doctrine*, eds. J. Eatwell et al. London: Macmillan.

Whitehead, Arthur. 1925. *Science and the Modern World.* New York: Macmillan.

Wilson, Edward. 1998. *Consilience: The Unity of Knowledge.* New York: Random House.

Wittfogel, Karl. 1957. *Oriental Despotism: A Comparative Study of Total Power.* New Haven, CT: Yale University Press.

5

The Political Economy of Economic Liberalization: Analytical Approaches from Economics and Political Science

Christopher Clague

Introduction

In the decades immediately following World War II, less-developed countries (LDCs) embarked on programs of industrialization and state-directed economic development, instituting economic policies that were, to put it mildly, at variance with the tenets of orthodox economic theory and advice. The familiar litany of "policy errors" includes the following: import quotas and prohibitions; excessively high and varied import tariffs; price controls on food and other measures discriminating against agriculture; detailed regulation of business activity; fiscal and monetary profligacy leading to inflation; regulations that repressed the financial sector, proliferation of inefficient state-owned enterprises, labor protection laws that reduced flexibility in the labor market, and failure to fulfill the state's essential functions of protecting property rights, enforcing contracts, and providing and maintaining physical infrastructure. Although some of these measures received limited endorsement from the new field of "development economics," the vast majority of economists trained at universities in the rich countries would, if they had examined the policies of typical LDCs, have been highly critical of the de-

This is a revised version of a paper prepared for the 1999 SABE Conference at San Diego State University, June 12–14, 1999. Thanks to Shoshana Grossbard-Shechtman for constructive comments.

gree of state intervention in the economy and the failure to achieve macro-economic balance.

In the last two decades, however, a remarkable change has occurred in direction in economic policies, particularly in Latin America, but also in other parts of the Third World. A large number of LDCs have undertaken "structural adjustment" programs, typically with guidance and funds from the International Monetary Fund (IMF) and World Bank; although many of these programs failed to achieve even modest goals, failure was often followed by renewed attempts, and quite a number of countries have enacted and implemented far-reaching economic reforms aimed at limiting government intervention and strengthening market forces. This chapter addresses these questions: Why have these reforms occurred? What has determined the political decisions affecting the occurrence or nonoccurrence of economic reforms? The topic has attracted a great deal of attention from both economics and political science. In keeping with the theme of this volume, I will try to characterize the differences in approach of the two disciplines.

Although investigators in both disciplines might take this question to be a reasonable starting point for a research project, they might have very different things in mind for a satisfactory answer. Many social science scholars, when observing a wave of policy changes such as this one, would study the individual cases and try to extract generalizations. This is an approach typically taken by political scientists. Other social scientists, typically but not exclusively economists, would scan the cases to compile a list of stylized facts and then see whether they can construct a model. The model would have to be consistent with the stylized facts, *and* with the assumptions of rationality, self-interest, and foresight. The construction of the model is regarded as the important accomplishment, as can be seen from the allocation of effort to that task, as opposed to the study of individual cases, and from the professional rewards allotted to the model builders.

Economists like to think of themselves as scientists, and their image of the scientific method is often derived from what they imagine goes on in the natural sciences. Scientists construct a formal model that is consistent with all the known observations; the model also has implications that have not been observed, and empiricists go into the laboratory to determine whether these implications are confirmed. Of course, in economics, this scientific approach is often a complete charade, in that the models, while consistent with the listed stylized facts, are often blatantly inconsistent with common-sense observations about the way people think and behave.

The judgment as to whether a model makes a scientific contribution is a subtle one. Models necessarily abstract from some aspects of reality, but they can advance the science by bringing to light factors that are not evident in the absence of the model. They can usefully guide further research, even when it is clear that they do not tell the whole story. To illustrate the point, consider the Heckscher-Ohlin model of international trade. The relationship between factor endowments and comparative advantage was sketched by the two Swedish economists who formulated the model early in the twentieth century. The model was worked out in mathematical form during the middle decades of the century, under extremely unrealistic assumptions. Although the model can be very misleading if these assumptions are applied inappropriately, most economists, nevertheless, would say that this model has proven to be very valuable because of its insights into the determinants of comparative advantage and the effects of trade on factor prices. The point is that these insights would not have been evident in the absence of the model. We shall apply this test to formal models of politics and policy reform: Do the models provide insight into real-world phenomena? Do they tell us something about these events that we did not already know?

As mentioned above, our focus is on the political decisions to carry out major programs of economic liberalization and stabilization, and on the insights to be obtained from different approaches to this research question. Several related topics lie outside the purview of this chapter. First, there is a vast economics literature on the appropriate role of government in a market economy, and a substantial literature on the economic effects of liberalization policies, including a very interesting branch on the sequencing of liberalization steps (McKinnon 1982, 1991). In my judgment, there is no question that formal economic models have contributed immensely to our understanding of these issues. One of the questions I pose in this chapter is whether one can say the same about the formal economic models addressing the political decisions to liberalize.

A second question that we shall treat only briefly here is whether economic liberalization along the lines recommended by the IMF and the World Bank is sufficient to produce economic growth in all poor countries. Market-based growth requires a government capable of providing some degree of security of property rights and contract enforcement, as well as physical infrastructure, and some less-developed societies may not be cohesive enough to do that. It may be that some countries' failure to liberalize is due to the correct perceptions of politicians and other policymakers that such policies will not work under present conditions. However, as I will argue below, even if such pessimism about the effects of liberalization turns out to be correct, that has not prevented political leaders from launching liberalization programs.

The rest of this chapter is organized as follows: The section that follows describes the evolution of economic policies in LDCs and presents a list of thirty examples of economic liberalization. This list is designed to illustrate the types of cases discussed in the literature and to present some characterization of the wave of policy reforms. Later sections describe three approaches to the analysis of economic liberalization: the comparative politics approach, the economic modeling approach, and approaches based on ignorance and learning.

Evolution of Economic Policies in Less-Developed Countries

In the years immediately following World War II, most LDCs embarked on government-directed programs of industrialization. The strong shift toward *dirigisme* (state economic planning and control) was certainly influenced by the prevailing ideology of the period, which reflected the world's experience in the Great Depression and the apparent success of the Soviet model of economic planning. In the typical pattern, countries with small public sectors and very little government regulation of economic activity began to increase import tariffs and to impose other import restrictions, to establish state-owned enterprises, and to regulate credit, labor, and goods markets. The import restrictions and budget deficits led to overvalued exchange rates, which hindered exports and discouraged agricultural production. Although these policies could be criticized (and they were, by mainstream economists such as Viner [1953] and Haberler [1959]), overall economic performance in the Third World was by no means bad in the 1950s, 1960s, and 1970s. There was apparently an "easy phase" of import-substituting industrialization, and during the 1970s the stagnation in exports could be offset by a rapid expansion in borrowing from the developed world.

Nevertheless, the policy regimes that emerged had severely harmful economic consequences. Krueger (1993a) describes how controls proliferated as simple regulations were modified to alleviate unintended harmful consequences, and to attempt to catch up with the inventive efforts of the private sector to evade the controls. At the same time, in many countries political mobilization led to dramatic expansion of public bureaucracies, while weak systems of taxation ensured structural budget imbalances. The extensive controls and high tax rates created temptations for bribery and sale of regulatory favors and tax exemptions. Policies that originated in ideological preference came to be buttressed by hard economic interests, in particular those of businesses receiving favors under the control regime, politicians allied with them, and government bureaucrats dispensing favors for cash. This nexus of interests contributed to delays in reforming policies that were clearly not working. Governmental corruption and incompetence fueled public cynicism toward politicians and undermined voluntary compliance with the rules. These weaknesses of the public sector took a terrible toll during the debt crisis of the 1980s.

Table 5.1

Economic Policy Reforms

Country, years	Inflation	Budget	Foreign exchange	Trade	Financial	Privatization	Tax	Labor	Other
Taiwan, early 1960s			X	X			X		
Korea, early 1960s		X	X	X	X				
Brazil, mid-1960s	x	X	X	X	X				
Singapore, late 1960s		X		x					
Indonesia, late 1960s	x	X	X	X	X				
Chile, mid-1970s	x	X	X	X	X	X	X	X	
Uruguay, mid-1970s			X	X	X				
Argentina, mid-1970s	x	X	X	X	X				
Sri Lanka, late 1970s			X	X					
Korea, late 1970s		X	X	X	X				
Turkey, early 1980s	x	X	X	X	X				SOE prices
Jamaica, early 1980s		X	X						
Indonesia, early 1980s		X	X	x	x				
Thailand, early 1980s		X	X		x				
Ghana, early 1980s		X	X	X	X				
Chile, mid-1980s		X	X	X	X	X			Pensions; deregulations
Bolivia, mid-1980s	X	X	X	X	X				
Israel, mid-1980s	X	X	X	x	X				
Gambia, mid-1980s		x	X	x	x				
Mexico, mid-1980s	x	X	X	X	X	X	X	X	SOE prices
Venezuela, late 1980s	x	X	X	X	X	x			Deregulations
Colombia, early 1990s			X	X	x				
Peru, early 1990s	X	X	X	X	x			x	
Argentina, early 1990s	X	X	X	X	x	X	X	X	
Egypt, mid-1990s		x			x	x			

Brazil, mid-1990s

Spain, early 1980s

New Zealand, mid-1980s

Australia, mid-1980s

Portugal, late 1980s

Definition of terms:

Inflation. This column indicates a dramatic reduction in the rate of inflation. Lower-case x means the reduction was less impressive.

Budget. Budgetary reforms are politically sensitive reductions in government expenditure and increases in tax rates. Reforms in tax administration are not included here. Routine adjustments in expenditure, in response to changing economic conditions, are not included here if they did not occasion major political battles.

Foreign exchange. Reform of foreign exchange system includes a politically sensitive devaluation of an overvalued rate (but not the routine adjustment of an adjustable peg) and removing exchange controls on current or capital account transactions. (The wisdom of opening up the capital account may be questioned, but at the time of these reforms, the dominant view of economists, and especially those in the IMF and World Bank, was that this was a desirable step.)

Trade. Trade reforms are reductions in tariffs and the lifting of quantitative restrictions on imports.

Financial. These reforms include raising government-controlled interest rates closer to market-clearing levels, liberalizing regulations on banks, denationalizing banks, and allowing foreign banks to enter. (Many of these reforms suffered from insufficient prudential supervision.)

Privatization. Refers to sale of state-owned enterprises (bank privatization is included in financial reforms).

Tax. Tax reform refers to strengthening of tax administration to increase collections. It does not include changes in tax structure.

Labor. Labor market reforms include lifting restrictions on conditions of employment, including restrictions on laying off workers.

Other. Pension reforms refers to Chile's new individual-account pensions. Deregulation refers to lifting of socially unproductive regulation of business activity. SOE prices refers to raising the prices charged by state-owned enterprises (SOEs) for such things as electricity, water, telephones, and gasoline.

In general, the policy reforms indicated here are those of stabilization of the macroeconomy and of removing excessive intervention in the microeconomy. I did not attempt to identify reforms in the delivery of public services (except for mention of reform of tax administration) or redistributive reforms (such as land reform).

Table 5.2

Political Characteristics of the Reforms

Country, years	Authoritarian government	Democracy	Military coup	Right government	Left government	Crisis	Reform campaign
Taiwan, early 1960s	X			X		X	
Korea, early 1960s	x		x			X	
Brazil, mid-1960s	X		X	X		X	
Singapore, late 1960s		x					
Indonesia, late 1960s	X		X	X		X	
Chile, mid-1970s	X		X	X		X	
Uruguay, mid-1970s	X		X	X		X	
Argentina, mid-1970s	X		X	X		X	
Sri Lanka, late 1970s		X		X			x
Korea, late 1970s	X			X		X	
Turkey, early 1980s	X		x	X		X	
Jamaica, early 1980s		X		X		X	X
Indonesia, early 1980s	X			X			
Thailand, early 1980s		x	X			X	
Ghana, early 1980s	X					X	
Chile, mid-1980s	X	X		X		X	x
Bolivia, mid-1980s		X		X	Pop	X	X
Israel, mid-1980s		X				X	
Gambia, mid-1980s		X				X	
Mexico, mid-1980s	X			X		X	x
Venezuela, late 1980s		X			X?	X	
Colombia, early 1990s		X				No	
Peru, early 1990s		x			X	X	x
Argentina, early 1990s		X			X	X	x
Egypt, mid-1990s	X					X	x

Brazil, mid-1990s	X	X	X
Spain, early 1980s	X	X	X
New Zealand, mid-1980s	X	x	X
Australia, mid-1980s	X	No	X
Portugal, late 1980s	X	No	X

Definition of terms:

Authoritarian government. Countries were classified as either authoritarian or democratic at the time of the launching and the early stages of the reforms. Lower-case letters indicate some ambiguity of classification. Fujimori in Peru was elected democratically in 1990 but staged an auto-coup in 1992.

Military coup. These cases indicate that a dramatic economic reform program followed fairly soon after a military coup. In all these cases, the economy was deteriorating sharply prior to the takeover. (Turkish reform was launched by democratically elected government in January 1980 but ran out of steam prior to military coup of September 1980. Reforms continued under democratically elected government in 1983.)

Right government, Left government. Governments were classified as to ideological orientation on economic policy. Blanks indicate the lack of a clear ideological orientation.

Crisis. In these cases there was a "perceived economic crisis."

Reform campaign. The two Xs in this column indicate that prior to any reform, the successful political party campaigned for market-oriented reforms. Lower case xs indicate cases where, after reforms had been launched, successful political parties campaigned for their continuation or extension.

The emerging field of public choice provided compelling explanations for the "perverse policy syndrome" in LDC (Olson 1965, 1982). The earlier view of the benevolent guardian state, which was implicitly assumed in the literature on economic planning, was replaced by a view of the state as captive of special interests or as the tool of a ruling elite. Formal economic models of special interests dominating economic policy provided explanations for the inability of countries to liberalize (Peltzman 1976; Wellisz and Findlay 1984; but see also North 1984). One of the questions posed in this chapter is how economists and political scientists have explained liberalizing reforms.

The Wave of Reforms

Table 5.1 describes thirty reform experiences in a variety of countries. The list is not exhaustive; it reflects the extent to which particular countries are described in the literature available to me. Table 5.1 identifies reforms in budgetary policies, foreign exchange regulations, trade restrictions, financial sector policies, privatization of state-owned enterprises, tax administration, labor market regulations, and other miscellaneous reforms (state enterprise [SOE] pricing, and deregulation of business activity). A separate column indicates stabilization of hyperinflation or very high inflation. Upper-case Xs indicate major reforms; lower-case xs indicate less impressive ones. Note that continuation of good policies does not count as policy reform: Labor markets in most Asian reformers have been quite free for the entire period, so these policies do not enter the table as reforms. Because the focus of this chapter is on policy reform in LDCs, most of the countries in Table 5.1 fall into that category. At the bottom of the table are four special cases: Australia and New Zealand, which are long-standing developed democracies, and Spain and Portugal, which might be considered less developed, but whose policy reforms were strongly influenced by the prospect of participating in European integration.

A striking feature of many of the reform episodes is the combination of macroeconomic stabilization with extensive liberalization of trade, foreign exchange, and banking regimes. Often these reforms have been implemented within a fairly short period of time. Privatization and labor market reforms are not usually part of the initial package, and they have been extensively implemented only in Chile, Mexico, Argentina, and New Zealand, which are four of the most dramatic reformers in the table. Tax administration reform has been crucial to fiscal discipline in these four cases. However, reform of the tax structure (broadening the base and lowering the rates, and introduction of a value-added tax) is not highly correlated with the cluster of reforms in other areas (Burgess and Stern 1993).

Table 5.1 conveys the impression of a spreading wave of reforms in the less-developed world, with a few reforms starting in the 1960s, quite a few more in the 1970s, and many more in the 1980s and 1990s.

Table 5.2 indicates some political characteristics of the reform episodes. The countries' governments were classified as either authoritarian or democratic, with some ambiguous cases in lower-case letters. The column for "military coup" indicates that the reform program was launched shortly after a military takeover. In all the cases listed in Table 5.2 (except Korea) the economy was deteriorating sharply prior to the coup. The countries were also classified according to their ideological orientation on economic policy (where such orientation was clear).

The first four columns in Table 5.2 display the move toward democratization in the 1980s and 1990s. In the 1960s and 1970s, economic reform was rather strongly identified with rightist governments, and several of the most dramatic turns in a market-oriented direction occurred under military governments following a coup. However, in the 1990s there is an impressive list of reforms launched under democratic governments, only one of which has been reversed due to popular resistance (Venezuela; Naim 1993). Moreover, from the late 1980s on there is a pronounced tendency for reforms to be launched by governments of a leftist political orientation. It is very rare, however, for candidates intending to launch a set of market-oriented economic reforms to campaign on such a platform. One such case, that of the Seaga campaign in Jamaica in 1980, turned out to have a rather high ratio of rhetoric to accomplishment. In eleven other cases (denoted by lower-case xs in this column of the table), candidates or parties campaigned for the continuation of reforms that had already been launched. Four of these involve the special cases mentioned above: two developed democracies (Australia and New Zealand) and two countries seeking access to the European Union (Spain and Portugal). Four of the others involve governments taking credit for ending hyperinflation (Bolivia, Peru, Argentina, and Brazil).

A commonplace in the literature on policy reform is its association with crisis. Some economists have criticized the "crisis hypothesis" on the grounds that the concept of a crisis is not clear, in that the economic circumstances that would be considered a crisis in one country would not be so considered in another (Rodrik 1996; Tommasi and Velasco 1996). Even if we refer to a "perceived crisis," the point is well taken, for the definition of a crisis is quite subjective. Thailand was described as having a sense of crisis when there was a mild run-up of foreign debt and some outflow of domestic capital (Doner and Laothamatas 1994, 420), whereas Ghana went through more than a decade of declining income, rapid inflation, and widespread smuggling of exports before economic reforms were launched. Recognizing the limitations of the concept, I have included a column in Table 5.2 indicating my subjective judgment as to whether the main political actors perceived the existence of a crisis prior to the launching of the reforms. In three cases observers stated that there was no crisis at the time the reforms were initiated, and in five others (the blanks in the crisis column in Table 5.2) there did not seem to be strong indications of a perceived crisis.

Thus, severe deterioration in economic conditions may lead to perceived crisis, which may lead to strong reforms, which may in turn become consolidated into a market-friendly equilibrium. In another pattern, some countries may avoid the *dirigiste* trap altogether. Four countries with low levels of *dirigisme* have not undertaken dramatic reforms, because their policies were not in need of such correction. Malaysia, Barbados, Botswana, and Mauritius have maintained sound market-oriented policies for at least three decades, without ever going through a *dirigiste* phase.

Styles of Explanation

In this chapter I do not attempt to survey the vast literature on the politics of economic liberalization. Instead, I will focus on several prominent strands in the literature: One is based on the conceptual framework and language of comparative politics; another consists of formal models of political and economic interactions; a third emphasizes ignorance and learning about how economic policy affects economic outcomes. In the comparative politics strand, the conceptual framework admits a wide variety of influences, including both society-centered and state-centered determinants of policy choices. The democratic or authoritarian nature of the regime, its class basis, the fragmentation of the party system, the administrative capacity of the government bureaucracy, the configuration of organized interests, the ideology and perceptions of leaders and followers, pressures and examples from abroad, recent experiences with particular policies—all these and others are relevant variables in the analysis. Much of the literature consists of comparing reform episodes and other country experiences with one another to see which influences seem most important. Political scientists are most prominent in this strand, but economists (especially those with field experience) have also made extensive use of this conceptual framework (e.g., see the essays in Haggard and Kaufman 1992; Williamson 1994; Bates and Krueger 1993).

The formal modeling approach to economic policy reform has its roots in public choice and the new political economy (see Meier 1991, especially the essays by Findlay and Grindle). The literature in the 1970s and 1980s provided explanations of policy choices that were individually rational but collectively harmful. As Grindle (1991) points out, this approach, based on a very cynical view of the motivations of politicians and government officials, is not very good at explaining the episodes of policy reform that have occurred. In the 1990s there has emerged a distinctive stream of articles employing noncooperative game theory and purporting to explain why urgently needed reforms are sometimes delayed and why they are sometimes adopted. Most of these reports construct models of economic interests negotiating with each other under rational expectations.

A third approach emphasizes the lack of understanding of how policies affect economic outcomes and the possible learning that may come from experience; Tommasi and Velasco (1996) call this the information-based approach. I include under this rubric both formal models of the process of learning and verbal accounts of how changed perceptions of the world have influenced policy reforms.

The Comparative Politics Approach

One of the interesting questions addressed in the literature on comparative politics is whether democracies or autocracies are better equipped to carry out economic policy reforms. In the 1960s and 1970s a common view was that, in LDCs, autocracies were in general better able than democracies to resist popular pressures and business special interests pushing for policies inimical to economic development. Several types of arguments were presented. Democratic governments were thought to be subject to pressures for government expenditures, especially on behalf of newly mobilized lower-income groups, at the expense of macroeconomic stability. Democratic politicians necessarily had to take a short-run view and please their constituents, whereas secure autocrats could take a longer view and impose the necessary sacrifices on the population. Economic stabilization, according to these common views, imposes short-run costs on workers and business interests, and these interests either prevent stabilization from being initiated or mobilize to impede its implementation. Apart from electoral punishment of reformist administrations, workers and other groups of the urban poor could take to the streets in protest against increases in the price of bread, fuel, or bus service, for example.

During the 1960s and 1970s, employment in government bureaucracies and state enterprises increased dramatically in many LDCs, as such employment was often used to reward party workers and supporters. Business interests benefiting from the import-substituting policies existed in symbiosis with bribe-taking government bureaucrats and party officials. In much conventional wisdom of the time, such a nexus of political and economic interests could be broken only by a modernizing, authoritarian government willing to implement pro-market reforms. Obviously not all authoritarian governments were bent on development, but it was commonly thought that authoritarian governments at least had a chance to implement market-friendly reforms. This conventional wisdom received support from the successes of strong governments in this period in Taiwan, Korea, Indonesia, Chile, and other cases listed in Tables 5.1 and 5.2.

However, careful empirical studies have shown that there was no systematic tendency for authoritarian governments to follow better economic policies than did democratic governments. This empirical finding even holds for the pre-debt-crisis period in Latin America (Remmer 1986). In the wake of the debt crisis, policy reforms have come to be associated with democratic governments more than with authoritarian ones (Remmer 1990, 1993).

The earlier image of the weakness of democratic governments in dealing with economic crisis was often based on society-centered models of politics, in which the state was the passive recipient of pressures coming from social classes and organized interests. This conception of the state is the traditional Marxist view, and it was also embraced by pluralists analyzing democratic politics in the developed democracies. About 1980, however, a movement in political science to "bring the state back in" began to gather increasing support, especially from studies of LDCs. This more state-centered view of politics helps to explain some of the otherwise puzzling experiences with economic liberalization.

In a review of several studies of economic policy reform in Latin America, Geddes (1995) draws three main lessons: (1) authoritarian governments have no advantage over democratic ones in dealing with economic crises; (2) the quality of the state bureaucracy is an important variable in successful implementation of reform; and (3) interest groups and societal pressures were less effective in resisting or promoting reforms than the society-centered models would have predicted.

Resistance to reform is often concentrated in the government administration and its close political supporters, both in democratic and authoritarian regimes. Thus, well-entrenched authoritarian regimes were as likely as democratic ones to persist in the old policy regime. Reform tends to occur when there is a change in regime, because the main losers from reform are no longer in power. This type of regime change can occur when authoritarian regimes replace democratic ones and when new democratic ones replace failed authoritarian ones. It can also arise when reformist elements take over ruling political parties and impose the costs of reform on the ousted elements of the parties (see Geddes 1995, 1999).

The new democratic governments that came to power in the wake of the debt crisis (and the collapse of communism) were expected by many observers to be too weak to cope effectively with the economic hardship being imposed on them. What has surprised many is that the new democracies have not only survived but have successfully implemented substantial economic reforms. Part of the explanation is that the new regimes were able to persuade the electorates to put the blame on the preceding regimes (Stokes 1996). Democracies also benefited from their inherent legitimacy, and the willingness of people to tolerate hardship owes something to the learning from the harsh lessons of the failed policies.

There has been a lively debate between two different perspectives on the route to reform of poorly functioning societies, one represented mainly by economists, and the other mainly by political scientists. The typical economist's perspective is to recommend getting on with the economic policy reforms by whatever political means are at hand. In support of this recommendation, the claim is typically made that successful implementation of the reforms will bring good economic performance that will provide political support for the new set of policies. The other perspective, advanced by *some* political scientists, is that democratic principles should always be respected, and that reforms should proceed with extensive consultation and, if necessary, compromise. This recommendation is often supported by the claim that reforms initiated and implemented by top-down methods will ultimately fail because of their lack of legitimacy.

These two different policy perspectives grow naturally out of the different foci of the two disciplines. Economists spend their days thinking about efficient economic policies and the obstacles to such policies erected by politicians and interest groups. They are aware from their study of the market economy that economic actors often have to accept unpleasant changes in constraints, but these changes are a necessary part of a progressive economy. If decisions to innovate or to close plants were made by consensus of all interested parties, progress would be impossible. Political scientists, in contrast, have spent time thinking about the conditions for social order and the circumstances under which order breaks down. They have seen that consultation and compromise are the essence of democratic politics. It should hardly be surprising that analysts' policy preferences influence the way they interpret the case-study materials.[1]

What light does recent experience shed on this ongoing debate? In my view, a great deal of experience supports the economists' view that macroeconomic policy reforms are not typically the product of prior consensus (Sachs 1994). Table 5.2 shows that a large number of reforms were launched and implemented under authoritarian governments; in virtually all of these cases, there was little consultation with interest groups until the reforms had passed the implementation stage. (Mexico is an exception to this statement, as the Pact for Economic Solidarity of 1987 was an important step in the implementation of the reforms there.) In the countries that were democracies at the time of the launching of the reforms, again it was rare for there to be consensus on the nature of the reforms. Only in Jamaica and possibly Sri Lanka did the reformist party campaign on a platform of market-oriented policies prior to the reforms. Parties did claim credit for stopping inflation in hyperinflation countries (Argentina, Brazil, Peru, Bolivia), and the Institutional Revolutionary Party (PRI) in Mexico took credit in 1994 for successful economic management (until the election!). In the four special cases at the bottom of Table 5.2 (Spain, New Zealand, Australia, Portugal), parties claimed credit for economic reforms after the fact. But the point remains that the launching of macroeconomic reforms was typically undertaken without a great deal of consultation among affected interest groups or the population at large, and in some cases the economic success of the reforms brought political support.

Conversely, in support of the political scientists' position described above, top-down macroeconomic reforms have often failed to produce economic progress and political stability. Violating the democratic norms of consultation and participation in the imposition of austerity and liberalization may not help economic performance, in countries where the basic institutions supporting market-friendly development are absent. Of course, in such countries it is not obvious that democratic processes of consultation and participation will produce progress, either, especially in an environment of *dirigisme* and macroeconomic instability.

This sample of insights from the comparative politics literature illustrates some characteristics of that literature. There are no clean generalizations to be made, as all general statements in this area have exceptions. The conclusions from the literature are derived from careful study of many individual cases and from comparisons among them. The case studies give rise to a change in emphasis on the variables that matter, and to moderate revisions in the theoretical lenses through which events are viewed. For example, the new emphasis on the state as an actor does not deny that interest groups and social class are sometimes powerful forces.

To summarize, politics is complicated. Outcomes depend on many factors: class structure, civil society, political institutions, ideology, experience in peer countries, recent country experience, international economic constraints and opportunities, administrative institutions, to name a few. Although political reality is complex, careful comparison of cases does produce insights.

The Economic Modeling of Policy Reform

Two excellent surveys of the economic modeling approach are Rodrik (1996) and Tommasi and Velasco (1996), and many of the most important papers are collected in the recent book edited by Sturzenegger and Tommasi (1998). It is interesting to see how the tillers of this particular field of inquiry describe their task. In their introduction, Sturzenegger and Tommasi state:

> What distinguishes these papers from the previous literature, as well as from the traditional political science literature, is the application of common standards of analytical rigor to economic and political behavior. That is, political agents and groups are assumed to be rational and forward-looking, with expectations that are consistent with the properties of the underlying model. Behavioral rules are derived by solving optimization problems with well-defined objective functions. . . .
>
> The political-economic outcome is derived as a Nash equilibrium in which each individual or group is doing the best it can given the actions of others. Consequently, reforms are viewed as the establishment of institutions that provide incentives for individual decisions makers to behave in ways that are collectively desirable. (pp. 2–3)

Drazen in an article section titled "The Road Not Taken" considers alternative approaches to the explanation of delayed reform. These approaches are based on the assumptions of ignorance of how to reform, lack of technical expertise to implement reforms, belief that benign neglect will solve the problem, and irrationality. Drazen acknowledges that each of these may have some relevance in particular situations, but explanations based on such assumptions are, in his view, unsatisfactory.[2] He states:

> Our *raison d'etre* as economists is to take phenomena which have resisted a logical explanation and explain them in a coherent, consistent framework. In the specific area of political economy, the goal is to show how policies which seem sub-optimal (hence, irrational in terms of basic welfare economics) can in fact be shown to be the result of the political mechanism under which the decisions of rational, self-interested agents are aggregated. (1996, 31)

These quotations illustrate very clearly what some economists regard as their job: to construct a model consistent with a set of stylized facts, and also consistent with the standard economist assumptions of self-interest, rationality, and foresight. Let us see what insights have come from this approach. In this section I consider models of conflicting economic interests negotiating with each other under rational expectations. In the section after that I shall consider approaches based on ignorance and learning.

The Interest-Based Approach

In a section on the political economy of macroeconomic cycles, Rodrik (1996, 21–25) observes that many countries have gone through repeated cycles of inflation and attempts at stabilization, with severely adverse consequences for the entire economy. A typical pattern is deficit spending, accompanied by an overvalued exchange rate, current account deficit and consequent buildup of foreign debt. The policies are clearly unsustainable and harmful. Why are they pursued? Rodrik criticizes Bates (1994) for assuming that all economic policies serve the interests of one powerful group or another, whereas these policies are not in the interests of anyone. He takes Ranis and Mahmood (1992) and Krueger (1993a) to task for explicitly or implicitly assuming that decision makers are myopic. The new literature confronts the challenge of explaining the persistence of unsustainable and harmful policies without resorting to myopia or ignorance on the part of decision makers. The much-cited paper by Alesina and Drazen (1991) presents a "war-of-attrition" model of two groups who understand the economic and political situation quite thoroughly, including the feasibility and desirability of agreeing on a stabilization program. The only uncertainty in the model is that each group does not know how much the other group is suffering as the delay continues. Agreement on stabilization comes when one group caves in and agrees to bear a disproportionate share of the costs of stabilization. Although the mathematics (which are quite complicated) can refer to any two groups and any policy issue, the paper reviews some of the inflation and stabilization experiences of Germany, France, and eastern European countries in the 1920s, where the two groups are identified as *capital* and *labor*. The model does fit several of the facts about these episodes; in successful stabilizations, parties representing capital have come to power. The model also predicts that stabilization will be delayed longer in more polarized societies; polarization is captured in the model by the degree of inequality in the sharing of the burden of stabilization.

An extension of this war-of-attrition model is in Laban and Sturzenegger (1994). They allow for "financial adaptation" by the rich; that is, the rich (but not the poor) can escape the inflation tax (at a fixed cost) by sending their money abroad. As inflation accelerates, the cost of the status quo increases more for the poor than for the rich, and the poor capitulate and agree to bear a large share of the stabilization burden.

There is also an ingenious model by Perotti (1992), in which there are three groups, the rich, the poor, and the middle class. The rich can escape the inflation tax through financial adaptation, and the poor pay the inflation tax but are too poor to be subject to ordinary direct or indirect taxation. The middle class cannot engage in financial adaptation and cannot escape direct and indirect taxation. In this model, the rich and the poor combine to enact populist policies that they know cannot be sustained, because the main costs of the ensuing stabilization will be borne by the middle class.

Notice that these economic theorists have been constructing a lot of society-centered models, at the same time that those working in the field of comparative politics (which includes some economists, as mentioned above) have been emphasizing the importance of the state. What have we actually learned from these interest-based models? We have learned that it is possible to construct models consistent with certain stylized facts. But does this fact persuade us that the variables in the models are more important than we had previously thought? Do they provide insight into the operation of these variables? We already knew that labor organizations and parties representing different social classes play some role in determining economic policy. Do these models advance our understanding of the circumstances in which their influences will be decisive? I believe the Perotti (1992) model very cleverly fits a number of stylized facts, but the political mechanism strikes me as very implausible. Which episodes of populism does this model illuminate?

I will illustrate my point with an analysis of the delayed stabilization model of Alesina and Drazen (AD) (1991). Although the authors describe a number of historical examples that display features that are consistent with their model, in my judgment the model fails to give substantial insight into these or other stabilization episodes. My first criticism is conceptual. What exactly do we mean by a *war of attrition*? We should distinguish a war of attrition from a rule-bound contest. In a *rule-bound contest*, one side emerges victorious according to the rules of the game, as in a sports contest or a vote in a committee or cabinet. A key feature of a war of attrition is that the struggle does not end until one of two things happens: one side concedes, or one side runs out of resources and is *unable* to continue fighting. Good examples of wars of attrition are labor strikes and guerrilla wars. But it is far from clear that stabilization struggles are wars of attrition. Programs are typically enacted following a political victory, either in an election or a political realignment without an election. To determine whether or not there is a war of attrition, we have to ask whether the losing side voluntarily conceded or was simply defeated according to the rules of the political game.

Next, there is the issue of the number of players in the contest. The AD model states that their model can be generalized to more than two players, but this aspect is not developed in their paper. In a footnote they mention that in a more general approach there could be n groups; if one group concedes, there is then a second war of attrition among the $n-1$ remaining groups. They say that they have not explored the implications of this model. But the conception raises the obvious problem: What prevents the group that concedes first from changing its mind while the others continue the struggle? More fundamentally, isn't it rather clear that in multiparty negotiations, no one party concedes until there is general agreement?

My third criticism concerns the nature of the players. In the stabilization struggles in France and Germany in the 1920s, the players included political parties, economic interest groups, and foreign powers (Maier 1975, 1987). The parties and the interest groups were composed of leaders and followers. The parties were relatively well organized, but of course they were not monolithic. Leaders could not count on delivering their followers. Moreover, it is quite clear that the information available to the leaders was more complete than that available to voters and party members. A classic problem facing political leaders in stabilization dramas is that seeking a compromise risks alienating one's followers (who do not appreciate the severity of the constraints) and being replaced by a more militant colleague. The AD model ignores this aspect of the situation by assuming that each side is monolithic.

The fourth point is to call attention to the enormous uncertainty surrounding stabilization dramas. The AD assumption that each side knows all the political and economic realities except for the cost of waiting on the other side is wildly off the mark. The historical episodes reveal that actors routinely fail to anticipate major economic and political events and mispredict the consequences of their own programs.[3] As events unfold, leaders and followers change their perceptions of the constraints and the opportunities. A common pattern is that when a particular party or leader or worldview is dominant for a time and is seen to have failed, people try alternatives.[4] While ignoring all of this uncertainty, the AD model assumes that the parties learn nothing from talking with one another; actions are all that matter, and each party makes its best choice given what it assumes about the decision function of the other party.

I think we already suspected that societies polarized by ethnic division and social and economic inequality are less likely to respond constructively to economic crisis. How has our understanding of this phenomenon been advanced by the fact that Alesina and Drazen were able to include a polarization parameter in their war-of-attrition model?

My purpose is not to discredit the construction of economic models. Even highly abstract models can provide insight not otherwise available, as illustrated by the example of the Heckscher-Ohlin model, and many other models in economics and political science. My point is to press forward a question that seems not to have been asked frequently enough: Does the model tell us something (about the real world) that we did not already know?

Approaches Based on Ignorance and Learning

Suppose we start from the assumption of widespread ignorance about the effects of specific economic policies. This assumption does not seem hard to justify. Economists may have confidence that market-friendly policies are conducive to economic growth in the long run, but the economy is driven by many factors over which policymakers have no control and limited ability to predict. Therefore, politicians, interest group representatives, and the general public are right to be skeptical of scenarios laid out by economist advisers. Some of these actors do have an understanding of some basic economic principles, but much of the general public remains woefully ignorant of them, even in the developed democracies where markets function well.

Under the assumption of widespread ignorance, it is highly plausible that economic policy decisions would be based on accidents of recent history. For example, a populist regime could lead the country to disaster, and a new government, by restoring economic growth with a stabilization program, could acquire the political support to implement structural reforms. Bhagwati has called this "learning by undoing" (cited in Meier 1991, 312).

An interesting example of the political effects of failed strategies is noted by Kiguel and Liviatan (1995, 390–391) in their study of stopping hyperinflation in Latin America. The stabilization plans in Argentina, Brazil, and Peru, launched in 1989 and 1990, all downplayed income policies and exchange-rate anchors, precisely because these were identified with prior failed programs.

The "Nixon in China" syndrome is a pattern that seems to be best explained by the information content of the politician's change of position. When a politician who has been strongly identified with a particular viewpoint reverses position, he sends a message to followers and opposition alike that he believes the new position will serve the country well. The public may quite rationally conclude that the politician has information not available to them and that he would not be changing his position were it not in the general interest. A model of this phenomenon is presented in Cukierman and Tommasi (1998). Table 5.1 lists quite a number of countries in which left-leaning or populist leaders in Latin America have initiated reforms: Paz Estenssoro in Bolivia, Perez in Venezuela, Fujimori in Peru, Menem in Argentina, and Cardoso in Brazil. In addition, it was the Socialist Party in Spain and the Labor parties in New Zealand and Australia that launched their reform programs.

Anyone who has been talking with Latin American economists over the past several decades is aware of the enormous change in Zeitgeist.[5] Views that were prominent in earlier decades—those favoring protectionism, restrictions on direct foreign investment, exchange controls,[6] government planning, self-sufficiency, economic autonomy—are seldom expressed any more by economists. Currently, the positions taken by the Economic Commission for Latin America and the Caribbean (ECLAC) on economic policy are not very different from those of the World Bank.

In earlier decades Latin American intellectuals were not interested in the success stories coming out of East Asia. Sebastian Edwards (1995, 321, footnote 7) observes that between 1960 and 1980 not a single article on East Asian experience appeared in *El Trimestre Economico*, one of Latin America's most prestigious economics journals. This parochialism has greatly diminished, as scholars in Latin America asked themselves why government-directed industrialization in their countries has turned out so differently from apparently similar programs in Asia.

Tommasi and Velasco cite the views of Mario Vargas Llosa, the Peruvian novelist, newly converted to free markets, who was defeated by Fujimori in the 1990 presidential election in Peru:

> [An] intellectual revolution has taken place in Latin America. For the first time in our history there is a broad consensus in favor of a predominant role for civil society and private enterprise: a consensus in favor of privatization not only in the economic sphere, but in the institutional life of society as well. (1996, 200)

In the late 1980s, Hernando de Soto's *The Other Path* (1989) became one of the best-selling books in Latin America. This work attributes the large size of the informal sector in Latin America to the cumbersome and corrupt system of regulation of the formal business sector. The author called for government agencies to pull back from excessive regulation and at the same time to strengthen and simplify property and contract registration so that small enterprises could take advantage of formal protection of their rights.

Of course, persuading the intellectuals is not the same thing as conquering the interest groups. All the major political parties seem to have accepted market-friendly policies in Chile, but in other countries there is room for doubt as to whether the reforms will be continued and deepened, or reversed. An interesting paradox of the market-oriented developed democracies is the lack of appreciation of economic principles in the general public. How do these countries manage to retain their liberal economic regimes? Why don't economic populists such as Pat Buchanan and Ross Perot have more impact than they do?

In my judgment, some economists have a tendency to exaggerate popular understanding of the effects of economic policies. As an example, let us consider the literature on the "electoral business cycle." The theory that politicians manipulate fiscal and monetary policy for their electoral advantage appeared in the 1970s, shortly before the notion of rational expectations took hold of the macroeconomics debate. The early models of the electoral business cycle found some evidence in its favor, but it did not come close to explaining actual policies in the developed democracies. Now a new literature (Alesina 1994; Alesina and Roubini 1997) claims to find evidence that supports rational expectations on the part of the public, so that politicians cannot successfully manipulate policy to their electoral advantage. I cannot criticize the econometrics, but I find this account hard to believe.

Some evidence against voter sophistication has been nicely summarized by Paldam (1997, 346), who describes five robust results on voter behavior in industrialized countries.

1. The responsibility hypothesis. Voters hold the government responsible for economic conditions, but this does not work in countries with many minority governments. It works in a two-party or two-block system.
2. The two important variables for voters are inflation and unemployment.
3. Voters are myopic. The effect of changing economic variables on voter choices is of a short duration. The period is generally less than a year.
4. Voters' expectations are retrospective. Studies have tried to determine whether voters react to expected economic conditions or past experiences, but such studies have always found that it makes no difference because voters' expectations are static.
5. To rule costs popularity.

Paldam goes on to point out that there is nothing nonrational about not acquiring information that is of no personal use. These voter characteristics would seem to be quite compatible with the original version of the electoral business cycle.[7] How then can we account for the weak evidence in favor of this model?

I would say that we should never have taken the model as the whole story of the determination of monetary and fiscal policies. The hypothesis would be more plausible if it were stated in this form: At times politicians will manipulate policies to their electoral advantage by taking advantage of the ignorance of the voters. However, even this hypothesis seems to be less true in the developed countries now than it was a few decades ago. I would guess that the explanation lies in the fact that political actors have come to have a greater appreciation of the desirability of economically sound policies, and as a result they have constructed political institutions that limit the ability of populists to gain electoral advantage. The creation of an independent Central Bank is an obvious example. Others are the Congressional Budget Office and commissions to close military bases.

The creation and maintenance of such institutions depends in part on the understanding and appreciation of economic principles, not by ordinary voters or party members, but by political elites, including leaders of interest groups and political parties. These political actors are in communication with one another, and on occasion they can reach a mutual understanding and bring their followers along. Reaching an agreement on sound economic policies is influenced by the prevailing ideologies of the day. The ideological environment was hostile to free markets in Peru in the early 1980s (according to Webb 1994), but it had clearly become much more favorable under Fujimori in the 1990s. In Bolivia, the ideological confrontation among the political parties gave way to a consensus on neoliberal reforms, following the collapse of alternative strategies.

This interpretation that a changed ideological climate played a contributing role in economic policy reform is consistent with the timing of the reforms (see Table 5.1). The reforms started mainly in Asia. The Latin American reforms in Brazil in 1964 and in the Southern Cone in the 1970s were tarnished by their identification with harsh military dictatorships. By the middle 1980s, *dirigisme* and fiscal imbalance had been thoroughly discredited by the punishment meted out in the debt crisis. Moreover, by this time, Chile's success had become apparent, and Asia had easily handled the external events that had triggered the debt crisis in Latin America.

Concluding Observations

Politics is a complicated business. It is no accident that formal models of politics are not as convincing as economists' models of the economy. At the heart of the complexity of politics lies the very uneven dispersion of information about what other political actors know and are planning to do. Much of the time political decisions are taken by very few people, who rely on the passivity of the general public and of members of organizations. But at specific moments, larger numbers of people take an interest in what is going on, and they weigh in with tremendous force.[8] Predicting such reactions is extremely difficult, as political experts and consultants concede.

The economy is also complicated, but I believe that specialized training in economics does help to understand and even predict the consequences of economic policies. Because most political actors, including the general public, lack this specialized training, their views on economic policies can shift dramatically as a result of experiences and interpretations of these experiences put forward by political leaders. Thus, as illustrated in the recent book on "technopols"[9] edited by Jorge Dominguez (1997), economists can play an extremely useful role in promoting economic reform by using both their communications skills and their economic expertise.

This chapter has suggested that part of the explanation for the wave of economic liberalization in the Third World is that some economic learning has taken place, both among the general public and among political leaders. This suggestion is not novel; for example, a chapter in Edwards (1995), "The Emergence of a New Latin American Consensus," describes the intellectual shift that has taken place there and its impact on economic policy. It is striking that a branch of the literature on economic policy reform models the process on the extremely unrealistic assumption that the actors are all well informed about the effects of different economic policies. In my judgment, not much insight has been contributed by this branch. Economist observers, along with political scientists, have conducted very useful studies of liberalization episodes and have contributed to a body of knowledge about their determinants. But as yet we are a long way from a formal theory of politics.

A recent survey of the impact of economics on political science (Miller 1997) concluded that, while economics had profoundly influenced political science by offering mathematical models based on rational choice, the substantive conclusions derived from the early economist models have not stood up well to subsequent empirical and theoretical analysis. Progress in both disciplines is now being made in understanding formal and informal institutions and the social norms and ideologies that support them. This type of research is likely to be the most promising avenue for further progress in understanding economic policy reform.

Notes

1. A few decades ago, political scientists as a group were much less convinced of the virtues of market-oriented policies than economists were. Some were even naïve enough about economics to praise the policies of economic populists, such as Roett did of Alan Garcia (Roett 1986). There are still many political scientists who are highly critical of the top-down imposition of Washington-Consensus type reforms (e.g., Smith, Acuna, and Gamarra 1994a, 1994b; Bresser et al. 1993). However, there is a group of prominent and influential political scientists who understand as well as anyone the pros and cons of the concentration of authority for the purpose of launching economic reforms, and who cannot be faulted for their lack of appreciation of markets (e.g., Bates, Geddes, Haggard, Kahler, Kaufman, Nelson, Stallings).

2. The assumption that economic and political actors have the same information on which to base expectations about economic and political outcomes underlies a branch of the literature on political business cycles. See Alesina and Roubini (1997).

3. Michael Bruno (1993) observes that everyone was surprised when real wages increased shortly after the launching of Israel's stabilization program in 1985.

4. In France in 1924 the policy of softness toward Germany was seen to have failed and its proponents were discredited.

5. The economic advisers to Alan Garcia upon his inauguration in 1985 believed that economic orthodoxy had been shown to have failed in Peru. They advocated extensive government intervention in the markets for goods, credit, and foreign exchange as a matter of principle. They also believed that fiscal deficits that transferred purchasing power to the poor would enable firms to lower unit costs, thereby reducing inflation. For more on their views and the resulting disaster, see Lago (1991).

6. Recent financial crises in Mexico in 1994 and Asia in 1997 have encouraged rethinking of the wisdom for LDCs of removing all barriers to the free movement of

international capital. But this revision of free-market doctrine is still a long way from the pro-exchange-control views common in the heyday of *dirigisme*.

7. Ames (1987) found ample evidence of electoral effects on fiscal policy in Latin America in the period from 1965 to 1975. Krueger (1993b, 359) remarks that in Turkey in the 1980s transfer payments increased several times, just prior to elections. Kaufman (1990, 110) observes that electoral cycles had a powerful impact on spending in Argentina, Brazil, and Mexico in the 1980s.

8. Hirschman (1974) has an interesting discussion of why political outcomes are so hard to predict. Preferences with regard to participation in public affairs are much more unstable than preferences regarding private goods, in part because the cost of participation may turn into a benefit, through the "happiness of pursuit."

9. A "technopol" is a technocrat who becomes a politician.

References

Alesina, Alberto. 1994. "Political Models of Macroeconomic Policy and Fiscal Reforms." In Stephan Haggard and Steven Webb, eds., *Voting for Reform*, pp. 37–60. New York: Oxford University Press.

Alesina, Alberto, and Allan Drazen. 1991. "Why Are Stabilizations Delayed?" *American Economic Review* 81: 1170–1186 (Reprinted in 1998 in Sturzenegger and Tommasi, *The Political Economy of Reform*).

Alesina, Alberto, and Nouriel Roubini. 1997. *Political Cycles and the Macroeconomy.* Cambridge, MA: MIT Press.

Ames, Barry. 1987. *Political Survival: Politicians and Public Policy in Latin America.* Berkeley: University of California Press.

Bates, Robert H. 1994. "Comment." In John Williamson, ed., *Political Economy of Policy Reform*, pp. 29–33. Washington, DC: Institute for International Economics.

Bates, Robert H., and Anne O. Krueger, eds. 1993. *Political and Economic Interactions in Economic Policy Reform: Evidence from Eight Countries.* Oxford: Basil Blackwell.

Bresser Pereira, Luiz Carlos, Jose Maria Maravall, and Adam Przeworski. 1993. *Economic Reforms in New Democracies.* New York: Cambridge University Press.

Bruno, Michael. 1993. *Crisis, Stabilization, and Economic Reform: Therapy by Consensus.* Oxford: Clarendon Press.

Burgess, Robin, and Nicholas Stern. 1993. "Taxation and Development." *Journal of Economic Literature* 31: 762–830.

Cukierman, Alex, and Mario Tommasi. 1998. "Why Does It Take a Nixon to Go to China?" *American Economic Review* 88: 180–197.

de Soto, Hernando. 1989. *The Other Path.* New York: Harper & Row.

Dominguez, Jorge I., ed. 1997. *Technopols: Freeing Politics and Markets in Latin America in the 1990s.* University Park: Pennsylvania State University Press.

Doner, Richard F., and Anek Laothamatas. 1994. "Thailand: Economic and Political Gradualism." In Stephan Haggard and Steven Webb, eds., *Voting for Reform*, pp. 411–452. New York: Oxford University Press.

Drazen, Allan. 1996. "The Political Economy of Delayed Reform." *Policy Reform* 1:

25–46 (Reprinted in 1998 in Sturzenegger and Tommasi, *The Political Economy of Reform.*)

Edwards, Sebastian. 1995. *Crisis and Reform in Latin America: From Despair to Hope.* Oxford: Oxford University Press for the World Bank.

Geddes, Barbara. 1995. "The Politics of Economic Liberalization." *Latin American Research Review* 30: 195–214.

———. 1999. "Douglass C. North and Institutional Change in Contemporary Developing Countries." In James E. Alt, Margaret Levi, and Elinor Ostrom, eds., *Competition and Cooperation: Conversations with Nobelists About Economics and Political Science,* pp. 200–227. New York: Russell Sage Foundation.

Grindle, Merilee S. 1991. "The New Political Economy: Positive Economics and Negative Politics." In Gerald Meier, ed., *Politics and Policy Making in Developing Countries,* pp. 41–68. San Francisco: ICS Press.

Haberler, Gottfried. 1959. *The Cairo Lectures: International Trade and Economic Development.* Reprinted 1988: San Francisco: Institute for Contemporary Studies.

Haggard, Stephan, and Robert R. Kaufman. 1992. "The Political Economy of Inflation and Stabilization in Middle-Income Countries." In Stephan Haggard and Robert R. Kaufman, eds., *The Politics of Economic Adjustment: International Constraints, Distributive Conflicts, and the State,* pp. 270–319. Princeton, NJ: Princeton University Press.

Hirschman, Albert O. 1974. "Exit, Voice, and Loyalty: Further Reflections and a Survey of Recent Contributions." *Social Science Information* 13: 7–26. (Reprinted in 1981 in Hirschman, *Essays in Trespassing: Economics to Politics and Beyond.* Cambridge: Cambridge University Press.)

Kaufman, Robert R. 1990. "Stabilization and Adjustment in Argentina, Brazil, and Mexico." In Joan Nelson, ed., *Economic Crisis and Policy Choice: The Politics of Adjustment in the Third World,* pp. 61–112. Princeton, NJ: Princeton University Press.

Kiguel, Miguel, and Nissan Liviatan. 1995. "Stopping Three Big Inflations: Argentina, Brazil, and Peru." In Rudiger Dornbusch and Sebastian Edwards, eds., *Reform, Recovery, and Growth: Latin America and the Middle East,* pp. 369–408. Chicago: University of Chicago Press.

Krueger, Anne O. 1993a. *The Political Economy of Economic Policy Reform in Developing Countries.* Cambridge, MA: MIT Press.

———. 1993b. "The Politics and Economics of Turkish Policy Reform in the 1980s." In Robert Bates and Ann Krueger, eds., *Political and Economic Interactions,* pp. 333–386. Oxford: Basil Blackwell.

Laban, Ricardo, and Federico Sturzenegger. 1994. "Distributional Conflict, Financial Adaptation and Delayed Stabilizations." *Economics and Politics* 6: 255–274.

Lago, Ricardo. 1991. "The Illusion of Pursuing Redistribution Through Macropolicy: Peru's Heterodox Experience, 1985–90." In Rudiger Dornbusch and Sebastian Edwards, eds., *The Macroeconomics of Populism in Latin America,* pp. 263–323. Chicago: University of Chicago Press.

Maier, Charles S. 1975. *Recasting Bourgeois Europe: Stabilization in France, Germany, and Italy in the Decade After World War I.* Princeton, NJ: Princeton University Press.

———. 1987. *In Search of Stability: Explorations in Historical Political Economy.* New York: Cambridge University Press.

McKinnon, Ronald I. 1982. "The Order of Economic Liberalization: Lessons from Chile and Argentina." *Carnegie-Rochester Series on Public Policy* 17: 159–186.

———. 1991. *The Order of Economic Liberalization: Financial Control in the Transition to a Market Economy.* Baltimore: Johns Hopkins University Press.

Meier, Gerald M., ed. 1991. *Politics and Policy Making in Developing Countries: Perspectives on the New Political Economy.* San Francisco: ICS Press.

Miller, Gary J. 1997. "The Impact of Economics on Political Science." *Journal of Economic Literature* 35: 1173–1204.

Naim, Moises. 1993. *Paper Tigers and Minotaurs: The Politics of Venezuela's Economic Reforms.* Washington, DC: Carnegie Endowment for International Peace.

North, Douglass C. 1984. "Three Approaches to the Study of Institutions." In David C. Colander, ed., *Neoclassical Political Economy: The Analysis of Rent-Seeking and DUP Activities,* pp. 33–40. Cambridge, MA: Ballinger.

Olson, Mancur. 1965. *The Logic of Collective Action.* Cambridge, MA: Harvard University Press.

———. 1982. *The Rise and Decline of Nations.* New Haven, CT: Yale University Press.

Paldam, Martin. 1997. "Political Business Cycles." In Dennis Mueller, ed., *Perspectives on Public Choice: A Handbook,* pp. 342–370. New York: Cambridge University Press.

Peltzman, Sam. 1976. "Toward a More General Theory of Regulation." *Journal of Law and Economics* 19: 211–240.

Perotti, Roberto. 1992. "Increasing Returns to Scale, Politics and the Timing of Stabilization." Unpublished paper, Department of Economics, Columbia University, New York.

Ranis, Gustav, and Syed Akhtar Mahmood. 1992. *The Political Economy of Policy Change.* Cambridge, MA: Basil Blackwell.

Remmer, Karen L. 1986. "The Politics of Economic Stabilization: IMF Standby Programs in Latin America, 1954–84." *Comparative Politics* 19: 1–24.

———. 1990. "Democracy and Economic Crisis: The Latin American Experience." *World Politics* 42: 315–335.

———. 1993. "The Political Economy of Elections in Latin America, 1980–1991." *American Political Science Review* 87: 393–407.

Rodrik, Dani. 1996. "Understanding Policy Reform." *Journal of Economic Literature* 34: 9–41.

Roett, Riordan. 1986. "Peru: The Message from Garcia." *Foreign Affairs* 64, no. 2 (Winter): 274–286

Sachs, Jeffrey D. 1994. "Life in the Economic Emergency Room." In John Williamson, ed., *Political Economy of Policy Reform,* pp. 501–521. Washington, DC: Institute for International Economics.

Smith, William C., Carlos Acuna, and Eduardo A. Gamarra, eds. 1994a. *Democracy, Markets, and Structural Reform in Latin America: Argentina, Bolivia, Brazil, Chile, and Mexico.* New Brunswick, NJ: Transaction Publishers.

———. 1994b. *Latin American Political Economy in the Age of Neoliberal Reform: Theoretical and Comparative Perspectives for the 1990s.* New Brunswick, NJ: Transaction Publishers.

Stokes, Susan C. 1996. "Introduction: Public Opinion and Market Reforms: The Limits of Economic Voting." *Comparative Political Studies* 29: 499–515.

Sturzenegger, Federico, and Mariano Tommasi, eds. 1998. *The Political Economy of Reform.* Cambridge, MA: MIT Press.

Tommasi, Mariano, and Andres Velasco. 1996. "Where Are We in the Political Economy of Reform?" *Policy Reform* 1: 187–238.

Viner, Jacob. 1953. *International Trade and Economic Development.* Oxford: Clarendon Press.

Webb, Richard. 1994. "Peru." In John Williamson, ed., *The Political Economy of Policy Reform*, pp. 355–375. Washington, DC: Institute for International Economics.

Wellisz, Stanislaw, and Ronald Findlay. 1984. "Protection and Rent-Seeking in Developing Countries." In David C. Colander, ed., *Neoclassical Political Economy: The Analysis of Rent-Seeking and DUP Activities*, pp. 141–54. Cambridge, MA: Ballinger Publishing.

Williamson, John, ed. 1994. *The Political Economy of Policy Reform.* Washington, DC: Institute for International Economics.

Part III

Comparing Ideas on the Firm

6

The Economic Approach
to Personnel Research

Michael Gibbs and Alec Levenson

Definition of an economist:
A person who knows all the answers,
but doesn't understand the questions.

—*The Humorous Dictionary of Economics,*
Moorman 1983

An economist (John) loses his keys while walking across a dark parking lot. His friend (Jane) happens upon him some time later.

> Jane: Hi John! What are you looking for?
> John: I lost my keys somewhere in this parking lot.
> Jane: Did you lose them under one of these streetlights?
> John: No, I checked those areas twice already.
> Jane: So why are you still looking under the streetlights?
> John: Because that's where the light is!

Prepared for the 1999 meetings of the Society for the Advancement of Behavioral Economics. We have benefited greatly from interactions with teachers, colleagues, and students over the years. A partial list of those whom we wish to thank includes George Baker, Gary Becker, Mike Beer, Susan Cohen, Joe Cooper, David Finegold, Ray Friedman, Cristina Gibson, Richard Hackman, Wally Hendricks, Bengt Holmstrom, Kathryn Ierulli, Mike Jensen, Ed Lawler, Eddie Lazear, Gary Loveman, Bentley MacLeod, Janice McCormick, Sue Mohrman, Kevin J. Murphy, Canice Prendergast, Dan Raff, Sherwin Rosen, Wim van der Stede, and Karen Wruck.

Introduction

The economic approach to personnel and organizations has grown greatly in scope and importance over the last decade or two. It is now recognized as a separate field within labor economics, responsible for as much as a third of papers in leading labor journals.[1] Business schools increasingly offer personnel economics courses, and they hire economists to teach human resource management and other organizational courses traditionally taught by noneconomists. Textbooks using, or strongly influenced by, the economic approach to organizations have appeared regularly for several years (e.g., Baron and Kreps 1999; Brickley, Smith, and Zimmerman 2000; Jensen 1998; Lazear 1998; Milgrom and Roberts 1992). Personnel and organizational economics has developed to such a great extent that there are now many excellent literature reviews that take stock of the contributions or criticize the approach. Aside from the citations in the text, the bibliography includes additional examples of surveys and recent textbooks.

A cynic might worry that the abundance of literature reviews indicates the imminent death of the field. At the very least, many observers criticize the economic approach to personnel. The criticisms often are those applied to all of economics, such as the assumption of rational behavior, crude specifications of individual and group psychology (Kaufman 1999 is the most sophisticated critique along these lines), and too-simple models of complex reality (Hirsch, Michaels, and Friedman 1987). Another common criticism is that the field focuses narrowly on incentives to the exclusion of other interesting and important topics.

Our purpose is not to provide another survey of the field. Nor is it to join in what Winship and Rosen (1988) term "tiresome debates" about methodology. Instead, we try to be constructive in other ways. One barrier to interdisciplinary communication is differences in language (Merchant, Van der Stede, and Zheng 2000). We use the language and viewpoints of both perspectives to try to decrease the language barrier. In the first section below, we briefly outline a way that many scholars outside of economics tend to view organizational design (see Fig. 6.1): the "systems" view of an organization. We interpret this view in economic language and use it as the skeleton for the rest of the chapter.

Our most important goal is to discuss research areas that we believe hold great promise for gains from integrating economic and behavioral approaches. In the spirit of the two quotes at the beginning of the chapter, economics is stronger at providing theory based on mathematical models, and pursuing topics that existing theory or databases most readily lend themselves to. Organizational scholars outside of economics give more emphasis to topics that are of empirical and practical importance, and they build theories accordingly, even where such theories do not lend themselves to formal (especially mathematical) modeling. We identify topics that have received great attention outside economics, little inside economics, and that might benefit greatly from the economic approach.

We do not provide a comprehensive review of topics in the management literature, with the objective of detailing how an economic approach can improve them, for two reasons. First, introducing the topics for economists is task enough for a single paper. Indeed, in many cases we give short shrift to topics that have received extensive coverage by behavioral researchers. Second, and perhaps more importantly, because many of the topics discussed here have been barely researched by economists, it is too soon to predict how taking an economic approach will improve the existing knowledge base. That said, we are confident that economics has much to add, as we point out below, and we look forward to a day in the near future when such a review will draw on a large body of research completed by economists.

The plan of the chapter is as follows. In the next section, we outline the systems view of organizational design, using it to compare economic and behavioral approaches. This also serves to bring out the main topics we pursue. In the third section we consider important organizational policies that behavioral scholars have studied extensively, but that economists have paid little attention to. In that section, our goal is to suggest interesting areas of research for economists to pursue, as well as to sketch some ideas about how that research might be pursued. Topics we discuss include intrinsic motivation, job design, decision making, organizational structure, and coordination. The fourth section takes a similar approach to topics in organizational dynamics. The fifth section provides a brief discussion of methodological and empirical issues, and the sixth section ends with brief concluding remarks.

The Systems View of Organizational Design

There are many ways to compare economic and behavioral approaches to organizational design. Here we highlight one difference that has not often been emphasized: Behavioral approaches tend to take more of a *systems* view than does the economic approach (e.g., Galbraith 1977; Senge 1990). Figure 6.1 illustrates the systems view of organizational design. It is adapted from a similar figure in Beer et al. (1984, Fig. 2–1). Similar ideas can be found in other writings throughout organizational research over many years. We modified the Beer et al. figure to make it more consistent with the language of economics.

Figure 6.1 **Systems View of Organizational Design**

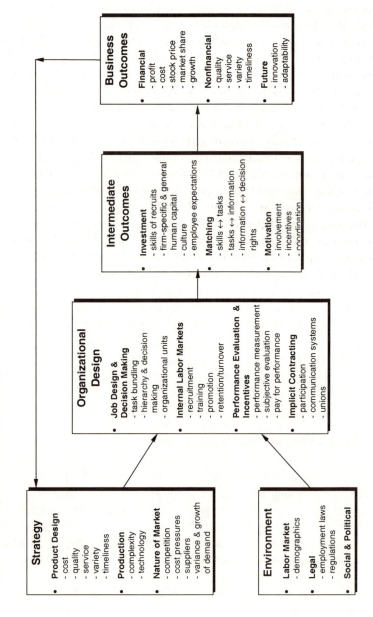

Source: Based on Beer et al. (1984).

"Organizational Design" represents firm design and personnel policies; these are the focus of personnel economics.[2] However, the systems view represents it as part of a larger process. By doing so, it encourages thinking about broader questions than by focusing only inside the Organizational Design box.

Behavioral scholars often view firms by first starting with the "Strategy" and "Environment." The firm chooses a strategy, product line, and product attributes (emphasis on cost, quality, timely delivery, customer service, innovation, etc.). This depends on the firm's constraints, including product and labor market conditions, legal considerations, social or political pressures, and competitor strategies. The strategy determines *what must be done* inside the firm to produce the product and implement the strategy, which then determines optimal organizational policies.

Organizational policies, in turn, produce "Intermediate Outcomes" (Fig. 6.1), which we have described in terms familiar to economists: investment, matching, and motivation. Personnel policies result in investments in firm-specific and general human capital, employee expectations, corporate culture, and so forth. They result in matching between employee skills and tasks, information and decisions, and other factors. They result in intrinsic and extrinsic motivation. These outcomes, combined with other firm inputs like capital, result in "Business Outcomes," which are measured in the same way as "Strategy" objectives: profit, product attributes, innovation, and so forth. Of course, this simplistic description makes the relationships seem more linear/causal than they really are. Intermediate and Business outcomes interact in complex ways, including feedback from business outcomes to intermediate outcomes.

External and Internal Fit

One thing the systems view highlights is that the firm's design should be *complementary*, or have *external fit*, with the firm's objectives and constraints. In other words, the Business Outcomes produced by the Organizational Design should ideally match the Strategy. Thus, in behavioral research, an interesting question is how personnel policies should vary with dimensions of the firm's product, technology, or strategy. By contrast, virtually all economic models have a single "product" with no dimension other than quantity (and sometimes quality). In an economic model, it typically is irrelevant whether the firm is producing a simple, low-tech, standardized product such as a tin can, or a complex, evolving product such as a semiconductor. It is irrelevant whether the firm is in manufacturing or white-collar work. In behavioral research, such distinctions are fundamental, and they lead to very different insights about optimal policies. We argue below that such distinctions may lead to important insights in personnel economics.

This is our first difference between the two approaches: economics tends to be vague about *what the firm is trying to do* beyond the abstract notion of "profit maximization." Because of this, economists have little to say about how policies should vary with different types of products, competitive environments, or technology, and how they might change over time.

The systems view also emphasizes *internal fit*, the idea that personnel policies may be more effective if they are designed to be mutually reinforcing (i.e., that they should be viewed as a *system*). For example, promotion-from-within is often said to be complementary with lifetime employment and deferred compensation. Team production and employee "empowerment" (decentralization of some decision rights) are often said to be complementary with enriched jobs. In Figure 6.1, this is the idea that the four types of policies in the Organizational Design box might be designed to work well together. At one level, this is trivial and obvious. At another, though, it may imply that there are *patterns* of organizational policies that firms tend to (and should) use together (Galbraith 1977; MacDuffie 1995; Lawler, Mohrman, and Ledford 1998; Baron and Kreps 1999).

Economists have recently shown interest in internal fit, drawing on the complementarities work of Milgrom and Roberts (1995). For example, Ichniowski and Shaw (1995) and Ichniowski, Shaw, and Prennushi (1997) investigated complementarity of personnel policies in steel finishing lines. In fact, their work was inspired by the behavioral literature's emphasis on internal fit among personnel policies. Gibbons and Waldman (1999) emphasized the value of integrative models designed to address patterns of empirical evidence. To do so, such models consider a broader set of policies as a system. We believe internal fit is an interesting idea that deserves more theoretical and empirical analysis.

Organizational Design

In the Organizational Design box in Figure 6.1, the middle two types of policies are by far the main focus of personnel economics. "Internal Labor Markets" involve recruiting, developing, assigning, and retaining the right worker skills. "Performance Evaluation and Incentives" are, of course, the essence of personnel economics. The economic approach has made substantial contributions to our understanding of these policies, and to describing the links between them and the three kinds of Intermediate Outcomes. If anything, economics has a comparative advantage here. It is the other two areas where economics has had less impact, and economists have placed less emphasis.

"Job Design and Decision Making" in Figure 6.1 encompasses the definition of jobs (bundling of tasks), teams, and information development and processing. It also includes macro-organizational structure, such as hierarchy, divisionalization, and coordination mechanisms. We make two observations here. First, the initial work in personnel economics, the first chapter of Adam Smith's *The Wealth of Nations* (1776), is on specialization in job design. However, there has been almost no work on job design in economics ever since. Second, much of the economic work on organizational structure has focused on the *boundaries* of the firm (Williamson 1975), rather than on what happens inside the boundaries. In contrast, job design and teams are large areas of interest among behavioral researchers. This research is often tied to discussions of "intrinsic" motivation, or ways in which jobs may be designed to make the work more motivating or less onerous. Decision making and organizational structure also have received much attention outside of economics, though less so than job design issues. We argue below that these are perhaps the most promising areas for future work in personnel economics.

A second major difference between the two research approaches is that personnel economics tends to be vague about *what employees do*. In economic models of assignment, training, or incentives, it is usually irrelevant to distinguish between blue-collar and white-collar jobs.[3] Workers are employed in generic "jobs" with abstract production functions. The only distinction between a manager and a worker is who is evaluating whom. Teams tend to be modeled as a group of workers with a common performance measure, but the reason for using teams in the first place is usually ignored. There is little analysis of different forms of hierarchy, coordination, or collaboration. All of these issues are fundamental to behavioral organizational research.

The last type of policy we call "Implicit Contracting" (Fig. 6.1). These practices go by many names, such as "psychological contracting," "employee voice," "culture," and "relational contracting."[4] We mean practices that firms use to facilitate implicit agreements with employees, for a variety of reasons, all arising from the inability to write perfect explicit contracts. A classic example is developing mutual trust to share investments in, and returns from, firm-specific human capital. Another is setting the implicit terms of the employment relationship between the firm and the employee at hiring. Another is investing in a reputation for fair treatment of employees, to facilitate subjective performance evaluations. These practices have received great attention outside, and some attention inside, of economics. The most common method for economic analysis of implicit contracting is game theory, with an emphasis on reputation and repeated games (Kreps 1990). Most of the work inside economics is theoretical, but most outside economics is empirical.

Organizational Dynamics

The final message in the systems view in Figure 6.1 is that organizational design is dynamic. An important topic in behavioral research on organizations is "managing change." Imagine that a firm has strong external and internal fit, so that the personnel policies are complementary and well adapted to the product, technology, competitive environment, and strategy. Now suppose that something changes in the environment (e.g., a new technology is developed that leaves old production methods outdated and relatively inefficient). In terms of Figure 6.1, this means that the Business Outcomes no longer match the Strategy. How does the organizational design change? Behavioral scholars often argue that organizational design is costly to change. This implies that the optimal change may involve not only changing the inside of the organization, but also reformulating the company's strategy to reflect constraints from the existing organization. This is why there is a feedback loop from Business Outcomes to Strategy in Figure 6.1. This topic has received little attention from economists.

The second sense in which an organization is dynamic is less reactive, and more proactive. It is possible to conceive of an organization being designed to be *adaptable* to future, unforeseeable environmental changes. Similarly, some personnel policies may foster continuous improvement in methods, innovation, learning, and so forth. These topics receive substantial attention outside, but very little inside organizational economics.

These two senses of organizational dynamics lead us to our third major difference between behavioral and economic approaches: Economics tends to take a *static view* of organizational design, which makes it difficult to consider issues of organizational change, or designing adaptable organizations.

Neglected Areas Inside the Black Box

In this section we discuss areas of organizational design that we believe hold promise for future research by personnel economists. Our first and most important topic is job design and intrinsic motivation. We contrast behavioral and economic approaches to job design (job enrichment vs. specialization). Combining the two perspectives makes the two seemingly very different approaches consistent. We suggest a way that economists can begin modeling intrinsic motivation. This discussion also highlights the potential benefits of considering not only complementarity between personnel policies (internal fit), but also external fit; we argue that the firm's optimal approach to job design depends importantly on the nature of its product, technology, and environment.

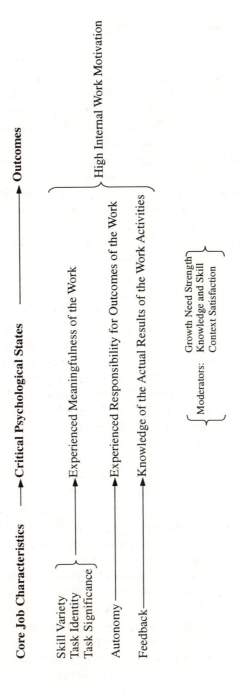

Figure 6.2 Hackman-Oldham Model of Intrinsic Motivation Through Job Design

Job Design and Intrinsic Motivation

In the first chapter of *The Wealth of Nations*, Adam Smith analyzes specialization in job design in a pin factory.[5] In what may be the first econometric
case study in personnel economics, Smith calculates that if a worker does
every task involved in making a pin, he can produce fewer than twenty pins
per day. Smith then estimates that if workers specialize on different tasks,
ten workers can together produce about 48,000 pins per day. Thus, in Smith's
example, specialization through narrow job design increases production by
about *24,000 percent*. This is an astonishing figure; even with a very large
standard error, it indicates the potential power of specialization as an approach to job design. Since then, a brief discussion of specialization (along
with comparative advantage) has been a staple of microeconomics textbooks.
There has been only a little work on job design in personnel economics since,
usually focusing on specialization (e.g., Rosen 1983; Becker and Murphy
1992).

Contrast this with the treatment of job design in behavioral research. The
classic works are Hackman and Lawler (1971), and Hackman and Oldham
(1980), widely cited as the most important studies on job design and intrinsic
motivation. Their approach is the exact opposite of Smith's: They argue that
job *enrichment* (adding complexity or more tasks) generates intrinsic motivation and increases productivity. The Hackman and Oldham (H&O) model
of job design (which builds off the foundation provided by Hackman and
Lawler) is so important outside economics that we describe it briefly here,
and focus our discussion around it. Figure 6.2 reproduces the diagram of
their model (1980, 83). Lawler (1986) provides an excellent treatment of job
enrichment.

Hackman and Oldham focus on designing jobs so that workers are more
intrinsically motivated. They argue that three "critical psychological states"
are required to achieve this: Meaningfulness, Responsibility for Outcomes,
and Knowledge of Actual Results. The more of each of these states that the
job design generates in the employee, the greater should be intrinsic motivation. These three states are determined by five elements of job design:
Skill Variety, Task Identity, Task Significance, Autonomy, and Feedback
(Fig. 6.2). Finally, three "moderators" (what economists would call "parameters") affect the strength of these effects: Growth Need Strength, Knowledge and Skill, and Context Satisfaction. Threaded through this section, we
explain these terms as we interpret the model as economists.

The most important element of the H&O model is making work "meaningful" so that workers become more "involved" in their jobs: are more
interested, pay more attention, think more carefully, and work more dili-

gently. The key aspect of job design that generates such involvement in work is Skill Variety: "the degree to which a job requires a variety of different activities in carrying out the work, involving the use of a number of different skills and talents of the person" (Hackman and Oldham 1980, 78). Hackman and Oldham argue that skill variety causes employees to "challenge or stretch their skills or abilities" (p. 78). They go on to say that this is a fundamental characteristic of human psychology, using the metaphor of newborn babies who are "wired in" to "explore and manipulate their environments" (p. 78). In this view, work is more interesting (less onerous) if it is more intellectually challenging. For this reason, they argue that job enrichment increases intrinsic motivation. Indeed, even Adam Smith recognized in *The Wealth of Nations* that specialization could lead to boredom and reduced productivity of workers.

Job enrichment is important empirically, for at least three reasons. First, there are observable patterns of specialization and job enrichment that are ripe for theoretical explanation. For example, management, "knowledge work," and jobs with higher levels of responsibility clearly tend to be defined with broader sets of tasks. Manufacturing jobs were historically defined with a narrower set of tasks. Second, and perhaps most interestingly, there appears to have been a recent trend toward job enrichment. Third, job enrichment is often associated with other policies such as job rotation, team production, and "empowerment." This is suggestive of the idea of complementarities or internal fit, and as such has attracted some economic researchers. However, this area has lacked a strong theoretical foundation for empirical work (Cappelli and Neumark 1999).

Given the importance of job enrichment in behavioral research and in practice, and the contrast with the economics focus on specialization, we believe that it is important for personnel economists to seriously explore this idea. We now outline how we believe economists could get a handle on this topic. By doing so, we present a different view of the H&O model that we hope illustrates the potential benefits of integrating economic and behavioral approaches.[6]

Modeling Intrinsic Motivation

Economists tend to avoid assuming things about the utility function, such as that certain types of work design raise or lower the onerousness of effort, unless this can be done in a way that produces empirically testable implications. Therefore, most economic work on intrinsic motivation sidesteps this issue in one way or another. One recent approach avoids the issue by assuming that a worker's actions affect not only the firm's profits but also the employee's utility; that is, the employee gets intrinsic motivation from the *output* (Murdock 1998).[7] Kreps (1997) focuses on how, in a multitask framework, intrinsic motivation on some tasks can be affected by extrinsic incentives on other tasks. Kreps does say, however, that perhaps it is time for economists to try to model intrinsic motivation more directly.

A simple starting point is the observation that job enrichment appears to increase intrinsic motivation. This might be done by assuming that the marginal cost of effort is lower if the worker is assigned more tasks. However, this runs the risk of assuming the result. Moreover, it does not capture the essence of the behavioral literature, namely that intellectual "stretch" or "challenge" is important. Therefore, a second possibility is to incorporate some notion of intellectual challenge about tasks by the worker. There are two senses that seem important. One is simply learning how to perform new tasks, or how to perform them better. The second is using intellectual or "thinking" skills on the job.

For the first sense of how work may be "challenging," one approach is to incorporate learning by doing (Lindbeck and Snower 2000). Learning would increase the worker's marginal product of effort, because the worker becomes more facile at the task. This is the standard economic approach. But the degree of learning by doing, perhaps modeled as the change in the worker's human capital stock in the task, would also affect (lower) the marginal cost of effort. That would reflect intrinsic motivation through learning.

Consider how implications might be derived from such a model. The firm would face a trade-off: More skilled workers are more productive, but less intrinsically motivated (holding characteristics of the job constant), because opportunities for further learning are diminished. It would not necessarily be the case that the best worker for a job is the one who is best trained for the job, as such a worker would have less to learn. This is different from the standard economic view that matching should be by comparative advantage. It is consistent with the evidence that many organizations using job enrichment also use job rotation: Workers are moved to new jobs periodically, even if they have mastered their old jobs. Ordinarily this would seem a puzzle to economists (especially as job rotation reduces gains from specialization even further).

Hackman and Oldham (Fig. 6.2) discuss two factors affecting intrinsic motivation through job enrichment—the "Growth Need Strength" moderator and the "Knowledge and Skill" moderator.[8] By growth need strength moderator, they mean that individuals respond differently to job enrichment. This is equivalent to saying that differences in marginal utility of learning affect how strongly a worker is intrinsically motivated. By knowledge and skill moderator, they mean the extent to which the worker has the requisite skills so that the job will not be too challenging. It is straightforward to incorporate this into an economic model: The worker's stock of human capital in the task may have nonlinear effects on intrinsic motivation. Very low levels of human capital may imply low intrinsic motivation because the challenge is too hard; very high levels of human capital may also imply low intrinsic motivation because the challenge is too easy. Thus, the optimal matching of worker to job may also imply some minimal level of training greater than zero.

There is a second sense of making the employee more involved in his or her work, beyond learning how to perform the job better: the extent to which the job is intellectually engaging. This is probably best modeled as a property of the work environment, or production function, not the worker's utility function, although it requires at least a rudimentary modeling of the idea that the intellectual nature of work may affect intrinsic motivation. Therefore, a second approach that we believe would be fruitful is modeling the information structure and intellectual nature of the production environment.

In addition, it is useful to distinguish between *job enrichment* and *job enlargement*. Job enlargement is a horizontal expansion of tasks without a commensurate increase in the intellectual nature of the job. Job enlargement can decrease boredom (and errors) by reducing repetition, but it does not necessarily increase other aspects of intrinsic motivation. For example, reducing the number of hours devoted to filing, substituting hours devoted to stuffing envelopes, can enlarge a file clerk's job. The job can be enriched by including the worker in decision making over what types of documents should be stored electronically versus in paper form.

Most economic incentive models use a metaphor that seems to be drawn from physical tasks: The firm wants the worker to provide more "effort." However, this is not quite what is needed for modeling intellectual work. In such jobs the firm does not want the employee to work "harder," but to think more carefully, collect more relevant information, perform analyses, and so forth. We encourage theorists to think more carefully about how to model these issues. Perhaps most interesting, though, would be for empirical economists to study the relationship between the intellectual nature of the work environment and the job design chosen by the firm.

Which Tasks Should Be Bundled Together?

To put further content on the idea of job enrichment, it is useful to consider which tasks should be bundled together. The clear answer to an economist is that more complementary tasks (larger positive cross-marginal products of production) should be bundled together. Unfortunately, this has little empirical content as stated, for it provides no way of thinking about which tasks are complementary. A second factor in the H&O model helps us begin to think about this issue: "Task Identity" (Fig. 6.2). Hackman and Oldham (1980, 78) describe Task Identity as "the degree to which a job requires completion of a 'whole' and identifiable piece of work."

An economic interpretation of Task Identity is constructive. Hackman and Oldham seem to be saying that it is important to *modularize* production into relatively discrete or separable subprocesses. There are three implications of such modularity. First, if production can be modularized, then it must be that the modules capture most of the important task complementarities *within* each module. Indeed, this is almost the definition of modularity. Thus, designing jobs with this concept of Task Identity in mind captures in a practical and implementable way the economist's notion of bundling complementary tasks together. Second, it gives guidance on how far to take job enrichment. The benefits of job enrichment are limited by the ability of the worker to learn and handle multiple tasks on the job. But the benefits are *also* limited by the nature of the tasks, in that bundling unrelated tasks together is less likely to increase productivity.

Third, modularity is consistent with our emphasis on designing work to increase *learning* on the job. When more closely related tasks are bundled together, it seems very likely that the employee will learn more about ways to improve production. For example, if an employee produces two parts that work closely together in a diesel engine, then the employee is likely to make both parts with higher quality, because the worker has a better understanding of how the parts will be used, how they fit with each other, and so forth. It also seems plausible that the worker will be more likely to figure out process improvements, because the production of each part may have implications for the effectiveness of the other part.

Where Is Job Enrichment Most Valuable?

This perspective helps us to understand trends toward adoption of job enrichment and related techniques. Under the traditional "Taylorist" approach, stemming from the work of Frederick Taylor (1923), industrial engineers worked out the "best" way to do work *ex ante*. They then designed narrow, specialized jobs, combined with mechanization, to repeat these best practices as much as possible; the goal was to *standardize* production to wring out variation and defects. This approach makes sense to the extent that the best production process can be figured out *ex ante* at reasonable cost.[9]

In many environments, figuring out the best approach to job design *ex ante* will be inefficient for several reasons. The more complex the product (in terms of number of parts, number of production tasks, or technology), the more difficult is the industrial engineer's optimization problem. Similarly, more complex product lines, with more variations in product design or more customization, imply costlier industrial engineering. More rapid technological change implies that the process must be redesigned more frequently. All imply lower returns to investing in *ex ante* industrial engineering, and thus less *ex ante* optimization of production methods.

The less effective is *ex ante* industrial engineering, the greater the scope for workers to learn process improvements. The greater the scope for workers to learn, the more beneficial will be job designs that encourage learning by workers. This helps explain why job enrichment and related policies are adopted more in some settings than in others. There has been a trend toward job enrichment in recent decades partly because firms increasingly use customization and techniques that facilitate more frequent changes in products and product lines (Milgrom and Roberts 1990). It is also likely that more rapid technological change in recent decades has fueled this trend; thus, such policies should be adopted more in settings where technological change is more important. Finally, under this view it is not surprising that adoption of job enrichment is closely associated with having workers emphasize continuous process improvement and total quality management; both are more important if the firm is less able to conduct effective *ex ante* process optimization.

This discussion suggests that economists think about modeling the information properties of the production environment so as to try to capture their effects on job enrichment and modularization. For example, theoretical and empirical researchers might consider incorporating ideas like the following into their models and data collection: how long the firm has been making a given product; how long it anticipates making the product without major changes in design or production technology; the complexity of the product, product line, or production process; the rate of change in technology in the industry; and whether the production process allows for frequent changes in products to accommodate customization.

Job Enrichment and Decision Making

If one of the primary benefits of job enrichment is that workers can learn and figure out process improvements, it follows that the firm will want workers to take initiative to some extent: come up with suggestions, and make some decisions about which to try and how to implement them. Two other parts of the Hackman-Oldham model address this.

Hackman-Oldham (1980) define "Autonomy" as "the degree to which the job provides substantial freedom, independence, and discretion to the individual in scheduling the work and determining the procedures" (p. 79). By Autonomy (Fig. 6.2), H&O do not really argue that workers get intrinsic motivation from being able to work independently (though that might be true). Instead, they emphasize giving the worker responsibility about procedures, in the sense of being able to try new methods (see Fig. 6.2).

"Feedback" is defined as "the degree to which carrying out the work activities . . . provides the individual with direct and clear information about the effectiveness of his or her performance" (p. 80). In other words, workers need to be provided information on the effects of their efforts, if the firm wishes to have workers come up with initiatives and test them (see Fig. 6.2).

Thus, decision making is an important element of job enrichment.[10] This explains why employee "empowerment" or "participation" is so strongly associated with job enrichment programs. We can think of the two as highly complementary practices in the following way. In addition to intrinsic motivation, job enrichment gives the worker a broad understanding of a set of strongly complementary tasks. The worker gains detailed and potentially sophisticated knowledge about the production process and sometimes the product design. Empowerment gives the worker the ability to make use of this information, trying new methods to improve the process and reduce defects.[11] Together they allow the worker and the firm to make improvements and more readily respond to changes in the environment. We now turn to a more detailed discussion of decision making.

Decision Making

Personnel economists tend to think of decisions as being made within hierarchies. But hierarchy models rarely have much element of decision to them; they are usually conglomerations of primitive production functions, with spans of control between supervisors and subordinates (Beckmann 1977; Calvo and Wellisz 1979; Rosen 1982).[12] Few models attempt to get a handle on decision making. Yet decision making is one of the most important functions of the internal organization of the firm. Location of decision-making authority (the degree of decentralization) is a major topic in behavioral fields. Moreover, decision making inherently involves both processing and strategically using information, which is a building block of economic theories of organization. It is therefore surprising that economists have had little to say about decision making.

Jensen and Meckling (1992), applying Hayek's (1945) analysis of markets to internal firm organization, provide a starting point. They emphasize a distinction between "specific knowledge," which is costly to communicate to someone else, and "general knowledge," which is not costly to communicate. If knowledge is general, decisions can be centralized to ensure coordination. The more that knowledge is specific, the more will the firm locate decision rights where the specific knowledge is generated. Jensen and Meckling apply this idea to discuss decentralization, which involves a trade-off between use of specific knowledge and coordination costs.[13]

We can enrich the idea of specific knowledge by thinking more specifically about what attributes of knowledge (information) make it more costly to communicate, and thus push the firm toward decentralized decision making (Milgrom and Roberts 1992; Brickley, Smith, and Zimmerman 2000). One attribute is whether the information is *perishable*. For example, information about a customer's immediate request for service must be acted upon quickly or it loses value. In such cases the firm is likely to decentralize service decisions because of the time involved in passing the information to a central decision maker.

Another attribute of information that makes it costly to communicate is *complexity*. If information has many dimensions (variables), with complex relationships among the variables, it may be costly to describe and convey to others. This helps to explain why participative decision making is used in complex work environments. A diesel engine plant is more likely to use job enrichment combined with empowerment than is a tin can factory: The engine has hundreds of interacting parts, whereas a tin can has at most half a dozen.

A third attribute of information that may make it costly to transfer is whether or not the information is *costly to understand* once received. Two examples come to mind immediately: *scientific or technical* information, and *subjective or experiential* information. In both cases, decisions that make use of the information will tend to be decentralized to workers who have the knowledge. For example, performance appraisals tend to be decentralized to supervisors despite problems of favoritism and influence costs (Prendergast 1999), because most jobs require subjective evaluations. These are hard to do without actually observing the employee on a day-to-day basis, and they are costly to communicate.

A more subtle issue of the cost of transferring subjective information is that it is more likely to be *manipulable* by the holder (performance appraisals again come to mind). But that does not necessarily imply that decisions should be decentralized to the potential manipulator! On the contrary, the opposite may sometimes be true. The possibility of gaming or manipulation of the information may alter the simple Jensen and Meckling story in interesting ways.

When information may be manipulated, we might call it *unreliable*. This is yet another category of attributes of information that could have important implications for the allocation of decision making. Another example is information that is noisy, or communicated with inaccuracy. "Garbling" (Geankoplis and Milgrom 1991) might also lead to decentralization of decision making.

A further notion is the degree of interdependence of the tasks needed to produce the output. Jensen and Meckling's (1992) framework is useful for considering at what level in a hierarchical organization decision making will be located. But it ignores the fact that tasks performed throughout the production process may be highly interdependent (Thompson 1967; Lawler 1986). Production of different parts of a car may be modularized and insulated from each other so that stoppages at one part of the process do not impact other parts. Decision making over each component can then be decentralized to subunits. A chemical production or oil refinery process, in contrast, has much more interdependent tasks, so there are large benefits from coordination. This leads into our next topic, organizational structure and coordination.

Organizational Structure

Behavioral scholars often distinguish between "micro" and "macro" organizational structure. *Micro* involves individual job design, as discussed above. *Macro* encompasses the firm's overall structure, including hierarchy and coordination mechanisms. (Decision making falls in between, as it makes sense to think about patterns of allocation of decision rights across the entire firm, but it is also an important part of individual job design.) Here we discuss macro organizational structure, long an important topic outside of economics, but not discussed much by economists.

A key insight in this literature by Lawrence and Lorsch (1967) is that "one size does not fit all." That is, there is not one ideal organizational structure, because improving the ability of a firm to perform along one dimension will diminish its ability to perform optimally along others. For example, producing at the lowest cost for a given product design can impede the firm's ability to respond quickly to changing demand conditions: The former implies minimal research and development (R&D), whereas the latter implies much larger R&D. Thus, along the lines of our discussions of external fit, a very interesting issue for economists to explore is how a firm's optimal organizational structure varies with its environment, technology, and related factors.

Much of the behavioral literature on structure can be crudely summarized as identifying conditions under which a traditional hierarchical functional organizational form is inappropriate (Galbraith 1977, 1995).[14] The traditional organization puts a premium on command and control mechanisms designed to overcome principal agent problems. Workers are organized in departments according to function (manufacturing, sales, R&D, human resources, accounting, etc.). This functional structure has several benefits: (a) it is clear which department is responsible for which tasks; (b) similar tasks are bundled into the same unit, facilitating specialization; (c) there are clear career paths requiring investment in only specialized skills; and (d) supervisors have knowledge of and experience with subordinate tasks, aiding supervision and performance evaluation. The hierarchical functional organization is a natural extension of the traditional Taylorist approach emphasizing specialization.

Important drawbacks exist to organizing along functional lines. A functional organization is best suited to firms that provide a single product or types of products that can be effectively managed centrally. Firms with highly differentiated products (e.g., laptop vs. mainframe computers; residential homeowner/car vs. business liability insurance) may find that creating separate divisions for each distinct category of products may be more efficient, because it allows for further specialization within organizational units.[15]

Specialization in a functional organization comes at a cost similar to the costs from specialization in individual job design: poorer integration, use of information, and learning across tasks. Consider a classic problem: product design, say, in a computer company. Sales and marketing personnel know a great deal about what trade-offs customers are willing to make among various features and cost; these employees have rich knowledge about customer demand curves. The R&D employees have technical and scientific knowledge about what designs are feasible. Production employees have technical knowledge about the implications of various design decisions on costs. All these kinds of knowledge are, to some extent, specific or costly to communicate to others. But all are important sources of information for product design decisions. Decentralizing product design decisions to any of these three groups will result in nonoptimal product design.

Thus, an interesting way to think about firm structure is to build on the idea of specific knowledge that is costly to communicate. But instead of thinking about the degree of decentralization, the key issue is that there are multiple "pockets" of specific knowledge located in various units in the firm. The firm would like to make combined use of these pockets of knowledge effectively. There are two general aspects of the firm's task (Lawrence and Lorsch 1967). The first is to *differentiate* the knowledge into different departments within the firm, so that departments specialize in developing (and to some extent) using the pockets of specific knowledge. The second is to *integrate* the various pieces of knowledge so that they can be used together. This is done through policies and processes that *coordinate* different units, allowing the pieces of knowledge to work together as needed.[16]

Integration could be achieved by centralization, with the usual costs emphasized by Jensen and Meckling. But it might be interesting for economists to explore more fully what those costs are, and how they may be mitigated (especially in modern times with extensive use of information technology). Integration could also be achieved by decentralization, combined with coordination mechanisms designed to get disparate decision-makers to work together. There are two general approaches that firms use, *incentives* and *coordination mechanisms*, which we now discuss briefly.

Incentives

The classic economic solution to coordination is *incentives*, used to motivate agents to work in concert with each other. One approach is to give organizational units incentives to maximize overall divisional or firm value, though this tends to have free-rider problems. Another is to incorporate the effects of a manager's actions on another division into his or her performance measure. Still another is some form of transfer pricing. In fact, firms frequently use these incentive approaches.

One point here is that performance measurement and structure (breaking up into organizational units) are intimately related. Consider the case of a divisional manager given discretion over personnel policies for the division. The manager's incentives will be strongly influenced by the divisional performance measure (e.g., cost center, revenue center, profit center, etc.). This should flow through to how incentives are structured for the rest of the division. Thus, the divisional performance measure has important implications for incentives in the entire division. Moreover, the divisional performance measure that the firm chooses will be closely related to how the division is defined; in fact, it will be almost determined by how the unit is defined. Definition of the unit defines how performance data (costs, revenue, headcount, etc.) are aggregated and computed. Therefore, the division of the firm into subunits immediately gives rise to certain performance measures and incentive effects.[17]

Unfortunately, it seems unlikely that the incentive approach to coordination will be completely effective in many situations, by the very nature of the problem. If knowledge is specific, or costly to communicate, it is hard to imagine how to develop performance measures (at least, *ex ante* and reasonably objective measures) that motivate agents who do not possess this knowledge to act in ways that take it into account (also see note 16 above). Therefore, other approaches are also likely to be important.

Coordination Mechanisms

An alternative for achieving coordination across pockets of specific knowledge is to use one of a plethora of structures that overlap traditional functional hierarchy. These structures may be permanent or temporary. One example, often used in product design, is a cross-functional team, with members from various units that possess information that can be combined productively. Another is a matrix organization, in which employees have two hierarchical assignments, one functional and one by product, project, and so forth. Galbraith (1995) describes a continuum of lateral coordinating mechanisms:

- Informal (or voluntary) processes occur spontaneously; they are not formally established by management.
- Teams are formal groups that are used to complement the informal voluntary processes; they are established by management.
- Integrators are full-time leaders who are appointed to lead the formal groups, and they are equivalent to cross-functional managers responsible for managing a product, project, brand, and so forth.

Galbraith (1995) describes "informal" organizations as those "characterized by voluntary coordination across units" (p. 49). He suggests that informal processes are usually preferable, because formal structures have to be designed and managed, with attendant principal-agent problems. However, this does not seem so clear to an economist. Informal mechanisms may clearly work against the firm's interests if the incentives of the initiators are not well aligned with firm objectives. In this sense Galbraith's definition of an informal organization assumes that the incentives induce only those voluntary actions that are aligned with firm objectives. A contrasting view (Lawler 2000), and one to which most economists are sympathetic, is that reward systems can create lateral interdependence by giving everyone the same fate (i.e., by explicitly aligning their financial interests with each other).

According to Galbraith, an organization can foster voluntary coordination by interdepartmental rotation, interdepartmental events, co-location, information technology, mirror image departments, and consistent reward and measurement practices. Is there a meaningful distinction between "voluntary" and "formal" coordination? If the only distinction is the definition within the organizational chart, then the distinction may be irrelevant. But if there is really something more, then economic tools like agency theory could help better define the distinction between informal groups formed voluntarily (via consistent reward systems) and formal teams set up by management using explicit team rewards.

Table 6.1

Determinants of Emphasis on Job Enrichment or Team Production
(Lawler)

		Technical Interdependence	
1. *Technological Requirements*		Low	High
Task	Low	Traditional job design	Traditional group design
Uncertainty	High	Job enrichment	Self-regulating teams

2. *Social/Psychological*			
		Social Needs	
Requirements		Low	High
Growth Need	Low	Traditional job design	Traditional group design
Strength	High	Job enrichment	Self-regulating teams

One insight from behavioral empirical research on coordination mechanisms (e.g., teams) is the relationship between the frequency with which a team meets and its design. If team members meet only infrequently, they can be a cross-functional team imbedded in a firm organized along traditional, functional lines. If they have to meet frequently, then it may be better to have team members' primary reporting relationship be with the team itself, and the secondary reporting relationship be with functional managers who help monitor the roles that specialists perform in teams. Specialization is preserved to some extent, but the efficiency of information flow between the different areas of specialization within the organization is improved and, consequently, so is the speed of responsiveness to the market. Thus, the extent to which a mechanism is permanent and emphasized, relative to the underlying functional structure, seems to depend on the relative importance to the firm of integration of the pockets of specific knowledge.[18]

In any case, this points to the basic trade-off in using coordination mechanisms: They reduce the employee's specialization and introduce monitoring and performance measurement costs, but they broaden the employee's view of tasks and facilitate learning and collaboration. In other words, optimal organizational structure, with functional hierarchy and coordination mechanisms, is based on much the same issues as is job specialization or enrichment.

Teams

Teams are a topic that has received considerable attention outside, but little inside, economics. Examples of different types include work, parallel, project, and management teams (Bailey and Cohen 1997). A large part of the literature is empirical, focusing on how teams can function effectively. Although the topics of this empirical literature are interesting (e.g., the role of interpersonal skills as a type of human capital), it is the theoretical role of teams that is relevant for the present discussion.[19]

Early work on teams was motivated by the sociotechnical literature, which examined how technology's effects on work organization are mitigated by the social structure and needs of the workers (Trist and Bamforth 1951; Miller and Rice 1967). This approach led to designing work to be performed by groups, to take advantage of the benefits of social interaction (Hackman and Oldham 1980).

Economists tend to view teams as a set of workers with a common task or performance measure, but they say little beyond such stylized representations. Clearly there is more to teams than that. For example, empirical evidence suggests that teams are more likely to be used when firms adopt job enrichment (MacDuffie 1995). Our discussion of job design suggests a possible explanation: Enriched jobs are designed to facilitate learning and continuous improvement by workers. Ideally, workers need to know all aspects of closely related tasks for this purpose (i.e., the job should be broadened up to the level of modularization of production). But in many cases that would imply job enrichment so broad that specialization and productivity would suffer. A balance between learning through job enrichment and specialization can be struck by using teams that work together.

There are several ways in which teams can facilitate learning. One is *cross-training*. Another is *information sharing*: One worker may have knowledge that can improve the productivity or decisions of another. A third is *collaboration*, in coming up with initiatives, testing them, and making decisions. An interesting avenue for modeling teams would be to explore the dynamics and incentives of collaboration in a group. The economic tools of information economics, agency theory, and game theory seem particularly well suited to the task.

According to Lawler (1986), the emphasis on teams versus individual job enrichment depends on both the technology and task uncertainty involved in producing the firm's output, and on the individual's needs for learning and social interaction (H&O's "Growth Need Strength" moderator); see Table 6.1 Thus, the firm needs to consider external fit, and there may also be internal complementarities between job design and personnel policies such as recruiting and training. Table 6.1 also suggests how characteristics of workers (bottom panel) interact with strategic objectives (top panel). If the firm wants to produce a product that requires a great deal of interdependent work, an assembly-line approach with narrowly defined jobs will not work. Two alternatives are having the product produced by teams or by individuals who do an entire "assembly" by themselves. Which is best depends on the technology and on the firm's ability either to mold the organization to the characteristics of the incumbent workforce, or to change those characteristics through training, restructuring, and turnover.

Organizational Dynamics

As noted in the introduction, the systems view of organizational design emphasizes that organizations are dynamic, evolving over time as their environments change. We now briefly discuss ways economists can think about organizational dynamics and design.

Organizational Evolution

In Figure 6.1, there is a feedback from Business Outcomes to Strategy. This captures the idea that the firm's existing design may limit its optimal strategy and ability to evolve. This is a strong theme in organizational research outside economics, where "Managing Change" is considered a fundamental topic. This literature is very large; here we focus on a few basic issues likely to be of greatest interest to economists.

Consider again our hypothetical firm with an existing strategy and design. Suppose the environment changes in some important way, such as a new technological development. If we were to consider the firm's optimal organizational design *ignoring* its existing organization, the problem would be unconstrained. But an interesting question is the degree to which the existing organization *constrains* the firm's ability to change or evolve. It is quite likely that this is the case, for several reasons.

The first constraint is that the firm has made organizational investments of various kinds, some of which are costly to change or abandon. For example, the firm has made investments in matching and developing appropriate employee skills. If there are turnover costs (say, because of the legal environment, severance provisions, or search costs), then changing to a new workforce with new skills may be prohibitively costly. Similarly, many firms invest in a reputation for how they treat employees. This facilitates implicit contracting over employment. Any organizational change may undermine this reputation, giving firms an optimal reluctance to change policies.

A second possible constraint on organizational change involves complementarity, or internal fit between personnel policies. If the firm has a bundle of policies that have been designed or evolved to work well together, and it wants to change one of them, it may find that they are no longer complementary. If so, the firm would face three options: (1) not changing policies, reducing external fit of the organizational design with the strategy; (2) changing the strategy to better match existing polices and practices; and (3) changing to a new bundle of complementary policies.

The problem with (1) is that it is likely to reduce the firm's competitiveness. The problem with (3) is that it may be costly to change multiple policies, structure, and processes simultaneously (or nearly simultaneously). In some cases, the firm may instead choose (2). In fact, this is essentially the core competence idea in the strategy literature (Prahalad and Hamel 1990): A firm should craft its strategy around what the organization is already good at. This is an intriguing argument that is worthy of careful theoretical (and especially empirical) research.[20]

A possibly even more intractable setting for organizational change involves two firms that decide to merge for strategic reasons. Both firms have existing job designs, structures, coordination mechanisms, decision making, employee skills, and implicit contracts. How are these two organizations to merge? If it is a merger of similar firms within an industry (i.e., a consolidation merger), this necessitates not just changing one organization, but two, and worse, *blending* them together. Blending is also necessary when firms in different industries merge. But the degree of blending in this case may be mitigated by the need to preserve unique aspects of the firms' original organizations in order to realize synergies. The costs of doing so effectively suggest that, in many mergers, one firm's organization will be left relatively intact, the other's largely abandoned (including its employees), and the customer lists merged. Casual empiricism suggests that this is often the case. This would be feasible for mergers that involve marketing synergies, but possibly not for other kinds of mergers. This issue potentially could be examined empirically by collecting personnel records for merging firms before and after the merger, to see which groups of employees survive.

Implicit Contracting

Economists have long recognized that implicit contracts play an important role in the labor market. The standard economic approach focuses on the limitations of formal contracts and what that means for how wages are set and how firms elicit optimal effort and investment from workers. Classic examples include risk sharing between the firm and workers over macroeconomic fluctuations, and sharing investments in firm-specific human capital. Another is the possible use of a wage premium to elicit effort that the employee might otherwise be reluctant to put forth (Akerlof and Yellen 1986).

Despite the rich variety of applications for which economists have used the notion of implicit contracts, they typically ignore organizational dynamics. For example, a key element of the "effort" that firms want to elicit from employees includes suggesting process improvements, which in some cases might eliminate the workers' jobs. This is a significant omission, given the importance of such feedback in optimizing product manufacturing and delivery mechanisms. Evidence from the behavioral literature on high-performance work systems shows that firms sometimes use job security provisions to elicit the desired information. Job security can never be an iron-clad explicit guarantee, so implicit contracts have a role to play.

Behavioral researchers have analyzed implicit contracts with renewed interest in recent years, under the heading of "psychological contracts" (Rousseau 1995). Two theoretical issues are particularly relevant. The first is that differences in the degree of uncertainty in the environment faced by organizations lead to different implicit contracts (the idea of external fit once again). A startup company (or division of a larger company) with uncertain market prospects cannot offer the same implicit long-term employment as can a company with a history of stable or growing demand for its product. A small company cannot offer the same career/skill development or promotion opportunities as can a large company.

The second interesting theoretical issue is an assertion (Rousseau 1995) that increases in the degree of uncertainty in the environment (say, due to increased competition or technological change) are likely to lead to *increased* reliance on "transactional" implicit contracts. Such implicit contracts emphasize the immediate benefits of exchange between the worker and firm. This is in contrast to the deferred benefits available from "relational" implicit contracts, which extend over longer periods (see below). For example, industries that previously were highly regulated and/or protected typically cannot offer the same level of job security after deregulation or the lifting of protection.

Working against this logic, however, is that an environment of increased uncertainty may make implicit offers by the firm less credible. Economists (usually game theorists) analyzing implicit contracting and corporate culture often emphasize the benefits of stability, consistency, long history, and related concepts in strengthening the *reputation* of the firm to employees (Kreps 1990; Camerer and Vepsalainen 1988). We can think about the employee's gauging of employer credibility over implicit promises as a statistical inference problem. Stability and consistency of how the firm has treated employees mean lower variance, or greater precision, of employee predictions about future treatment. Similarly, longer history implies more data, and therefore more accurate predictions. When the environment changes suddenly, the firm may lose much of its reputational capital.

Rousseau (1995) uses two dimensions to frame the discussion of implicit contracts: expected job duration and whether there are explicitly specified performance terms for the contract. This leads to four types of contracts:

- *Relational:* long employment duration, performance terms not specified explicitly. Examples include technical and professional employees, and managers;
- *Balanced:* long duration, performance terms specified. Examples include "core" blue collar and office support occupations;
- *Transactional:* short duration, performance terms specified. Examples include temporary employees, contract employees, and consultants;
- *Transitional:* short duration, performance terms not specified. Examples include transactional employees who are auditioning for long-term employment (e.g., temp-to-perm), and employees of an organization (both relational and balanced) undergoing restructuring and/or implementing significant head-count reductions.

It has been widely noted that increased uncertainty in the environment has led many companies to decrease fixed labor costs by converting relational and balanced jobs into transactional and transitional jobs. Anecdotal evidence includes the end of "lifetime employment" at traditionally stable companies (such as IBM and General Motors), the removal of entire layers of middle management, and increased use of temporary and contract labor for jobs that formerly were staffed by "core" employees.

An interesting issue is whether such changes impact a firm's ability to deliver the product dictated by its strategy, because of problems with external fit. If the majority of the firm's employees were hired under a regime of implicit contracts that promised long-term job security, those same workers might not be happy with the conversion to transactional or transitional status. At the extreme, if the resistance to implicit contract changes by incumbent workers is too strong, a firm might not be able to make the transition to a new technology or process for organizing work without suffering a significant drop in productivity. The alternative is to open an entirely new site and to staff it with new hires and incumbent workers who opt for the new implicit contract. This is consistent with Ichniowski and Shaw's (1995) evidence on the greater use of the complete set of changes that make up high-performance work systems by new sites; older sites, in contrast, are more likely to adopt only a subset of the changes.

Knowledge Management

At the intersection of implicit contracts and organizational evolution is the issue of *knowledge management.* In intellectual work, employees develop specific knowledge that is not entirely firm-specific, but is a form of intellectual capital or trade secrets that are valuable to the firm.[21] For example, a software engineer might develop techniques that would be beneficial to the firm's competitors. The problem arises because of possible employee turnover. First, can the firm create effective incentives to encourage the transmission of the specific knowledge by the employee before he or she leaves? Second, can the firm protect its investments in intellectual capital from expropriation by the departing employee? Here we focus on the second issue, as personnel economics has a long history of thinking about ways to reduce turnover (see Lazear 1998).

Both knowledge management and retention of key employees have received much attention within the management literature (and among consultants) for two reasons. The first is the current relatively high demand (and low unemployment rate) for highly skilled technical and professional employees. This has greatly increased labor market opportunities for these workers, leading to increased turnover. The usual way to reduce turnover is to offer deferred compensation that is not vested, but this is harder for firms to do successfully if the employee's outside alternatives rise rapidly. This is bound to be a transitory phenomenon, because markets will adjust eventually.[22]

Second is the more relevant issue regarding the long-run trend toward more knowledge-intensive work. How can a firm protect its intellectual capital? One possibility is to recognize the difficulty of preventing the employee from leaving and taking the knowledge. In this view, the intellectual capital is simply a form of general human capital. But the issue becomes more difficult if the employee's knowledge is in the form of trade secrets, as seems likely in the case of R&D employees. The optimal legal environment, restricting the employee's post-firm employment rights, is far from obvious. The issues are somewhat similar to those of patents in general. But general reluctance of employment law to restrict individual employee rights makes it more difficult for firms to protect their part of investments in such intellectual capital.

Designing in Adaptability

The discussion of organizational evolution hinged on the case where the firm's environment changes unexpectedly. But there is another sense in which a firm can think about evolution. It can design personnel policies with adaptability in mind, recognizing that the environment is likely to change (in some ways that are partially foreseeable, like future technology changes, and in some ways that are not foreseeable). This focuses on "Intermediate Outcomes," or attributes of personnel policies, that economists do not usually consider. Here we briefly mention some attributes that are likely to facilitate organizational adaptability.

First, our discussion of job design above emphasized the development and use of knowledge through job enrichment and related practices. Thus, job enrichment and, in some cases, decentralization of decision rights to employees, are ways that firms can develop some adaptability. Job enrichment facilitates continuous improvement by employees, which is more beneficial in settings where the firm's product, product line, or production technology change more rapidly.

"Empowerment" of certain decision rights allows the firm to tap into suggestions that may flow out of new information that comes to employees. This builds in a way for the firm to react to and exploit useful specific knowledge that arises in various pockets throughout the organization. This is especially true when what Fama and Jensen term (1983) "decision management" rights are decentralized. These are the rights to suggest new initiatives, and to decide how to implement new initiatives that have been chosen. Thus, we predict that decision management is more likely to be decentralized, the greater the change in the industry (in the sense of unpredictability, technology, competition, regulation, etc.).[23]

Another approach to adaptability is to invest in more adaptable employees (Lindbeck and Snower 2000). It is usually argued that giving workers a broader set of skills (either more skills, or including intellectual as well as physical skills) allows them to be redeployed more readily.

Implicit contracts with employees are clearly very important to adaptability. The firm would like to motivate employees to suggest new ideas, reveal specific knowledge, and be willing to be redeployed as circumstances change. To some extent these can be motivated by incentives and other practices, but they are likely to be affected to a great extent by implicit contracts. Thus, a firm culture that encourages suggestions, collaboration, some risk taking, and flexibility by employees would seem desirable in most cases.[24] Countering this is the problem of how to encourage employees' willingness to share knowledge in those cases where the firm is not able to offer plausible long-run employment promises.

Methodological and Empirical Issues

Complementarities?

Personnel economists have recently become very interested in *internal fit*, or complementarities among organizational policies. Much of this interest has been theoretical, stemming from Milgrom and Roberts's (1990, 1995) application of lattice theory. There has also been a strong interest in empirical work on internal fit in recent years, both inside and outside personnel economics (Ichniowski, Shaw, and Prennushi 1997; Levine 1995; MacDuffie 1995; Cappelli and Neumark 1999). Of course, at some level, it is inarguable that a firm should design personnel policies taking other policies into account, *ceteris paribus*. The real question is whether complementarity (or substitutability) between two or more specific policies has important effects on firm objectives like productivity.

We believe that economists' interest in complementarities is warranted. If the view that internal fit among policies can be an important source of organizational efficiency is correct, then this is important for us to understand and teach. Moreover, behavioral scholars have argued for decades that this part of the systems view is important. Much of their argument is based on case studies and on their experiences working with real organizations. This is not the kind of source for empirical insights that economists are used to using. However, many instances exist where economists have learned of important empirical insights or topics from other fields in this way (in the spirit of the first quote at the beginning of this chapter). Given the strength of this thread through the behavioral literature, economists should take this idea seriously.

Some surveys have argued that strong evidence now exists for the impact of internal fit on organizational effectiveness. Although we believe that existing evidence is provocative and promising, we remain somewhat more skeptical, and we argue that we have some way to go before we can be confident about the empirical validity of this concept. Consider, for example, the case of Lincoln Electric Co. (Berg and Fast 1975), the best-selling Harvard Business School case of all time. Economists often describe Lincoln Electric as an example of the value of internal fit. Lincoln makes extensive use of piece-rate incentives. The company also has other policies designed to deal with classic problems with piece rates, such as poor quality, lack of cooperation, and others. In particular, Lincoln's success is often attributed to its ability to use complementary implicit contracting practices that ensure effective subjective performance evaluations (Baker, Gibbons, and Murphy 1994). These practices are said to be especially effective because of Lincoln's long and consistent history. Indeed, Lincoln has experienced strong economic success, and few of the classic incentive system problems, for many years.[25]

However, consider another case study on piece-rate incentives, namely Safelite (Lazear 2000). Safelite instituted piece rate incentives for automobile windshield installers. Lazear's analysis indicates that productivity skyrocketed 20 percent to 40 percent, depending on how the effects of worker selection are estimated. These numbers are similar to the productivity differentials attributed to Lincoln's set of personnel policies. Yet Safelite did not obviously institute a system of complementary policies of the form seen at Lincoln. Nor did the company have strong implicit contracting and subjective performance evaluation, or a long history of consistent treatment of workers on which to base implicit contracts.

The disparity between these two case studies immediately makes one wonder how important complementarities really are to the effectiveness of personnel policies. Of course, these are only two observations, and the Safelite case was not written with a broad description of other policies in mind. Much preferred would be systematic empirical research with larger data sets, such as the works cited above.

One problem with empirical research on complementarities stems from the lack of strong theoretical analysis of the issues. Unless we can develop a convincing *ex ante* theory of precisely what policies are supposed to be complementary with each other, empirical work has little guidance for what set of policies to look for. Suppose that, following the literature on strategic human resource management, we observe that firms using a certain set of policies together tend to have higher productivity, lower costs, lower turnover, and so forth.[26] Are we to conclude that these policies exhibit complementarity or internal fit? Another possibility is simply that the policies are correlated with something else. Perhaps the policies just are often intelligent ones to use, so their use in practice is driven by correlation with managerial talent. Another possibility is that they are driven by some environmental variable. Perhaps a number of policies are all well adapted to certain production environments, but are not complementary with each other per se. Then a firm that uses this bundle of policies will have higher productivity, but not because of internal fit.

Therefore, before further empirical work on complementarities is done, we urge economists to think more carefully about the theory behind it. We need to develop more rigorous theories of exactly which policies are complementary with each other, and why. We also need to think more carefully about how to disentangle complementarities empirically from other effects that might drive mutual adoption of a set of policies (though consistency of empirical patterns with a well-respected theory would be a substantial step in that direction).

One way for theorists to tackle this problem is to consider Baron and Kreps's (1999) assertion that internal fit can lead to *patterns* of organizational design. If we can develop a theory that suggests that policies A, B, and C should be observed together, while policies D, E, and F should be observed together, but that firms should rarely use A, B, or C with D, E, or F, this would be an interesting and new test.[27] But that still begs the question of what determines whether a firm adopts one pattern or another. An even stronger theory would yield predictions on this dimension, so that we could test whether the incidence of any observed patterns (if there are such organizational design patterns) varies as predicted.

Thus, we also need to think about factors that might drive patterns of policies. We believe the answer here is to consider external fit. For example, our discussion of job design suggested that there might be two rough patterns, enrichment (with decentralization of some decision making) or specialization. It also suggested that the enrichment approach is more valuable in information-rich environments, where there is large scope for on-the-job learning. We described several examples of when a firm might have that kind of environment; for example, when a firm has made less use of industrial engineering; if the product line is relatively new; the product is complex; or technology is rapidly changing. These are testable predictions about the relationship between the firm's environment and the adoption or effectiveness of a pattern of personnel policies.

Empirical Research

Personnel economics is a productive and empirically relevant field. Great strides have been made, particularly in developing a theoretical structure that provides a rich framework for analyzing organizational issues. However, empirical work in the field is sparse and too narrowly focused. There are a large number of empirical studies of careers and compensation, but there is limited work on most other topics. For personnel economics to continue to grow and be influential, it is paramount that researchers focus more on empirical research.

There has been growing interest in collecting new types of data, especially personnel databases (e.g., Medoff and Abraham 1980; Lazear 1992; Baker, Gibbs, and Holmstrom 1994a, 1994b; Lazear 2000). Such databases are rich sources of information on the internal workings of firms. However, they have two limitations. First, these data sets are usually collected from a single or small number of firms, so generality of findings is an issue (though matched worker–firm data sets are starting to be collected, especially in Europe; see Abowd and Kramarz 1999). Second, by their nature, personnel databases focus on some variables (those collected for personnel computer systems) but exclude others.

The most common approach to solving the generality problem is to collect personnel data across a large sample of firms, typically in the same industry (Ichniowski and Shaw 1995). This substantially reduces the problem, though it does not entirely eliminate it if the data are from only a single industry. Unfortunately, such data collection is difficult and expensive, for it involves contacting and collecting data from many firms at once. Nevertheless, we hope to see more projects along these lines in the future.

A second problem with existing empirical work by economists is that it tends to ignore a wide variety of important and interesting issues, such as those discussed above. Some of the most interesting empirical work will require collecting *new kinds* of variables. Many of these variables are difficult to measure by traditional means. Others are subjective by nature. Nevertheless, it is important for economists to find ways to collect and analyze such data systematically, instead of leaving this area solely to behavioral researchers.

The most likely way to collect such data sets would be to write and administer surveys. Survey research is standard in most fields outside economics.[28] By using surveys, economists can begin to do empirical work on decision making, job design, organizational structure, implicit contracting, and so forth. For example, Cooper (1998) used survey techniques to measure employee cooperation, linking that to compensation contracts and other variables.

Behavioral researchers have developed a variety of methods to measure subjective dimensions of employment. For example, job satisfaction and commitment measure worker perceptions of the employment relationship; organizational citizenship behaviors (OCBs) measure the ways that they express their perceptions by taking actions that help the organization even if there is no immediate monetary reward (Mobley 1982; Hom et al. 1992). It would be interesting to interpret such data from the perspective of economic theories of implicit contracting, corporate culture, and repeated games. More generally, an extensive body of work by behavioral researchers links motivation and both effort and job performance (e.g., Whyte et al. 1955; Steers and Porter 1991). It might be interesting to relate such variables to how incentive contracts are designed, along the lines of typical economic studies that link incentives to quantitative output and cost measures.

Conclusion

Economics has added much to our understanding of personnel management and organizational design, as have behavioral approaches. Economics uses formal mathematical modeling more than do other fields. Such modeling has the benefit of providing a systematic way to derive conclusions about topics that otherwise might be too difficult to analyze formally. In the process, though, economics sometimes ends up throwing out much that is interesting. It does this in two ways. First, economic theory may be applied in areas where economists have already developed extensive insights. Thus, we have a vast literature on incentive theory. Second, empirical work in economics tends to follow traditional econometric methods and to focus on traditional econometric databases. Unfortunately these rarely have much interesting within-firm information.

Behavioral researchers tend to take a systems view of organizational design, which is one reason why they approach the field differently from economists. In recent years, economists have shown increasing interest in part of this view, namely *internal fit* (which they term "complementarity"). This is an important concept that deserves careful scrutiny. However, economic work on the idea of complementary has far to go. Empirical work is suggestive, but hardly conclusive. The theoretical underpinnings are scant. This issue would benefit from more thorough mathematical modeling and from more data collection.

To make progress, a logical starting place would be to bring in the related concept of *external fit.* It is sometimes argued that complementarities imply *patterns* of organizational design. Presumably, each pattern would be more useful for some purposes than for others. Thus, a useful way to begin modeling internal fit might be to consider how a firm's policies help achieve various intermediate outcomes, such as learning, adaptation, cost reduction, and others.

Economic theory of the internal design of firms would benefit from a richer view of *what actually happens inside firms.* Economic theory is highly abstract about jobs and other features of organizations. Of course, this has great value in developing generalizable insights. However, it means that economists have little to say about a great many important and practical topics. Economics could learn from other fields by paying attention to what behavioralists have found to be interesting topics.

We described several areas of organizational research where there is (yet) little economic work. These include intrinsic motivation, job design, decision making, coordination, and more specificity about implicit contracting. Notable about this list is how fundamental these issues are to organizational design. Moreover, most of them have to do with information, communication, and incentives. Economists should have much to say about these topics; we sketched only a few starting ideas.

Our discussion of how to conceptualize the firm had a theme: It is useful to view the firm as a *developer and processor of knowledge.* Many economic models use a physical task metaphor (such as the emphasis on eliciting "effort" in incentive models). Yet much of what is interesting about organizations is intellectual. If firms can effectively invest in industrial engineering, perfecting the process in advance, and if the product and market are stable, then it is reasonable for the firm to use a Tayloristic approach. The firm should then look much like Adam Smith's pin factory. But that does not apply to the majority of firms. There are fascinating and fundamental issues involved in collecting, processing, learning from, and communicating information within the firm. These issues are also important in understanding how organizations adapt and evolve.

The most interesting progress in personnel economics is likely to occur in empirical research. There are many important and interesting topics about which we still know little to nothing empirically. And, as Lazear (1999) argues, personnel economics must be empirical to be relevant in the long run. We need to *collect more data*. We need to *collect more interesting data*. To do so, we also will sometimes need to employ less traditional data-collection methods, such as surveys. These are not always easy or low cost tasks, but the returns can be enormous.

Notes

1. We are thinking about several overlapping fields. Lazear's (1999) definition of personnel economics is best for our purposes: "The use of economics to understand the internal workings of the firm."
2. Behavioralists distinguish between "policies" and "practices." The former indicates norms that are formally codified as officially sanctioned, whereas the latter indicates norms that may or may not be formally codified. Economists do not make such distinctions. We use either term to refer informally to both.
3. A notable exception is the long line of research in labor economics that tries to explain why workers with easily identifiable characteristics (union status, exempt status, race, ethnicity, gender) have different observed outcomes (wages, turnover, training). The motivation for this lies primarily with governmental policies on collective bargaining, overtime, benefits, and antidiscrimination laws. However, this objective has led economists to use nationally representative data sets to the virtual exclusion of within-firm analysis. Naturally, exceptions exist, such as Doeringer and Piore (1971) and Levine (1995).
4. Of course, "policies" themselves can be explicit or implicit, and intentional, historical, ad hoc, or accidental.
5. The "pins" were actually nails. Interestingly, Smith's analysis of specialization may trace back to Persia 900 years ago (Hosseini 1998).
6. As we were completing this draft, Lindbeck and Snower (2000) published a very interesting analysis of multitask job design that is closely related to our arguments. Their analysis provides a modeling framework for thinking about these issues, and it shows how changes in four factors can lead to greater use of job enrichment: changes in production and information technologies that promote task complementarities, changes in worker preferences, and advances in human capital that make workers more versatile. The first two are most closely related to our arguments. Our analysis is complementary to theirs in several ways. They present a stylized, technological view of multitask production, whereas we provide some theoretical underpinnings about intrinsic motivation, learning on the job, and what might specifically drive task complementarities. Our emphasis on learning and complexity of the work environment also more fully fleshes out an explanation for why there has been a recent trend toward job enrichment.
7. Hackman and Oldman (H&O) have a related idea in their model, "Task Significance," which they do not emphasize. This can mean several things. They describe it as "the degree to which the job has a substantial impact on the lives of other people"; obviously, this might affect the worker's utility function through altruism. Task Significance could also mean the degree to which the job affects utility directly

(Murdock 1998). An economist might add that a task could be significant to the worker if output affects the worker's pay, through incentive compensation.

8. It is worth noting that there is a debate over the causal factors behind intrinsic motivation; see Ryan and Deci (2000) for a (brief) review. According to Ryan and Deci, self-determination theory holds that intrinsic motivation is an innate propensity of the individual that can only be enhanced or diminished by external factors. According to this view, "all expected tangible rewards made contingent on task performance . . . undermine intrinsic motivation" (p. 70). If indeed this were the case, then job enrichment undertaken to enhance intrinsic motivation would be doomed to failure.

9. In the Tayloristic approach, workers are a source of variation and error; thus, they lead to quality problems and cost increases. In its ideal form, industrial engineering squeezes humans out of the process and uses mechanization instead. This is in striking contrast to the more modern view: Workers can be a source of ideas for improvement, quality, cost reduction, and so forth.

10. Note that it has nothing to do with intrinsic motivation and psychology. Further, the kind of intrinsic motivation that H&O argue is increased by job enrichment (mental involvement in the work) is ideal for decentralization and learning by workers. Thus, the H&O model overall has less to do with psychology than might initially seem apparent.

11. For an interesting economic view of Total Quality Management (TQM) programs (which usually employ "quality circles" or other forms of teams) as attempts to have workers engage in the scientific method to develop process improvements, see Jensen and Wruck (1994). In our view TQM is a special case of more general job enrichment methods designed to get employees to generate and use knowledge to improve quality and efficiency.

12. See Garicano (2000) for an interesting approach emphasizing costs of processing and transmitting knowledge.

13. Fama and Jensen (1983) provide an interesting extension, distinguishing between different types of decisions. They describe a four-stage process: generating ideas or initiatives; choosing/ratifying initiatives; implementing choices; and monitoring of implementation. They term the first and third processes "decision management" and, the second and fourth processes "decision control." The distinction provides a richer way of thinking about decision making and decentralization, but space limits prevent us from exploring it here. As a quick point, note that firms tend to use relative centralization of decision control to improve coordination, combined with relative decentralization of decision management to improve use of specific knowledge.

14. Galbraith (1995) provides a light treatment targeted toward practitioners, sufficient for an overview. Galbraith (1977) offers a more academic treatment.

15. Firms often organize along lines other than functional (e.g., product, geographical, or customer divisions). However, such structures almost always have a strong element of functional hierarchy within them. Breaking up into subhierarchies in this sense appears to be due to limitations on the optimal size of a hierarchy, such as communication costs, garbling of information, limits of managerial talent, and other factors.

16. The need to integrate economic activity across several decentralized agents with specific knowledge could be one reason for the existence of firms instead of markets. Price mechanisms might be inadequate for coordination when pockets of knowledge are costly to communicate but need to be integrated. This same logic suggests that incentives (internal substitutes for the price system) are unlikely to fully

achieve coordination inside a firm. If they could, it would beg the question of why the activity is internalized instead of using markets.

17. See Lawler (2000) for a discussion of the trade-offs involved.

18. At the extreme, if such cross-functional teams perform a majority of the critical work of the organization, then they may become the principal unit that defines the organizational structure (Mohrman, Cohen, and Mohrman 1995).

19. See Bailey and Cohen (1997) for a detailed review of the empirical literature.

20. A flip-side to this argument is that if organizational investments are costly or time-consuming, they might be a source of competitive advantage (a barrier to entry) if they are well matched to the firm's environment. For example, firms with long histories in relatively stable industries should have competitive advantages against new entrants, *ceteris paribus*.

21. Thus, the intellectual capital is firm-specific in the sense that it involves specific knowledge of the firm's technology, organization, methods, or products. But it is general in the labor market sense that it increases the employee's outside market value because competitors can benefit from learning this knowledge. It is different from the usual general human capital case because the benefit to the departing employee or competitor comes at the expense of the firm. Thus, there may be an efficiency loss when the employee departs, similar to firm-specific human capital. In this way it is similar to the transferable skills described by Stevens (1996).

22. David Finegold (personal communication) points out that, in the specific case of the demand for technical workers in the United States (especially software programmers), rapid and substantial rises in hourly wage rates during the 1990s did not lead to an adequate supply response. Lags and rigidities in the education system and immigration policy are the most likely reasons.

23. The method of evaluating initiatives also has implications for the firm's adaptability, as it affects the number of projects that are evaluated, the percentage that are accepted or rejected, the likelihood of Type 1 and Type 2 errors, and the overall "creativity" of firm projects (Sah and Stiglitz 1986).

24. Not all of these elements are desirable in all circumstances. For example, encouraging suggestions on process improvements from the cleaning staff at a factory producing explosive chemicals can be beneficial; but encouraging risk taking among these same staff could be quite detrimental. Similarly, changes to the production process at such a factory are only valuable if they can be codified and replicated (through the identification of best practices). So it may be optimal for management to limit the number and duration of times during which suggested deviations from standard operating procedures are vetted.

25. Though the Lincoln Electric case is now twenty-five years old, it remains relevant to the company's U.S. operations today. The policies in place in the United States as late as 1998 were almost identical to those described in the case. Though Lincoln had substantial difficulty in its overseas operations in the last decade or so, for a variety of reasons, its U.S. operations continue to operate with very high productivity.

26. Huselid (1995); MacDuffie (1995); Lawler et al. (1998); Guthrie (2001).

27. An additional test would be to look for cases of organizational change, and see if firms adopt theoretically complementary changes simultaneously, or whether doing so increases effectiveness of the change. Thus far, this approach has yielded mixed support for the theory of internal fit (Ichniowski and Shaw 1995; Lazear 2000).

28. In fact, most large data sets used in labor economics are also collected by government surveys, but economists have been insulated from the data-collection process.

References

Abowd, John, and Francis Kramarz. 1999. "The Analysis of Labor Markets Using Matched Employer–Employee Data." In Orley Ashenfelter and David Card, eds., *Handbook of Labor Economics.* Amsterdam: North Holland, vol. 3B, chap. 40, pp. 2629–2710.

Akerlof, George, and Janet Yellen. 1986. *Efficiency Wage Models of the Labor Market.* Cambridge: Cambridge University Press.

Bailey, Diane E., and Susan Cohen. 1997. "What Makes Teams Work: Group Effectiveness Research from the Shop Floor to the Executive Suite." *Journal of Management* 23(3): 239–290.

Baker, George, Robert Gibbons, and Kevin J. Murphy. 1994. "Subjective Performance Measures in Optimal Incentive Contracts." *Quarterly Journal of Economics* 109: 1125–1156.

Baker, George, Michael Gibbs, and Bengt Holmstrom. 1994a. "The Internal Economics of the Firm: Evidence from Personnel Data." *Quarterly Journal of Economics* 109(4): 881–919.

———. 1994b. "The Wage Policy of a Firm." *Quarterly Journal of Economics.* 109(4): 921–955.

Baron, James, and David Kreps. 1999. *Strategic Human Resources: Frameworks for General Managers.* New York: Wiley.

Beckmann, Martin. 1977. "Management Production Functions and the Theory of the Firm." *Journal of Economic Theory* 14(1): 1–18.

Becker, Gary S., and Kevin M. Murphy. 1992. "The Division of Labor, Coordination Costs, and Knowledge." *Quarterly Journal of Economics* 107(4): 1137–1160.

Beer, Michael, Bert Spector, Paul Lawrence, D. Quinn Mills, and Richard Walton. 1984. *Managing Human Assets.* New York: Free Press.

Berg, Norman, and Normal Fast. 1975. The Lincoln Electric Company, Case # 376–028. Boston: Harvard Business School Press.

Brickley, James, Clifford Smith, and Jerold Zimmerman. 2000. *Managerial Economics and Organizational Architecture.* New York: McGraw-Hill.

Calvo, Guillermo, and Stanislaw Wellisz. 1979. "Hierarchy, Ability, and Income Distribution." *Journal of Political Economy* 87(5): 991–1010.

Camerer, Colin, and Ari Vepsalainen. 1988. "The Economic Efficiency of Corporate Culture." *Strategic Management Journal* 9: 115–126.

Cappelli, Peter, and David Neumark. 1999. "Do 'High Performance' Work Practices Improve Establishment-Level Outcomes?" National Bureau of Economic Research working paper 7374.

Cooper, Joseph. 1998. "The Effect of ESOPs on Effort and Cooperation." Working paper, Tuck School, Dartmouth University, Hanover, NH.

Doeringer, Peter B., and Michael J. Piore. 1971. *Internal Labor Markets and Manpower Analysis.* Lexington, MA: D.C. Heath.

Fama, Eugene, and Michael Jensen. 1983. "Separation of Ownership and Control." *Journal of Law and Economics* 26: 301–326.

Galbraith, Jay R. 1977. *Organization Design.* Reading, MA: Addison-Wesley.

———. 1995. *Designing Organizations: An Executive Briefing on Strategy, Structure, and Process.* San Francisco: Jossey-Bass.

Garicano, Luis. 2000. "Hierarchies and the Organization of Knowledge in Production." *Journal of Political Economy* 108(5): 874–904.

Geankoplis, John, and Paul Milgrom. 1991. "A Theory of Hierarchies Based on Limited Management Attention." *Journal of the Japanese and International Economies* 5(3): 205–225.

Gibbons, Robert, and Michael Waldman. 1999. "Careers in Organizations: Theory and Evidence." In Orley Ashenfelter and David Card, eds., *Handbook of Labor Economics*. Amsterdam: North Holland, vol. 3B, chap. 36.

Guthrie, James P. 2001. "High Involvement Work Practices, Turnover and Productivity: Evidence from New Zealand." *Academy of Management Journal* 44(1): 180–190.

Hackman, J. Richard, and Edward E. Lawler III. 1971. "Employee Reactions to Job Characteristics." *Journal of Applied Psychology* 55(3): 256–286.

Hackman, J. Richard, and Gene R. Oldham. 1980. *Work Redesign*. Reading, MA: Addison-Wesley.

Hayek, Friedrick von. 1945. "The Use of Knowledge in Society." *American Economic Review* 35(4): 519–530.

Hirsch, Paul, Stuart Michaels, and Ray Friedman. 1987. "'Dirty Hands' Versus 'Clean Models': Is Sociology in Danger of Being Seduced by Economics?" *Theory and Society* 16: 317–336.

Hom, Peter W., Fanny Caranikas-Walker, Gregory E. Prussia, and Rodger W. Griffeth. 1992. "A Meta-Analytical Structural Equations Analysis of a Model of Employee Turnover." *Journal of Applied Psychology* 77(6): 890–909.

Hosseini, Hamid. 1998. "Seeking the Roots of Adam Smith's Division of Labor in Medieval Persia." *History of Political Economy* 30(4): 653–681.

Huselid, Mark. 1995. "The Impact of Human Resource Management Policies on Turnover, Productivity, and Corporate Financial Performance." *Academy of Management Review* 38(3): 635–672.

Ichniowski, Casey, and Kathryn Shaw. 1995. "Old Dogs and New Tricks: Determinants of the Adoption of Productivity-Enhancing Work Practices." *Brookings Papers: Microeconomics* 1–65.

Ichniowski, Casey, Kathryn Shaw, and Giovanna Prennushi. 1997. "The Effects of Human Resource Management Practices on Productivity: A Study of Steel Finishing Lines." *American Economic Review* 87(3): 291–313.

Jensen, Michael. 1998. *Foundations of Organizational Strategy.* Cambridge, MA: Harvard University Press.

Jensen, Michael, and William Meckling. 1992. "Specific and General Knowledge and Organizational Structure." In Lars Werin and Hans Wijkander, eds., *Contract Economics*. Oxford: Blackwell, pp. 251–274.

Jensen, Michael, and Karen Wruck. 1994. "Science, Specific Knowledge, and Total Quality Management." *Journal of Accounting and Economics* 18(3): 247–287.

Kaufman, Bruce E. 1999. "Expanding the Behavioral Foundations of Labor Economics." *Industrial and Labor Relations Review* 52(3): 361–392.

Kreps, David. 1990. Corporate Culture and Economic Theory." In James Alt and Kenneth Shepsle, eds., *Perspectives on Positive Political Economy.* Cambridge: Cambridge University Press, pp. 90–143.

———. 1997. "Intrinsic Motivation and Extrinsic Incentives." *American Economic Review Papers and Proceedings* 87(2): 359–364.

Lawler, Edward E. 1986. *High-Involvement Management.* San Francisco: Jossey-Bass.

———. 2000. *Rewarding Excellence: Pay Strategies for the New Economy.* San Francisco: Jossey-Bass.

Lawler, Edward E., Susan Albers Mohrman, and Gerald E. Ledford, Jr. 1998. *Strategies for High Performance Organizations—The CEO Report.* San Francisco: Jossey-Bass.

Lawrence, Paul, and Jay Lorsch. 1967. *Organization and Environment: Managing Differentiation and Integration.* Boston: Harvard Business School Press.

Lazear, Edward. 1992. "The Job as a Concept." In William Bruns, ed., *Performance Evaluation and Incentives.* Boston: Harvard Business School Press, pp. 183–215 .

———. 1998. *Personnel Economics for Managers.* New York: Wiley.

———. 1999. "Personnel Economics: Past Lessons and Future Directions." *Journal of Labor Economics* 17(2): 199–236.

———. 2000. "Performance Pay and Productivity." *American Economic Review* 90(5): 1346–1361.

Levine, David I. 1995. *Reinventing the Workplace: How Business and Employees Can Both Win.* Washington, DC: Brookings Institution.

Lindbeck, Assar, and Dennis Snower. 2000. "Multi-Task Learning and the Reorganization of Work: From Tayloristic to Holistic Organizations." *Journal of Labor Economics* 18(3): 353–376.

MacDuffie, John Paul. 1995. "Human Resource Bundles and Manufacturing Performance: Organizational Logic and Flexible Production Systems in the World Auto Industry." *Industrial and Labor Relations Review* 48: 197–221.

Medoff, James, and Katherine Abraham. 1980. "Experience, Performance and Earnings." *Quarterly Journal of Economics* XCV: 702–736.

Merchant, Kenneth, Wim Van der Stede, and Liu Zheng. 2000. "Disciplinary Constraints on the Advancement of Knowledge: The Case of Organizational Incentive Systems." Working paper Marshall School of Business, University of Southern California, Los Angeles.

Milgrom, Paul, and John Roberts. 1990. "The Economics of Modern Manufacturing: Technology, Strategy, and Organization." *American Economic Review* 80(3): 511–528.

———. 1992. *Economics, Organization and Management.* Englewood Cliffs, NJ: Prentice-Hall.

———. 1995. "Complementarities and Fit: Strategy, Structure, and Organizational Change in Manufacturing." *Journal of Accounting and Economics* 19(2–3): 179–208.

Miller, Eric J., and A.K. Rice. 1967. *Systems of Organization: The Control of Task and Sentient Boundaries.* London: Tavistock Publications.

Mobley, William H. 1982. *Employee Turnover: Causes, Consequences, and Control.* Reading, MA: Addison-Wesley.

Mohrman, Susan A., Susan G. Cohen, and Allan M. Mohrman, Jr. 1995. *Designing Team-Based Organizations: New Forms for Knowledge Work.* San Francisco: Jossey-Bass.

Moorman, Jere. 1983. *The Humorous Dictionary of Economics.* San Diego: Crane Publications.

Murdock, Kevin. 1998. "Intrinsic Motivation and Optimal Incentive Contracts." Working paper, Stanford Business School, Stamford, CA.

Prahalad, C.K., and Gary Hamel. 1990. "The Core Competence of the Corporation." *Harvard Business Review* 68(3): 779–792.

Prendergast, Canice. 1998. "What Happens Within Firms?" In John Hultiwanger, Marilyn Manser, and Robert Topel, eds., *Labor Statistics Measurement Issues* (NBER Working Paper). Chicago: University of Chicago Press.

———. 1999. "The Provision of Incentives in Firms." *Journal of Economic Literature,* 37(1): 7–63.

Rosen, Sherwin. 1982. "Authority, Control, and the Distribution of Earnings." *Bell Journal of Economics* 13(2): 311–323.

———. 1983. "Specialization and Human Capital." *Journal of Labor Economics* 1: 43–49.

Rousseau, Denise M. 1995. *Psychological Contracts in Organizations: Understanding Written and Unwritten Agreements.* Thousand Oaks, CA: Sage.

Ryan, Richard M., and Edward L. Deci. 2000. "Self-Determination Theory and the Facilitation of Intrinsic Motivation, Social Development, and Well-Being." *American Psychologist* 55(1): 68–78.

Sah, Raaj, and Joseph E. Stiglitz. 1986. "The Architecture of Economic Systems: Hierarchies and Polyarchies." *American Economic Review* 76(4): 716–727.

Senge, Peter M. 1990. *The Fifth Discipline: The Art and Practice of the Learning Organization.* New York: Currency Doubleday.

Smith, Adam. 1776. *The Wealth of Nations.* Reprinted by Modern Library.

Steers, Richard M., and Lyman W. Porter, eds. 1991. *Motivation and Work Behavior,* 5th ed. New York: McGraw-Hill.

Stevens, Margaret. 1996. "Transferable Training and Poaching Externalities." In Alison L. Booth and Dennis J. Snower, eds. *Acquiring Skills: Market Failures, Their Symptoms and Policy Responses.* Cambridge: Cambridge University Press, pp. 19–40.

Taylor, Frederick. 1923. *The Principles of Scientific Management.* New York: Harper & Row.

Thompson, James D. 1967. *Organizations in Action: Social Science Bases of Administrative Theory.* New York: McGraw-Hill.

Trist, Eric L., and Ken W. Bamforth. 1951. "Some Social and Psychological Consequences of the Longwall Method of Coal-Getting." *Human Relations* 4: 3–38.

Whyte, William Foote, Melville Dalton, Donald Roy, Leonard Sayles, Orvis Collins, Frank Miller, George Strauss, Friedrich Fuerstenberg, and Alex Bavelas. 1955. *Money and Motivation: An Analysis of Incentives in Industry.* Westport, CT: Greenwood Press.

Williamson, Oliver. 1975. *Markets and Hierarchies.* New York: Free Press.

Winship, Christopher, and Sherwin Rosen. 1988. "Sociological and Economic Approaches to the Analysis of Social Structure." *American Journal of Sociology* 94: S1–S16.

For Further Reading

Baron, James and Michael T. Hannan. 1994. "The Impact of Economics on Contemporary Sociology." *Journal of Economic Literature* 32(3): 1111–1146.

Gibbons, Robert. 1998. "Game Theory and Garbage Cans: An Introduction to the Economics of Internal Organization." In *Debating Rationality: Nonrational Aspects of Organizational Decision Making,* ed. Jennifer Halpern and Robert Stern. Ithaca, NY: ILR Press.

———. 1999. "Taking Coase Seriously." *Administrative Science Quarterly* 44: 145–157.

———. Forthcoming. "Firms (and Other Relationships)." In *The Twenty-First Century Firm: Changing Economic Organization in International Perspective,* ed. Papul DiMaggio. Princeton: Princeton University Press.

Lazear, Edward. 1991. "Labor Economics and the Psychology of Organization." *Journal of Economic Perspectives* 5(2): 89–110.

Simon, Herbert. 1991. "Organizations and Markets." *Journal of Economic Perspectives* 5(2): 25–44.

7

Household Work and Market Work: Toward a New Model of Worker Absenteeism

Richard Peter Audas and John Graham Treble

Estimates of the cost of worker absenteeism are enormous. For the British economy, the annual (but flawed) survey sponsored by the Confederation of British Industry regularly produces a number in excess of £10 billion. Despite this, economists' studies of absenteeism are somewhat thin on the ground. Instead, empirical work on the topic has been dominated by researchers with a background in applied psychology. These studies pose questions that can be summarized as: Why do employees sometimes absent themselves from work?

The main contention of the present chapter is that, though it is important to answer this question, it is only a small part of a bigger and potentially more revealing one: What determines the rate at which employees are absent from work? A second contention of the chapter is that the bigger question can only be answered by expanding the field of inquiry beyond the bounds of psychology. Of course, this observation is not new. Researchers in the field have long recognized that the context of absenteeism is of importance.[1] What we believe to be novel about our proposal is the idea that the rate of absence and a variety of properties of the work and household situation are

Revised version of a paper prepared for the 1999 SABE Conference at San Diego State University, June 12–14, 1999. This chapter draws heavily on our own recent work, and that of several other researchers, especially Tim Barmby, Melvyn Coles, and Marco Ercolani. Support from the ESRC (Contract No. R000222401) and the Leverhulme Trust is gratefully acknowledged. Responsibility for errors and omissions remains with us.

all *codetermined.* This codetermination can be summarized parsimoniously in the context of an economic, market model of employment contracts and the division of labor in the household.

Psychology deals with the motivation of employees confronted with a specified environment. It does not have a great deal to say about the way in which that environment is formed. And yet that environment is the outcome of the decisions of governments, of employers, and of health systems faced with a productive resource whose supply is unavoidably unreliable. Here economists' skills in analyzing markets and contracts have a great deal to contribute, as does work from a variety of intellectual traditions (including economics) dealing with the structure, behavior, and dynamics of households.[2]

Recent studies in the economics of absenteeism have made some progress in extending the bounds of the field of inquiry. The thrust of the work has been to concentrate on the bigger of the two questions. Researchers have also utilized new sources of data with which to study absenteeism and related phenomena. The goals of this chapter are to outline an economic theory within which the psychological ideas can be embedded; to indicate how this theory can be used to explain phenomena that cannot easily be explained on a psychological basis alone; and to outline where future research may helpfully be directed.

Psychological Research

The influential paper by Steers and Rhodes (1978) remains the leading theoretical vehicle for the study of absenteeism by psychologists, despite having been heavily criticized by (among others) its authors (Steers and Rhodes 1984). The first Steers/Rhodes paper offered a unifying theoretical model to synthesize the large volume of existing empirical research. Despite the vintage of the paper and its acknowledged imperfections, it remains an important source for those wishing to take a systematic approach to explaining employee absenteeism.

Steers and Rhodes' main idea was to examine the variety of empirical perspectives that had been taken on absenteeism in the literature and to develop a single theoretical framework within which the empirical literature could be understood. Steers and Rhodes noted that at the time they wrote their article, much of the existing work on absenteeism had been focused on using it as a measure of "withdrawal" from the work situation and viewed it as a potential predictor of turnover at some point in the future. Thus, absence was viewed as the manifestation of people's dissatisfaction with their present job.

Steers and Rhodes' process model posits that absence is a function of people's *motivation* to attend (work) and their *ability* to attend. They break down these two key factors into seven broad influences on work attendance. These are:

1. *The job situation.* This captures most of the attributes of the job. The researchers argue that job scope, job level, the degree of stress induced by the job, the size of the work group, the leadership style used by those who supervise the individual, the relationship the individual has with his and her coworkers and the individual's opportunities for advancement comprise the job situation. Empirically, they note that job content (what the individual actually does) plays a much bigger role in predicting absence than does job context (the work environment).

2. *Employee values and expectations.* In modeling absenteeism, it is not sufficient simply to describe the job situation, since different individuals may perceive it differently. Steers and Rhodes' idea of values and expectations is that every individual, when taking on a job, will form a set of criteria (regarding the attributes of the job) upon which they will evaluate the job.

3. *Personal characteristics.* Steers and Rhodes assert that the individual's expectations about the job will be largely influenced by personal characteristics. In particular, they note that education, tenure, age, gender, and family size can all influence the expectations one has about one's job. For instance, they argue that individuals with university degrees would expect jobs of a broad scope and with opportunities for advancement.

4. *Satisfaction with job situation.* Here the two researchers refer to the extent to which the attributes listed above actually meet the individual's expectations of their job. This is something of a theme for Steers, as he and Porter (1973) go to great lengths to discuss the idea of "met expectations," arguing that the extent to which a job does not meet the individual's expectations, the individual will be more likely to be absent from it. From an economist's perspective, this sounds like a matching story. They argue that individuals in "poor" matches (poor to the extent that they do not meet the individuals' expectations) are more inclined to be absent.

5. *Pressure to attend.* Steers and Rhodes argue that in addition to matching, there is a second class of factors exerting influence on the attendance decision, which they refer to as "pressure to attend." These include:

    • *The economic environment.* In times of high unemployment, individuals will have greater incentives to attend since losing one's job in a recession is more likely to lead to a lengthy spell of unemployment.

- *Incentive systems used by employers to reward good, or penalize poor, attendance.* The evidence discussed by Steers and Rhodes suggests that positive rewards for good attendance tend to have a stronger effect than does penalizing poor attendance.
- *Work group norms, or the pressure to attend exerted on a worker by coworkers.* This is often thought of as a function of the level of cohesiveness in the group. An economist might think of cohesiveness as being akin to worker complementarity (Rotemberg 1994), in which case the greater the cohesiveness (or complementarity) the greater the impact absence has on the productivity of other individuals in that work group.
- *Individual's personal work ethic (the individual's inherent value system) and organizational commitment.* This is defined by Steers and Rhodes (1978, p. 399) as "an agreement on the part of the employees with the goals and objectives of an organisation and a willingness to work towards these goals."

6. *Attendance motivation.* In the process model, attendance motivation is a function of the individual's satisfaction with the work situation (i.e., the extent to which the job meets the individual's expectations) and the pressure to attend from sources outside. A high level of satisfaction could be offset if the pressure to attend is low. This implies a highly satisfied worker in an organization that has few rewards for good attendance (or sanctions for poor attendance) would be more inclined to take absence than would an employee with a similar level of satisfaction facing greater rewards for attendance (or penalties for absence).

7. *Ability to attend.* An individual's ability to attend work is viewed independently from the person's motivation to attend. It incorporates factors such as health, family circumstances (which are a function of the individual's personal characteristics), and transportation problems. Health is clearly important. An individual could be as satisfied as possible with his or her job and also face significant external pressure to attend and still not be physically well enough to attend. Family circumstances, such as the presence of sick children, could inhibit a parent's ability to attend on a given day.

Attendance, in the Steers/Rhodes view, is determined by the interaction between one's motivation to attend and one's actual ability to do so. *Ability* to attend is driven by an individual's personal characteristics and the state of the person's health on any given day. *Motivation* to attend is a function of job satisfaction, which is determined by the extent to which the job in which they work meets the expectations that the individual has from employment. Steers and Rhodes argue that the expectations that one has of one's job are determined by personal characteristics. Pressure to attend can either be *internal* (commitment and work ethic) or *external* (work group norms, economic environment, rewards and penalties based on attendance).

From an economist's perspective, the Steers and Rhodes approach is interesting as it incorporates both labor supply and labor-demand factors. Hitherto, absence had been considered largely from the perspective of the individual's decision to supply labor.[3] It is also interesting in that it attempts to take a comprehensive view of the individual's decision to supply effort in the form of attendance. To this point, there had been no integrated theory or framework to examine the absence phenomenon, making the Steers and Rhodes model a landmark in the study of absenteeism.

The model has not gone uncriticized. Steers and Rhodes, in trying to incorporate virtually every hypothesis ever directed toward employee attendance, produce a model that lacks the rigor to make the findings sufficiently robust. Steers and Rhodes themselves point out that many of the studies used to build the process model use simple bivariate correlations, which may not hold up to a more sophisticated statistical analysis. Another problem that seems to receive little attention is the potential for endogenous relationships within the model. This is alluded to earlier with particular reference to motivation and work ethic, which are seen as independent from the extent to which an individual is satisfied with one's job. One other key criticism of this model is the extent to which it is testable. Many factors that are included in the model, such as measures of health, organizational commitment and work ethic, and the extent to which individual's expectations about the job are met, are very difficult to quantify.

In light of the criticism their model faced and the empirical evidence that emerged after its publication, Steers and Rhodes (1984) offered several ways in which their model could be improved. In particular, they suggested that more could be done to incorporate work-group norms explicitly, although they point out that there remains little empirical justification for the claim that these are important predictors of absence. They also note that job involvement appears to be a better predictor of absence than does job attitudes, and they suggest that this requires a further explanation. Finally, they note that "perceived" ability to attend might be more important than "actual" ability to attend, and they believe this to be a critical distinction.

They also answer some of the criticisms that have been leveled against their model. Steers and Rhodes maintain that in many ways their model has been misinterpreted, and they argue that in several respects the criticisms of it are unjustified. They do take some of the blame for this lack of clarity and offer a simplified schematic flow diagram which asserts that attendance motivation is a function of work-related attitudes, economic and market factors, organizational control systems, personal factors, and absence culture and work group norms. Attendance motivation interacted with perceived ability to attend determines absence.

Steers and Rhodes also arrive at a conclusion with relevance for what follows in the rest of the present chapter: The reduction of absenteeism may not always be efficient. They state:

> It is possible, however, that some absenteeism may in fact be healthy for organisations in that such behavior can allow for temporary escape from stressful situations (perhaps through the provision of personal days off), thereby potentially contributing to the mental health of employees. . . . In fact, rigid efforts to ensure perfect attendance (such as through behavior modification) may lead to unintended and detrimental consequences on the job, such as reduced product quality, increased accidents, and so forth. Hence, it would be helpful if future studies could examine the extent to which changes in absence rates have adverse consequences for other aspects of organisational effectiveness. If reduced absenteeism is accomplished at the expense of product quality, accident rate, strike activity, or employee mental health, serious cost-benefit questions must be raised concerning the desirability of initiating efforts aimed at reducing such behavior on the job. (1984, 265–266)

A virtue of the model outlined later in this chapter is that it shows under what conditions costly monitoring and control of absenteeism are inefficient.

Steers and Rhodes thus take issue with the view of much psychological literature that absence, lateness, and turnover all share similar roots and are manifestations of a single phenomenon—withdrawal. The key test of this idea on which the literature has focused is that turnover and absence behavior should be linked. However, the withdrawal school itself seems to be unsure about what the implications of withdrawal are. In a fairly recent survey, Mitra, Jenkins, and Gupta (1992) divide the withdrawal literature into three separate strands. Each strand forms a different prediction of the relationship between absence and turnover:

1. Absence and turnover may be positively related because withdrawal leads to increased levels of both.

2. They may be negatively related because absence and turnover are alternative means of expressing withdrawal.
3. Absence and turnover may not be related at all.

The third strand is typified by Porter and Steers (1973), who criticize the withdrawal school as follows: "Too often in the past absenteeism has been considered an analogue of turnover, and too often it has been assumed, without sufficient evidence, that the two shared identical roots."

They argue that absenteeism can be distinguished from turnover along three dimensions:

1. The negative consequences (for the individual) of absenteeism are much less than those associated with turnover. They argue that in a regime of complete or near complete replacement of wages with sick pay benefits, the employee can take absence at a relatively low cost, while turnover implies a complete severance of the employment relationship.
2. Absenteeism is more likely to be a spontaneous and easy decision, while quitting one's job must, generally, require much more serious consideration.
3. Absenteeism may represent a form of temporary avoidance and as such be a substitute for turnover, particularly when alternative employment might not be readily available.

Their line of reasoning suggests that absence and turnover may emanate from the same basic cause (dissatisfaction with one's job). However, the differences in the relative severity of the two actions mean that it may be possible to observe a considerable amount of individual absence without necessarily observing the same individuals quitting their job. They also point out that absence may be a result of a variety of other phenomena that have very little to do with withdrawal. Although an association might exist between absence and turnover, they argue that an observed increase in absenteeism does not necessarily (or even regularly) lead to a correct prediction of turnover.

Our own view, which is summarized in more detail below, coincides in many respects with the Steers/Rhodes model, although we believe that their emphasis on motivation and ability to attend is misplaced. Our argument is that psychology alone is inadequate to explain the observed rate of absence, which is best seen as arising from a conflict between the demands of household and market production on a single resource—time.

This view is not entirely new. The work of Chadwick-Jones, Nicholson, and Brown (1982) stressed the importance of working conditions in generating observed patterns of absence, and a large number of later studies have attempted to use classifications of working conditions to resolve the pattern of absence, turnover, and job satisfaction measures. This work broadens the focus, but it does not explain why there exists a variety of different types of working conditions or attitudes toward absence. Such factors are, at least partially, in control of managers, and effective management will choose an absence culture appropriate to its operation and its organizational goals.

The tools that managers have available to influence the absence culture are many and varied. They include hiring standards, incentive pay systems, provision of leisure facilities, and the intensity and type of monitoring and measurement methods used for absence. The idea of a contract as an all-embracing description, not only of what workers are paid, and the hours they are expected to work in return, but also of the conditions of work, fringe benefits, and systems of work-group norms and so forth has gained ground considerably in recent years[4] among labor economists, who have developed new tools for their analysis.[5] At the same time, the program of the New Home Economics, according to which households should be viewed as productive units, suggests that similar problems arise in the household context as arise in the workplace. According to this view, households have production systems, reward systems, and conditions of work in much the same way as firms do (Mincer 1962, 1963).

In the theory, the outlines of which are described below, we take this parallelism seriously, and we believe that it provides a more useful framework than do any of the previous approaches, all of which are, we believe, more partial in nature.

A Contracting Theory of Absenteeism

Our main purpose here is to outline an economic theory of absenteeism. This has been under development for some time, and it is now showing signs of yielding dividends in the form of new empirical possibilities and insights. The development of the model has been accompanied by the creation and exploitation of large data sets of various kinds that have permitted identification of a variety of effects, with a greater degree of confidence than data on workers alone will permit. The central point of the argument is that the difficulty experienced in pinning down relationships between absenteeism and turnover is due to what econometricians call an "identification problem." This can only be resolved by construction and estimation of models that embrace both company and worker decisions.

Identification problems are endemic in empirical market analysis. Suppose that workers in a particular firm for some reason decide they want to take more absence. The absence rate will rise. The firm may decide to take managerial action leading to a decline in the rate. These two movements in the absence rate have been identified as being a consequence of a demand shift and a supply shift, respectively. Usually, though, an investigator will not know which side of the market is generating a particular shift and will have to find ways of pinning down whether a given change was generated by a demand side shift or a supply-side shift, or possibly both.

The idea of time "allocation" is an important feature of modern labor economics. The ideas in the path-breaking articles by Mincer (1962,1963) and Becker (1965) now pervade both macro- and microeconomics. Becker's paper presents a rigorous analysis of the household as an organization that uses its budget of time and market-purchased commodities to produce goods which its members consume themselves. Market purchases are financed by selling time in the labor market.

We can view the firm in much the same light, except firms are generally thought of as purchasing *all* inputs in markets, and selling *all* outputs. There are two differences between a household and a firm in this view of the world:

1. Membership of a household is, at least in the short term, fixed,[6] so that the time available to the household can be treated as fixed, while firms can grow to an optimum size.
2. Households consume their own product, firms sell theirs. This difference is not very profound. Households show considerable flexibility in shifting the mix of outputs that are produced and consumed internally and those that are purchased from outside. Consider, for instance, the history of domestic service in the twentieth century, which shows a swing away from the market between the end of World War I and sometime in the 1970s and a resurgence in market purchases of cleanliness, cooking, and child-rearing since. These movements can be viewed as arising from changes in technology and the value of time, combined with the constraint implied by item 1.

Various models of labor supply arise from the Mincer/Becker framework in a natural way. Each household allocates its fixed endowment of time between market and home production. The outcome of this process depends on relative prices and the relative productivities of household members in the two production processes. Thus, the development of labor-saving household technology increases productivity in the household, enabling the production of a fixed level of output with less labor input. Although such a change will generate both a scale effect and a substitution effect, the substitution effect is likely to dominate. Hence, households and clothing have become cleaner since the invention of the vacuum cleaner and the washing machine, and women's labor supply to the market sector has also increased.

We can construct a model of absenteeism from this framework in a number of ways, but they all rely on the difficulties inherent in writing a contract of employment that accommodates rigidities in the market and household production functions. Indeed, if there were no such rigidities, absenteeism would not be an issue.

One popular way of introducing rigidity is simply to assume that employees' hours of work are fixed exogenously. This gives rise to a simple labor supply interpretation of absence, in which the marginal rate of substitution (MRS) between income and leisure at the fixed number of hours is not equal to the wage rate. This amounts to saying that the wage is set insufficiently high to generate labor supply equal to the fixed hours of work. Symmetrically, one can use this idea to produce a theory of overtime working.

Such a simple model begs the question of why an employer would propose a contract that is suboptimal for the employee, and also why an employee would accept it. One way of resolving these issues, discussed in Barmby and Treble (1991), is to observe that in many workplaces there are economies in uniformity. These are a consequence of complementarities in production, which imply that increased productivity can be achieved by simultaneous working. If workers are heterogeneous, then it may be cheaper for a firm to propose a uniform contract, and to allow workers to select into the contract if that is the optimal thing for them to do. Given that there will be a finite number of potential employers within the labor market, some workers will choose to sign contracts that do not exactly equalize their MRS and the wage. The observed incidence of absence will then arise from these workers.

This model leads to the conclusion that, given that the wage is too low, larger deviations from MRS imply higher rates of absence. This kind of model forms the basis of the empirical studies by Youngblood (1984) and Fichman (1988, 1989), both of whom measure deviations between MRS and the wage rate and relate them to observed absence patterns.

A somewhat different approach is to assume that marginal rates of substitution are subject to random shocks. In this version of the model, we think of workers as signing a contract that has MRS equal to the wage "on average." In this version, all workers are at risk of taking absence from time to time, but they can differ in the variance of that risk. Then it is workers who have high variance who take more absences. This kind of model was first introduced by Barmby, Orme, and Treble (1991), and has been adopted subsequently by Barmby, Sessions, and Treble (1994), Brown, Fakhfakh, and Sessions (1999), and Coles and Treble (1993, 1996).

The last of these papers develops an explicit contracting model in which firms offer job contracts specifying a wage and an acceptable absence rate. The outcome is a proposition similar to one in Allen (1981) in which hetero-geneous workers sort among heterogeneous firms, so that workers with high propensities for absence sign contracts with firms whose production is not highly dependent on worker reliability. The model implies that there should be a negative relationship between absence rates and the wage, but this arises for reasons different from those highlighted in the pure supply model. There, absenteeism arises because workers cannot find a contract that suits them exactly. Here, workers are absent because their contract allows them to be. They are able to negotiate such a contract because of their willingness to take a reduced wage in exchange for a greater degree of flexibility in working hours.

What determines the observed rate of absence in a model of this sort? The sorting equilibrium is determined in the usual way (see Rosen 1986), with workers who value absence highly being employed in firms with technology that is relatively independent from absenteeism. In particular, we show that firms with complementarities in production have less elastic demand for re-liability than do firms whose labor works independently. The reason for these patterns is that when production is linear in the input of a worker, the value of the marginal product is equal to the profit-maximizing wage rate. When there are complementarities, the value of the marginal product is greater than the wage rate. This implies that for firms whose technology is "lumpy," an absence is more expensive, *ceteris paribus*, than for firms with linear tech-nology. The separating equilibrium also implies the existence of a wage pre-mium (or compensating differential) for reliability.

The main characteristics of the equilibrium in the Coles/Treble model can be summarized as:

- Workers' marginal rate of substitution between permissible absence and remuneration is set equal to the cost to the firm of the marginal absence.
- Firms' iso-profit lines are, in general, nonconcave; this means that mul-tiple equilibria are possible, and also that there is likely to be consider-able instability in the cost to the firm of the marginal absence.
- The cost to the firm of the marginal absence varies with the degree of complementarity in production. In particular, a production function in which the process does not work at all unless sufficient workers are present to form a complete team ("assembly line" production) yields a larger cost of absence than does a linear technology.
- Sorting of workers between firms reflects both their tastes and the tech-nology used by the firm. An assembly line firm will employ low absence workers at higher wage rates than will a firm with linear technology.

- Firms with nonlinear technologies will in general find it profitable to employ a larger workforce than the minimum required by the technology.

Because the Coles/Treble (1996) model is a pure selection model, it does not consider the moral hazard aspects of absenteeism.[7] *Moral hazard* is a term arising from the insurance industry, where it refers to the tendency for persons to run greater risks when insured than when they are not. An excellent example of the problem in the context of absence is given by the work of Denerley (1952) and Buzzard and Shaw (1952) who observed a doubling of the absence rate when a new sick pay scheme was introduced.

The problem of absence control is the focus of an enormous amount of managerial effort, is heavily influenced by a variety of government social policies, and deserves to be taken seriously. Coles and Treble envisage a permissible level of absence, but how this is enforced is unexplored by them, and it is an important current research question. Morally hazardous behavior has been observed in absenteeism studies ever since the early studies of Vernon and co-workers (1928, 1931). It appears in numerous anecdotes about worker behavior and is responsible for the extraordinary creativity demonstrated by management in the design of monitoring, recording, and incentive systems. This is especially true in Britain where state-mandated levels of sick pay are far from generous.

The separation of selection effects and moral hazard suggests a useful analytical distinction between strategies designed to mitigate the impact on profits of absenteeism, and those designed to control the level of absenteeism itself. A striking feature of the Coles/Treble model is its prediction that firms will maintain a stock of workers as a buffer. Many firms do this, but there are several other ways in which the impact of absenteeism on profit can be diminished (e.g., by rescheduling work and reassigning tasks, or by selecting workers). These are probably best viewed as features of the production technology. As far as we are aware, there are no systematic studies of this aspect of corporate behavior.

We have argued that there will be a compensating differential paid to reliable workers by those firms who find unreliability expensive. This argument applies equally to households. There will exist an implicit premium that compensates reliable household workers for attending to household production where it is not robust to be absent.[8] This explains why absence is higher for workers who have children than for those who do not. But it also has other implications. In a household with two adults, both of whom may choose to participate in market production as well as household production, a feasible solution to the joint time allocation problem is for one partner to specialize in reliable labor supply to the market, while the other specializes in reliable labor supply to the household. In this way, the household can earn both premiums. In future work, we intend to develop this idea, which we conjecture will go some way toward explaining the observed pattern of absenteeism both within and between households.

Such a model has other enticing features: It predicts the emergence of primary and secondary workers in the market sector (and in the household sector). The main characteristic of the primary worker is reliability in market labor supply. With that goes higher remuneration, greater job attachment, more training opportunities, and many other characteristics that have been associated with primary workers in the dual labor-market literature. The main characteristic of secondary workers is unreliability in market labor supply: with it go low remuneration, low job attachment, few promotion and training opportunities, and other traditional characteristics of secondary workers. The other side of this coin is that unreliability in *market* labor supply can be a consequence of reliability in *household* labor supply. It is not possible to be perfectly reliable in both if there is any uncertainty in the system at all. What the Coles/Treble theory does not achieve is a satisfactory explanation of why the division of labor should be gendered. However, it has the potential to make that phenomenon easier to understand, because of the symmetry in the theory.[9]

The efforts of firms to reduce absentee levels have been the subject of extensive study by management specialists (e.g., Confederation of British Industry 1994). There exists a bewildering variety of schemes, some providing rewards for good attendance, others imposing punishments for poor attendance. Often, schemes will link attendance to some aspect of remuneration. Two schemes with particularly interesting dynamic structures include the experience-rated sick pay scheme described in Barmby et al. (1991) and a scheme that links absence dynamically to overtime entitlement (Barmby, Brown, and Treble 1997).

How Do the Theories Handle the Evidence?

In two recent papers, Barmby, Ercolani, and Treble (1999, 2000) have extracted from the Labour Force Surveys (LFS) a consistent series of absence rates for Britain at monthly, quarterly, and annual frequencies, and for several other countries at annual frequencies. The series for Britain are available for the period from 1971 to 1997, and because they are derived from surveys of individuals, they can be disaggregated by a number of different characteristics of individuals and their jobs. The data are also suited to multivariate analysis. Audas (1999) has undertaken a similar exercise for the

Figure 7.1   Absence Rate by Quarter, Great Britain

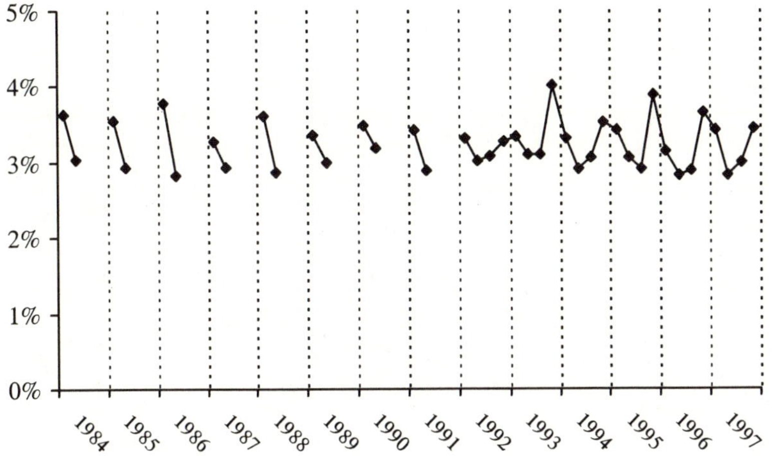

Source: Barmby et al. (1999).

United States with data from the Current Population Surveys, and it seems likely that similar data for other countries can be extracted.

In this work, the absence rate is defined as the hours reported absent due to illness expressed as a proportion of contracted work hours. The plots displayed below are for Great Britain, but similar pictures can be generated relatively easily for other countries. A plot of the quarterly absence rate series for Britain is given in Figure 7.1.[10] The key features of the series are that the long-term trend is flat and that there exists a strong seasonal element, with the absence rate being higher in the first and fourth quarters of each year.

As an example of the possibilities of the LFS, we decompose the absence rate in Britain by age and gender. The decomposition by age is presented in Figure 7.2. The absence rate increases for both genders from the age of twenty to retirement age. After retirement age the absence rate is low, which is almost certainly due to a selection effect. People who choose to continue to work after retirement are more reliable.

A decomposition by gender and year shown in Figure 7.3 indicates that the absence rate for women is systematically higher and that the gap seems to have increased with time, especially since 1988.

Decompositions of the absence rate dependent on the respondent working in the private or public sector are shown in Figure 7.4. The public sector experiences a systematically higher absence rate than does the private sector.

How would the idea of withdrawal explain these observations? The seasonal patterns seem more likely to be associated with temporary sickness (or

Figure 7.2   **Decomposition of Absence Rate by Age, Great Britain, 1984–1997**

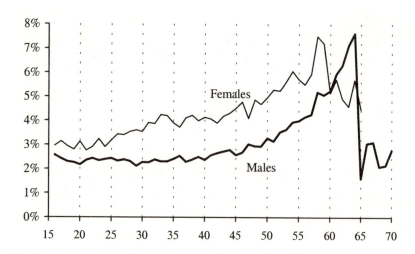

Source: Barmby et al. (1999).

Figure 7.3   **Absence Rate by Year and Gender, Great Britain, 1984–1997**

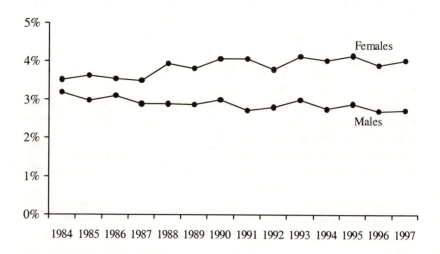

Source: Barmby et al. (1999).

Figure 7.4   **Absence Rate by Year and by Private/Public Sector Workers, Great Britain**

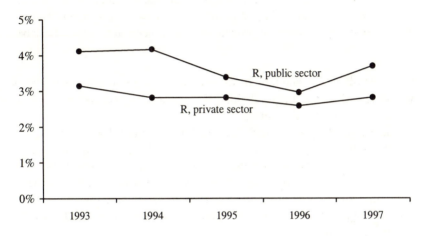

Source: Barmby et al. (1999).

other seasonal changes in tastes) than with a permanent withdrawal. The observed difference between public and private sector employees might be explained by more frequent, more severe, or more widespread withdrawal in the public sector than in the private sector. If that is the case, then we would like to know why, and what the implications for public sector budgets may be. Is it because the characteristics of individuals who seek public sector jobs are different, or because the management of the public sector is less rigorous in controlling absence?

Consider now the changing rates of absence across genders. To explain these using the idea of withdrawal, one would need to argue either that women were withdrawing in larger numbers, or that those women who displayed withdrawal behavior were withdrawing to a greater extent over time or that for some reason the withdrawal has become increasingly more likely to be expressed as absence behavior over time. Of course, some or all of these effects may be present simultaneously, and for men one would need to argue the opposite.

Suppose one could show that women are withdrawing in larger numbers, then two further questions are raised: Why? and Why have firms continued to employ women in ever greater numbers in the face of such apparent lack of attachment? As to why women might be withdrawing in greater numbers, there are two important possibilities:

1. A genuine behavioral change has been taking place, perhaps because the nature of the relationship between firm and household has changed; or
2. The observed pattern is due to composition effects as the female workforce has enlarged during the last two decades, and women with higher absence propensities have been drawn into the labor market.

The question of why and how firms can tolerate increasing absence rates is not addressed within the psychological paradigm, as firms are not seen as subjects for psychological study.

Theories of the psychological motivation for work alone are inadequate to explain the data. At the very least a theory of a firm's attitudes to absence is needed, for without such a theory, we cannot explain why there exist apparently consistent differences in absence rates across different type of firms. In addition, it is probably necessary to understand how households moderate absence. Is the contracting theory outlined above able to provide convincing explanations?

Before we can be sure that it can, much more research must be done. However, we can describe here the outline of how these observations might be explained by the theory. In the Coles/Treble view of the world, different firms and industries can have different absent rates for several reasons. These are all associated with the idea that management's incentive to control absence is linked to the costs of control and the potential benefits from doing so. It seems likely that these incentives differ consistently across private and public sector firms, with absence being either cheaper to control, or more expensive as a source of lost profits in private industry than in public.

Changes in the male and female rates of absence are almost certainly associated with other broad features of changing labor markets at the turn of the twentieth century. Female participation continues to rise, and an explanation of the pattern observed in the raw data would be based primarily on the consequences of this for the kinds of jobs that women do, and second on associated and interlinked changes in household structure and behavior. It would seem impossible to handle all these issues without a model that deals with both household and firm production, such as the one proposed above.

Conclusion

At the center of the new approach to the study of absenteeism proposed here is the idea that a person cannot be at two places at once. Attendance at work implies absence from the household. The idea that worker absenteeism arises from a tension between the demands of household and market production is not an especially surprising one. conversely, the idea that withdrawal on its own is a useful lens through which to observe absence behavior seems inconsistent with the evidence.

The Steers and Rhodes' division of the problem into motivation and ability to attend to work is more useful. But it also draws attention to the shortcomings of a purely psychological approach. Workers' ability to attend is determined by many aspects of their lives, including the structure of their households and the nature of household responsibilities. To think of a worker's motivation outside the context of their chosen contract of work fails to take account of an employing firm's interest in controlling behavior.

Our argument here is that contract structure is a mechanism for moderating the interests of households and the interests of firms, and with it the pattern of absenteeism behavior. It also replaces the Steers and Rhodes' notion of "process" (which involves a feedback from behavior to motivation) with a market model of observed attendance at work and in the household, in which this behavior is codetermined with a variety of other aspects of the work situation.

As Kaiser (1998, p. 82) so neatly puts it: "[T]he distinguishing feature of the management literature is the assumption that the motivation to be absent (or attend) is determined internally within a given individual." We believe that emphasis needs to be placed much more heavily on analysis of the institutional structure within which household and market work are carried out, and that such a change of emphasis has great potential for further insights.

Finally, it should be stressed that the apparently abstract modeling issues in this chapter have important practical implications for the conduct of human resources management. We draw attention to just one here: the error of "benchmarking." The idea of a benchmark rate of absence is that it reflects "best practice" in the industry or sector to which the firm belongs. The minimum rate in the sector is often chosen as a benchmark. The theory outlined above implies that neither comparison with other firms nor a choice of a low rate as target is a necessarily efficient procedure. All other things being equal, an efficient rate of absence for a firm whose technology is robust to absenteeism will be higher than the efficient rate for firms with less robust technology, and devoting resources to hitting an inefficiently low absence target leads to lower profits, not higher ones.

Notes

1. For a concise and readable survey, see Kaiser (1998).
2. "Household" throughout this chapter should be broadly construed. Prior to the development of the factory system, the conflict between household and market work

was less clear-cut as much market production took place in the household. Modern technology appears to be creating conditions in which the spatial conflict stressed in this chapter can once again be eased by a resurgence of cottage industry.

3. A notable exception is Deardorff and Stafford (1976).

4. See Lazear (1993) for a comprehensive statement of this case.

5. For an introduction to this literature, see Milgrom and Roberts (1992).

6. That is, exogenous to this model. In concentrating on reliability of labor supply, we need to narrow the focus of inquiry to some extent.

7. Coles and Treble (1993) present a moral hazard argument. Current work includes melding these two aspects of imperfect information.

8. Because household work is rarely explicitly paid, these premiums are unlikely to take a monetary form. Nonetheless, the provision of reliable child-care clearly has a utility value not only to the child, but also to the parents. Grossbard-Shechtman (1993) introduces and investigates the concept of the spousal wage.

9. The symmetrical treatment of household and firm in the model is one of its most attractive features. See Stewart and Golubetsky (1996).

10. Between 1984 and 1991, British LFS data exist only for the first quarter of the year.

References

Allen, Steve. 1981. "An Empirical Model of Work Attendance." *Review of Economics and Statistics* 63: 77–87.

Audas, Rick. 1999. *Essays on Absenteeism.* Doctoral dissertation, University of Wales, Bangor.

Barmby, Tim, Sarah Brown, and John Treble. 1997. "Absenteeism and Overtime: A Dynamic Model with Endogenous Constraints." Mimeograph, University of Newcastle-upon-Tyne.

Barmby, Tim, Marco Ercolani, and John Treble. 1999. "Sickness Absence in Great Britain: New Quarterly and Annual Series from GHS and LFS, 1971–1997." *Labour Market Trends* August: 405–415.

———. 2000. "Sickness Absence: An International Comparison." http://www.bangor.ac.uk/~abs003/main.htm.

Barmby, Tim, Chris Orme, and John Treble. 1991. "Worker Absenteeism: An Analysis Using Microdata." *Economic Journal* 101: 214–229.

Barmby, Tim, John Sessions, and John Treble. 1994. "Absenteeism, Efficiency Wages and Shirking." *Scandinavian Journal of Economics* 96: 561–566.

Barmby, Tim, and John Treble. 1991. "Betriebliche Fehlzeiten und Arbeitsvertrage." *Mitteilungen aus der Arbeitsmarkt- und Berufsforschung* 24(3): 595–604.

Becker, Gary. 1965. "A Theory of the Allocation of Time." *Economic Journal* 75: 493–517.

Brown, Sarah, Fathi Fakhfakh, and John Sessions. 1999. "Absenteeism and Employee Sharing: An Empirical Analysis Based on French Panel Data 1981–91." *Industrial and Labor Relations Review* 52: 234–251.

Buzzard, R.B., and W.J. Shaw. 1952. "An Analysis of Absence Under a Scheme of Paid Sick Leave." *British Journal of Industrial Medicine* 9: 282–289.

Chadwick-Jones, J.K., Nigel Nicholson, and Colin Brown. 1982. *Social Psychology of Absenteeism.* New York: Praeger.

Coles, Melvyn, and John Treble. 1993. "The Price of Worker Reliability." *Economics Letters* 41: 149–155.

———. 1996. "Calculating the Cost of Absenteeism." *Labour Economics* 3: 169–188.

Confederation of British Industry. 1994. *Managing Absence—In Sickness and In Health.* London: Centre-File, Quality Business Solutions.

Deardorff, Alan, and Frank Stafford. 1976. "Compensation of Co-operating Factors." *Econometrica* 44: 671–684.

Denerley, R.A. 1952. "Some Effects of Paid Sick Leave on Sickness Absence." *British Journal of Industrial Medicine* 9: 275–281.

Fichman, Mark. 1988. "Motivational Consequences of Absence and Attendance: Proportional Hazard Estimation of a Dynamic Motivation Model." *Journal of Applied Psychology* 73: 119–134.

———. 1989. "Attendance Makes the Heart Grow Fonder: A Hazard Rate Approach to Modeling Attendance." *Journal of Applied Psychology* 74: 325–335.

Grossbard-Shechtman, Shoshana. 1993. *The Economics of Marriage.* Boulder, CO: Westview Press.

Kaiser, Carl. 1998. "What Do We Know About Employee Absence Behavior? An Interdisciplinary Interpretation." *Journal of Socio-Economics* 27: 79–96.

Lazear, Edward. 1993. *Personnel Economics*, Cambridge, MA: MIT Press.

Milgrom, Paul, and John Roberts. 1992. *Economics, Organization and Management.* Englewood Cliffs, NJ: Prentice-Hall.

Mincer, Jacob. 1962. "Labor Force Participation of Married Women: A Study of Labor Supply." In *Aspects of Labor Economics*, ed. H.Gregg Lewis, pp. 63–97. Princeton, NJ: Princeton University Press.

———. 1963. "Market Prices, Opportunity Costs and Income Effects." In *Measurement in Economics*, ed. Carl Christ, pp. 67–82. Stanford, CA: Stanford University Press.

Mitra, Atul, G. Douglas Jenkins Jr., and Nina Gupta. 1992. "A Meta-Analytic Review of the Relationship Between Absence and Turnover." *Journal of Applied Psychology* 77: 879–889.

Porter, Lyman, and Richard Steers. 1973. "Organizational, Work and Personal Factors in Employee Turnover and Absenteeism." *Psychological Bulletin* 80: 151–176.

Rosen, Sherwin. 1986. "The Theory of Equalizing Differences." In *Handbook of Labor Economics*, vol. 1, eds. Orley Ashenfelter and Richard Layard, pp. 641–692. Amsterdam: North Holland.

Rotemberg, Julio. 1994. "Human Relations in the Work Place." *Journal of Political Economy* 102: 684–717.

Steers, Richard, and Susan Rhodes. 1978. "Major Influences on Employee Attendance: A Process Model." *Journal of Applied Psychology* 63: 391–407.

———. 1984. "Knowledge and Speculation About Absenteeism." In *Absenteeism*, eds. P.S. Goodman and R.S. Aitken, pp. 229–275. San Francisco: Jossey-Bass.

Stewart, Ian, and Mark Golubetsky. 1996. *Fearful Symmetry.* London: Penguin Books.

Vernon, H.M., and T. Bedford. 1928. "A Study of Absenteeism in a Group of Ten Collieries." London: Medical Research Council, Industrial Fatigue Research Board No. 51.

Vernon, H.M., T. Bedford, and C.G. Warner. 1931. "Two Studies of Absenteeism in Coal Mines." London: Medical Research Council, Industrial Health Research Board No. 2.

Youngblood, Stuart. 1984. "Work, Nonwork and Withdrawal." *Journal of Applied Psychology* 69: 106–117.

Part IV

Comparing Ideas on
Family and Church

8

The Economics and Sociology of Marriage: Historical Trends and Theories of In-Marriage Household Labor

Shoshana Grossbard-Shechtman

The economics of marriage includes the application of economics to studies of marriage formation and dissolution, type of marriage, and decision making within marriage. In turn, decisions made by married couples can cover a wide range of topics, from labor-force participation and division of household labor to contraceptive use and savings. The economics of marriage applies to all these topics. The entry of economists into this field of application of economics started when Gary Becker published his economic theory of marriage in 1973. This path-breaking analysis was one of the reasons why Becker was awarded the Nobel Prize in 1992. But economic concepts penetrated into the study of marriage before economists moved into this field: Sociologists of marriage had been importing economic concepts at least since the 1930s. This chapter presents a history of the application of economics to the study of marriage, including an assessment of the impact of Becker's theory of marriage. The chapter then makes some comparisons between the economics of marriage and the economics of fertility, and between the economics and sociology of marriage. Particular differences between a sociological and economic approach to marriage are emphasized via the example of two theories of division of labor within marriage: the dependency model

I am grateful to Michael Brien, Xuanning Fu, and Evelyn Lehrer for helpful comments.

developed by sociologists and an economic model of Work-In-Marriage (WIM) markets that is in the New Home Economics (NHE) tradition.

Within academia, there continues to be a long-standing division of labor between economists and sociologists, with economists more involved in studying monetized transactions and sociologists maintaining a grip on the study of most nonmonetized transactions, including marriage. It is hoped that this chapter will help readers address the following questions: Is this academic division of labor optimal? What could be gained if more economics was imported into the field of marriage research?

Early Uses of Economic Concepts in the Sociology of Marriage

Traditionally, marriage is a topic that has been studied mostly by sociologists, social anthropologists, and social psychologists (they will all be called "sociologists" here). Sociologists did not wait for Becker to open their eyes to the applicability of economic concepts to the study of marriage; they started applying these concepts as early as 1937. Two assumptions dear to economists—rational choice and bargaining among potential spouses—can already be found in an article on dating published by Willard Waller as early as 1937. A major figure among the functionalists, sociologist Robert Merton (1941) wrote about intermarriage in terms of "compensatory reciprocal exchange." In such exchange, individuals belonging to a less desirable group compensate their mate by bringing higher levels of desirable personal resources such as wealth or beauty. Such reasoning is totally in line with more recent market analyses of intermarriage (such as Grossbard-Shechtman 1983a, 1993). So are sociological studies of marriage market effects on intermarriage, such as done by David Heer (1962), Erich Rosenthal (1970), Sergio Della Pergola (1976), and Wesley Fisher (1980).

Theories of exchange in marriage were contributed by J.W. Thibaut and H. H. Kelley (1959) and Robert Blood and Donald Wolfe (1960), and a social exchange theory of divorce was contributed by George Levinger (1965). About the same time, sociologists George Homans (1961) and Peter Blau (1964) were offering theories of social exchange that analyzed situations of bargaining not only in marriage but also in other social contexts.

The basic reasoning in these social exchange theories is similar to that found in the bargaining theories of marriage contributed by Marilyn Manser and Murray Brown (1980) and Marjorie McElroy and Mary Jane Horney (1981).[1] Not only did these early sociologists discuss bargaining and negotiations within marriage, but many of them also recognized that marriage market conditions influence individual husband/wife bargaining results; for example, Thibaut and Kelley (1959), Homans (1961), Heer (1963), Blau (1964), and Levinger (1965).

Sociologists have also preceded economists in writing about how marriage market circumstances affect many other kinds of behavior. Sex ratio—the ratio of men to women in a marriage market—is a determinant of marriage market conditions that is particularly easy to measure, and therefore marriage market analyses often look at sex ratios. Early examples of sociological analyses of the effects of sex ratios on marriage rates include P. Karmel (1946), Louis Henry (1966, 1975), and Paul Glick, John Beresford, and David Heer (1963).[2] In addition, sociologists have investigated the effect of sex ratios on husband/wife differences in age and education (Graham Spanier and Paul Glick 1980), suicide (Marcia Guttentag and Paul Secord 1983), and crime (Guttentag and Secord 1983; Katherine Trent and Scott South 1989), topics that so far have not been treated by economists. As for sex ratio effects on premarital sex, out-of-wedlock births, and cohabitation, they were analyzed independently by an interdisciplinary team (Heer and Grossbard-Shechtman 1981) and sociologists Guttentag and Secord (1983).[3]

Most economic analyses of marriage are based on assumptions regarding the division of labor within a marriage. Becker (1981) assumes that wives engage in household labor more than do husbands (i.e., they specialize in household production). The assumption that wives specialize in household production can also be found in the writings of Talcott Parsons (1942), a major figure in the so-called functionalist school in sociology.[4] At the same time, sociologists have recognized that women may be motivated by a desire for independence from traditional family norms regarding intrahousehold division of labor (Valerie Oppenheimer 1970). Women's wages relative to men's were analyzed as contributing to married women's independence in decision making, including labor force participation, in the works of sociologists before similar arguments were made by economists trained in bargaining theories.

The sociological theories of exchange did not just reinvent economics independently: Homans, Blau, along with Karen Cook and Richard Emerson (1978), explicitly acknowledge their debt to economic theory. The impact of economic concepts on Homans and other early sociologists should be seen as part of more general trends in sociology as a discipline related to economics. From the start, sociology was inspired by economics. One of the founders of sociology, Max Weber, was a professor of economics in Germany (see Reinhard Bendix 1962). Another founder of sociology, whose writings date back to the nineteenth century, Emile Durkheim (1949), placed the economic concept of division of labor at the center of his conceptual framework. It has been claimed that in the United States, sociology departments were created to deal with issues that economists were neglecting.

Though social exchange theory can be considered as an economic theory, some other sociological writings on marriage that have been called "theories" would not be considered as theories by most economists and have not been called that way by some sociologists, including Homans, who stated:

> Not until one has properties, and propositions stating the relations between them, and the propositions from a deductive system—not until one has all three does one have a theory. (1964, 812)

Propositional inventories considered as theories by Parsons (1942), Hill, Katz, and Simpson (1957), or Burr, Hill, Nye, and Reiss (1979) do not qualify as theories following Homans' standards or standards used by economists.

Even in the case of social exchange theory, the sociologists who adapted this version of price theory did not fully take advantage of market analysis, the core of microeconomics. Like most of his contemporaries, Homans (1961, 68) did not realize that the concepts of market and price are applicable to nonfinancial social interactions. He thought that "economics only considers the exchange of commodities for money in a perfect market." Right around that time, in 1960, Mincer presented his famous paper on women's labor force participation at a conference of the National Bureau of Economic Research. To a standing ovation he had argued for the application of economic analysis to the study of nonmonetized interactions occurring inside households. That was the beginning of the New Home Economics (NHE). Later, Becker developed his economic theory of marriage, improving substantially on social exchange theories of marriage by applying the standards of microeconomic theories to the analysis of marriage.

The New Home Economics and Becker's Theory of Marriage

Becker brought the economic analysis of marriage to the intellectual marketplace.[5] Becker's contribution was an integral part of the New Home Economics (NHE) started by Jacob Mincer (1962, 1963).[6] Following Mincer, Becker's theory of marriage also assumes that households are like firms—they produce goods and services. Some households are lone individuals, and other households are marriages. Mincer and Becker also assumed that women specialize in household production. Becker (1981) derived that result from other assumptions regarding gender differences in productivity in household production and in the labor force, formalizing some of the ideas found in functionalist sociology. However, the validity of most NHE contributions, and of Becker's theory of marriage in particular, does not depend on the assumption that women specialize in household production.

The first NHE theories assumed that decisions are made not by individuals but by households (Mincer 1962, 1963) or that *households* maximize a utility function (Becker 1965; Lancaster 1966). In contrast, in Becker's (1973) theory of marriage, a fundamental assumption is that *individuals* are rational utility maximizers, where utility is their own personal utility. Individuals then rationally choose a household type—marriage or single status—that suits them better. The decision rule regarding marriage formation and dissolution is based on an individual comparison between the total amount of goods (market goods and home-produced goods) that can be produced alone and the total amount of goods that can be produced in marriage. If individuals can negotiate with each other before and after marriage, what matters is a comparison of the total they can produce alone with the total they can produce together.

Becker further assumes that marriages are heterosexual, and that substitution is possible: Some men can be substituted for each other, and some women can be substituted for each other. Consequently, a marriage market exists. Becker's theory of marriage recognizes two alternative mechanisms by which the allocation of potential mates into couples may occur: a market process involving prices, or a nonprice matching mechanism.[7] A market equilibrium is obtained to the extent that men and women participating in the same marriage market compete with each other, where competition is defined in the same sense that economists define competition in markets for goods or labor. Becker also realizes that if marriage markets operate with a price mechanism, they do so within a given institutional framework consisting of laws, regulations, and other institutions.

According to Becker's (1973, 1981) marriage market model, an individual's price in the marriage market can be reflected in that person's share in the consumption of goods produced in the marriage. Becker considers the possibility that individuals may bargain over prices (i.e., bargain regarding access to marital goods), especially if there is not a single price at which the marriage market clears. While Becker's theory of marriage does not use the term *bargaining*, it discusses the division of gains from marriage and the *negotiability* of various arrangements dividing the gains from marriage. Economists often use the terms "negotiations" and "bargaining" interchangeably when they write on the division of profits in the context of a firm. The two terms are also interchangeable in the context of a marriage.

Those who have mistakenly inferred that Becker's economic theory of marriage ignores intrahousehold bargaining have approached game-theoretical models of bargaining in marriage such as Manser and Murray Brown (1980) or McElroy and Horney (1981) as alternatives to Becker's theory of marriage. Instead, bargaining theories of marriage should be viewed as complementary to Becker's, for they specify mechanisms influencing the division of goods inside a marriage when the market mechanism is not sufficient.[8] Assumptions such as the existence of a Nash equilibrium do not add much to the explanatory power of Becker's theory of marriage.[9] Most of the predictions derived from these game-theoretical models can also be derived from the marriage market model contained in Becker's theory of marriage and other competitive marriage market theories based on Becker (e.g., Grossbard-Shechtman 1984, 1993). For instance, all these economic models lead to the predictions that (1) sex ratios affect the relative well-being of husbands and wives, and (2) wife's income relative to that of husband's is likely to influence each spouse's individual access to marital goods.

Assessing the Impact of Becker's Theory of Marriage

Becker's theory of marriage has been very influential, especially since it was published as part of the *Treatise on the Family* in 1981. Exactly how influential it was on either economics or sociology is hard to assess systematically. My impressions are that today (1) sociologists analyzing marriage very frequently cite Becker's theories, and (2) relatively few economists are taking advantage of the many insights found in Becker's theory of marriage.

Impact on Sociologists

Initially, Becker's theory of marriage did not have much impact on sociologists and social psychologists, even if they were Becker's colleagues at the University of Chicago. The following episode is an indication of the limited penetration of Becker's economic theory of marriage in the late 1970s. Becker and Fred Strodtbeck, a leading University of Chicago social psychologist studying marriage, had not communicated much. It was not until a local TV program included both professors that the two specialists on marriage started a dialogue (Grossbard-Shechtman 1981).

Also, published six years after the appearance of Becker's theory of marriage, the 668-page-long *Contemporary Theories About the Family* (Burr et al. 1979) did not contain a single reference to the economic analysis of marriage. The few sociologists who cited Becker's theory of marriage in the 1970s include Andrew Cherlin (1977), Michael Hannan, Nancy Tuma, and Lyle Groeneveld (1977), and John Richardson (1979). The turning point in sociologists' attitude toward Becker's ideas on marriage occurred some time after the publication of his *Treatise* in 1981.

Within twenty years, this situation has been reversed. In 2001, most sociological research on marriage contains references to Becker's *Treatise on the Family*. In fact, sociologists often seem eager to cite Becker's theory of marriage rather than an earlier source in sociology, even when the same idea is found in both Becker's and earlier sociological writings. A case in point is the assumption of a traditional division of labor in marriage, an assumption very commonly made by sociologists in the functionalist tradition, such as Talcott Parsons. But Becker is often cited for presenting that idea in recent writings by sociologists, whereas Parsons barely gets cited. Another example is what has long been called the "independence effect" in sociological literature: the idea that women who earn higher wages are less likely to marry and more likely to divorce. Although that sociological literature predates Becker's theory of marriage, many sociologists who discuss the relationship among women's earnings, marriage, and divorce cite Becker (1981) rather than earlier sociological sources. Becker is cited in the following extract from a paper on divorce that sociologists Constance Gager and Laura Sanchez (1999, 2) recently presented at the annual meetings of the Population Association of America:

> [M]uch of the prior research derives from an economic perspective, often viewing marriage as a system of exchange relations, while largely ignoring the emotional side of marriage (Becker 1981).

Reading contemporary sociological analyses of marriage and divorce, one thus obtains the erroneous impression that Becker introduced the idea that economic variables influence exchange in marriage and therefore divorce decisions. Within twenty years, sociologists switched from not citing Becker's theory of marriage at all to citing that theory too much, not giving sufficient credit to earlier social exchange theories such as George Levinger (1965).

Impact on Economists

Even though at the time that he published his theory of marriage Becker had already acquired the reputation of a first-rate economist, the economics profession initially gave his models of love and marriage a lukewarm reception. An indication of the slow response to Becker's theory of marriage can be found in the limited number of journal articles published by economists in the 1970s that cite Becker's first 1973 article on marriage. Among the few articles that I am aware of are (in chronological order): my own article on polygamy that appeared in *Current Anthropology* (Grossbard 1976), a *Journal of Political Economy* article on divorce by Becker, Elizabeth Landes, and Robert Michael (1977), Michael Keeley's (1977, 1979) articles on search and age at marriage, and an article on female headship that economist Sheldon Danziger and a number of his colleagues published in *Journal of Marriage and the Family* (Katherine Bradbury et al. 1979).

Another possible indication of such limited interest can be found in the few doors that opened for Becker's students who wrote doctoral dissertations on the economics of marriage in the 1970s. The career path of Michael Keeley is a case in point. A top student at the University of Chicago, Keeley specialized in labor and econometrics, eventually writing a book on labor supply (Keeley 1981) that was published in a series edited by economist Jim Heckman, winner of the 2000 Nobel Prize in economics. Keeley was on the job market for economists in 1974, about the time that he was completing his doctoral dissertation on the economics of marriage under the principal guidance of Becker. Keeley's thesis contained an important theoretical innovation: an application of search theory to the marriage market.[10] Based on up-to-date econometric techniques, Keeley's thesis obtained interesting counterintuitive results regarding the demand for marriage among various categories of Americans. There may be many explanations as to why Keeley was not hired by a leading university. It is not far-fetched to include lack of interest in the economics of marriage, the topic of Keeley's dissertation, among these explanations. Soon after he completed his Ph.D. degree, Keeley became a senior investigator at Stanford Research Institute, where he continued to do more research in labor and population economics. In part as a result of the messages that the market for such research was sending him, Keeley switched to other applications of economics.

I entered Chicago's graduate program two years after Keeley and had the opportunity to learn from his experience. In addition, Jim Heckman explicitly warned me of the widespread lack of interest in the topic of marriage in the economics profession. But by the time of this warning, I had developed such a passion for the economics of marriage that I decided to continue my dissertation on the economics of polygamy, even if it involved paying a price in terms of job market success.[11] Though I expected a cold shower when I entered the job market for economists in 1976, I did not expect the shower to be so cold. During a number of job interviews I distinctly sensed how any serious interest on the part of an academic department disappeared when the conversation turned to the topic of my dissertation. When I reported my disappointment to him, Becker communicated his confidence that it was only a matter of time before his ideas about marriage would catch on. Becker's confidence was justified.

The 1980s saw an increase in applications of Becker's theory of marriage. Two factors made a big difference: the publication of Becker's *Treatise on the Family* and that of bargaining theories of marriage (Manser and

Brown 1980; McElroy and Horney 1981). Since then, many economists' applications of Becker's ideas on marriage were inspired by an interest in game theories such as these bargaining theories. Much of this literature deals with the study of consumption, including individual consumption in less developed countries. In the last twenty years, applications of economic analyses of marriage have spread in many directions.

Assessing Applications of Economics to Research on Marriage

Overall, Becker's economic theory of marriage opened the door to a wide range of research. Applications of economics that currently use economic theories of marriage and that are performed mostly by economists include:

- applications of bargaining theories of marriage to the study of consumption and economic development (see a survey by Frances Woolley, Forthcoming).
- studies of marriage formation (see a survey by Michael Brien and Michelle Seran, Forthcoming) and divorce (see a survey by Evelyn Lehrer, Forthcoming), including studies of the effect of fiscal policies on marriage and divorce (see a survey by Leslie Whittington and James Alm, Forthcoming).
- studies of the characteristics of individual spouses and how type of matching is related to other kinds of individual behavior. For instance, how are husband's relative age and possible compensating differentials in marriage related to wife's labor supply (Grossbard-Shechtman and Neuman 1988, Grossbard-Shechtman and Xuanning Fu 2001), or how does husband and wife religion and religiosity relate to marital stability (Lehrer and Carmel Chiswick 1993). Here the concept of spouse-specific marital human capital and the distinction between general and specific human capital have been useful (see Becker et al. 1977; Chiswick and Lehrer 1990; Lehrer 1995, 1996).
- studies of poverty and welfare policies (see, e.g., Nancy Folbre 1994; John Fitzgerald, Forthcoming), including studies of child support payments by noncustodial parents (see, e.g., Andrea Beller and John Graham 1993).
- studies of allocation of time to the labor market and to household labor. A survey of economic literature dealing with marriage and household labor can be found in Joni Hersch (Forthcoming), and a number of examples of labor supply studies using Becker's theory of marriage are found in Grossbard-Shectman (Forthcoming a).
- studies in the law-and-economics of divorce laws (see survey in Whittington and Alm, Forthcoming).

Most of these topics are also studied by noneconomists who are mostly sociologists. In the case of law-and-economics, the noneconomists are mostly legal scholars. These noneconomists have also been influenced by economic theories of marriage, especially Becker's. A number of observations can be made regarding these various applications of economics to the study of marriage. In comparison to other applications of economics, this research is characterized as follows:

1. *More Empirical Than Theoretical.* In most fields of economics, we are used to a blend of theory and empirical work that includes a substantial dose of theoretical research. Much of the marriage-related literature is of an empirical nature. This is certainly the case of the demographic literature on marriage formation and dissolution produced by economists, which is mostly of an empirical nature and is often indistinguishable from similar literature produced by sociologists. In that respect the economics of marriage is similar to labor economics, another field that tends to emphasize empirical applications rather than theory, at least in the last twenty-five years. Exceptions include theoretical contributions in the field of (a) consumer studies based on game theories of marriage (e.g., Manser and Brown 1980; McElroy and Horney 1981; Woolley 1988; Chiappori 1992; Lundberg and Pollak 1993), (b) labor supply (Grossbard-Shechtman 1984), and (c) models of determinants of marriage and cohabitation (e.g.; Grossbard 1976; George Akerlof, Janet Yellen, and Michael Katz 1996; Theodore Bergstrom and Mark Bagnoli 1993; Hanan Jacoby 1995; Lina Edlund 1999), and (d) divorce (e.g., Yoram Weiss and Robert Willis 1985).

2. *Interdisciplinary Cooperation.* Quite a few demographic studies of marriage have been jointly produced by teams of economists and sociologists. Dual-discipline teams include Heer and Grossbard-Shechtman (1981), sociologist Neil Bennett and economist David Bloom (e.g., Bennett, Blanc, and Bloom 1988), sociologist Linda Waite and a number of coauthors who are economists (see, for instance, Waite and Arleen Leibowitz 1988, 1991; Waite and Lee Lillard 1991; Lillard and Waite 1993; Brien, Lillard, and Waite 1999; Leibowitz, Jacob Klerman, and Waite 1992), economist Irwin Garfinkel with sociologist Sara McLanahan (e.g., Cynthia Miller, Garfinkel, and McLanahan 1997), and sociologist Lisa Greenwell with economists Leibowitz and Klerman (Greenwell, Leibowitz, and Klerman 1998).

3. *More Impact of Sociological Concepts.* In the area of marriage, economists have often used concepts or theories introduced or developed by sociologists. For instance, economists Evelyn Lehrer and Carmel Chiswick have expanded the theories of sociologist Larry Bumpass about the effect

of inter-religious marriage on marital instability (see Bumpass and Sweet 1972; Lehrer and Carmel Chiswick 1993), and Grossbard-Shechtman (1984, 1993) imported the concept of "marriage squeeze" from demography.

Are these three features typical of all demographic economics? An interesting comparison consists of juxtaposing the economics of marriage with the economics of fertility. Making such comparison can help us identify some of the underlying reasons for these characteristics of the economics of marriage and the relations between the economics and sociology of marriage.

A Comparison with the Economics of Fertility

Becker and Mincer were also among the founders of the "economics of fertility," an application whose development was intricately related to the growth of the New Home Economics (NHE) in the 1960s. The economics of fertility preceded the economics of marriage by about ten years (see Becker 1960, 1965; Mincer 1963). In the case of both research on fertility and research on marriage, the econometric standards that dominate in economics have been adopted by most researchers, irrespective of the department where they were trained. But I see a *difference in adoption of theoretical constructs in these two demographic applications of economics.* In the case of fertility and population growth, basic economic theory started being used in demographic discussions soon after the start of the economics of fertility. From the start of the economics of fertility there was more of a blend of economic theory and empirical work than in the case of the economics of marriage.

By the mid-1970s, economists were playing a prominent role in discussions on fertility at the Population Association of America (PAA, the national organization of demographers) and concepts such as demand and supply of children or contraceptive technology were found on many lips, including those of demographers trained in sociology. By the mid-1970s, economists were obtaining large portions of the grants available for research on fertility, they were holding top positions in the PAA, and they were publishing substantial fractions of the articles in top-rated demography journals (see Grossbard-Shechtman 1981).

In contrast, even today, economic theories of marriage do not play a major role in PAA sessions on marriage, cohabitation, or divorce. Even though sociologists and demographers who have attended marriage-related sessions at the PAA in the years between 1977 and 2001 often mention marriage markets and Becker's theory of marriage, one hears few presentations involving economic theory, including simple theory such as the theory of demand and supply. This lack of interest also applies to most of the economists who participate in these sessions: They seem more interested in measurement and estimation issues than in the development of new predictions based on economic theories of marriage and divorce.

The use of economic theory is also minimal in recent journal articles dealing with the demography of marriage. For instance, there are plenty of sociologists' empirical contributions regarding the measurement of marriage market imbalances, such as Daniel Lichter et al. (1992). Much of the recent economic literature on this subject also deals with measurement issues (e.g., Robert Wood 1995; Brien 1997). The amount of mathematical formulations and applications of demand and supply analysis found in most articles on marriage formation that have appeared in demographic and labor journals in the 1990s is low relative to that found in articles on fertility published by economists in similar outlets in the 1970s and 1980s (such as Ronald Lee 1977, 1980). In part, this reflects a trend within labor economics, from an emphasis on theory to an emphasis on econometric techniques. In the early 1970s, labor economists who are also econometricians were a rarity. In the 1990s, they were the norm.

The relatively higher weight on economic theory in the study of fertility than in the study of marriage is also related to other differences between the two applications. As mentioned in points 2 and 3 above, economists of marriage often seem to cooperate with sociologists and to cite sociological literature. It is my impression that economists of fertility have been less likely to coauthor studies with sociologists,[12] and that they are less likely to cite sociologists than is the case of economists of marriage.

These three differences between the economics of marriage and the economics of fertility are related to each other and to other differences between the economics of marriage and the economics of fertility: Relative to the penetration of economic theory into studies of fertility, the penetration of economic theory into studies of marriage proceeded (1) at a slower pace, and (2) more often via the adoption of economic concepts by sociologists than via the entry of economists into the study of a particular aspect of marriage.

What explains the relatively limited use of economic theory in most contemporary studies of marriage is not the lack of applicability of the tools of economic analysis. It is certainly not the case that these tools—including demand and supply analysis—are not applicable to the theoretical study of marriage. In fact, given that there are very limited markets for babies, these tools are more applicable to research on marriage than to research on fertility.

Better explanations for why little economic theory is being used in studies of marriage include the dominance of nonquantitative sociologists in the study of marriage, and the breadth of topics that theories of marriage need to deal with.

The Role of Quantitative Skills

When the economics of fertility appeared on the scene in the late 1960s and 1970s, the sociologists/demographers who studied fertility and were trained in sociology tended to be more quantitative and prone to economic analysis. At that time zero population growth was a big priority, and both foundations and the U.S. government were pouring dollars into empirical research on the determinants of fertility, research requiring quantitative skills. There seemed to be enough funding for everyone who had some empirical skills, whether they were trained in economics or sociology. As a result, economists entering the field of fertility faced little opposition on the part of sociologists. Much of the interaction between economists and sociologists of fertility occurred within the discipline of demography, a discipline with an interdisciplinary tradition (see Ronald Lesthaeghe 2001) and a heavy emphasis on quantitative skills. In contrast, until recently most specialists on marriage who were trained in sociology had a relatively weak background in quantitative methods.

Even though quantitative methods have experienced a tremendous growth in the social and behavioral sciences in general, especially with the exponential growth in computer capacity and data availability, one gets the impression that the *Journal of Marriage and the Family* has been late at adopting quantitative methods and the mathematical thinking that goes with it. This reflects the training of most specialists on marriage. Many of them were trained as counselors and psychologists, specialties less compatible with economics than with demography.

The relatively low level of mathematical sophistication among specialists in the field of marriage and family helps explain why there has been a limited demand for economic theories of marriage in the literature on marriage. I learned this lesson soon after the publication of my first article—a study of polygamy—in *Current Anthropology* in 1976. One of my findings was that women who are at an optimal age from the point of view of reproductive strength (between ages twenty and thirty) had fewer co-wives than women who were either younger than twenty or older than thirty. The result was based on a regression of number of co-wives using senior wife's age and a quadratic term of that age. The editor, the late Sol Tax, also published a sociologist's discussion of that article. Clearly unacquainted with quadratic regression functions, the discussant decried the use of a square term as utter nonsense (Remi Clignet and Joyce Sween 1977).

The emphasis on quantitative methods among sociologists and psychologists of marriage has increased significantly in recent years, and one observes rapid change in this matter. One is encouraged by the success of sociologists of marriage who have worked with economists and respect our discipline, as is the case of Linda Waite, director of Population Studies at the University of Chicago. The fact that many marriage and divorce specialists continue to be trained as counselors or lawyers, and tend to lack quantitative and mathematical skills, is expected to be an obstacle to further growth of the economics of marriage.

Marriage: A Broad Field of Study

Children are basically just one of the possible products of marriage. Marriage is a broader topic than fertility. It is easier to apply economic theory to a well-defined and relatively narrow question such as the optimal number of children than to a broad set of questions such as the effect of the institution of marriage as opposed to some of its alternatives such as cohabitation and divorce. The study of marriage and its alternatives has been a core specialty of sociology for decades, and the top sociology journals have been publishing articles on marriage formation, matching of spouses, alternatives to marriage, household production, and many topics related to marriage. Sociologists have their way to examine these questions, their textbooks, their courses. For economic concepts and models to replace the existing concepts currently driving sociological analyses, the economic models need to apply to all these aspects of marriage. It is more likely that a general economic theory of marriage will make it worthwhile for specialists of marriage to replace their existing theories and adopt economic concepts than will a series of separate theories of marriage, divorce, matching, intrahousehold allocation, and so forth.

It took an intellectual leader such as Gary Becker, one of the greatest economists alive, to make a difference. To have an impact on the large field of marriage and the family, Becker devoted many years of his life to the writing of a treatise on the family, a treatise of a general nature covering many aspects of marriage. He purposefully chose a title for this *magnum opus* not containing the word "economic." Becker also became a professor of sociology as well as economics. Even so, the penetration of economic ideas about marriage was relatively slow in comparison to the rapid spread of economic ideas about fertility in the 1970s. Becker's influence on the study of marriage seems to have grown since he received the Nobel Prize in 1992. This influence may take another leap, for in 2000, Becker became the only recipient of the National Medal of Science in the Behavioral and Social Sciences.[13]

The breadth of the field of study discourages supply of adequate economic models by most economists. Economists may be hesitating about whether they should enter a new field that is complex and already being cultivated by large numbers of sociologists, anthropologists, psychologists, and others.

It does not help the popularity of economic models of marriage that some sociologists, wanting to guard their territory, might be fighting the influence of economics. In the case of marriage there may thus have been (and still be) more people who are unhappy about the entry of economic analysts in their field than had been the case when the economics of fertility invaded demography. It is a broader field, and there are more sociologists who are poorly trained in math and statistics and stand to lose from competition than was the case when the economics of fertility arrived on the scene.

This interpretation also helps explain why the penetration of economic ideas and theories into the field of marriage more often takes the form of sociologists adopting economic ideas than the form of economists entering the field of marriage, whereas the opposite was the case with the economics of fertility. Even if sociologists of marriage willingly absorbed all the interested economists in their midst, the sheer number of practicing sociologists of marriage makes it difficult for economists to be a significant presence in the field of marriage. Furthermore, economists of marriage tend to be a heterogenous grouping, which weakens their influence as a group, and therefore the influence of their ideas.

The economists of marriage who are also demographers are the most successful at penetrating the field of marriage. These economists of marriage who are also demographers and regularly attend PAA meetings are more in communication with their counterparts in sociology. Demography, whose interdisciplinary tradition helped promote the economics of fertility, continues to act as a good channel of communication between economists and sociologists with the quantitative skills appreciated in demography, including most of the economists and sociologists of marriage who have cooperated on joint projects and articles (see above). This institutional/organizational constraint reinforces the empirical nature of the economics of marriage.

The economists of marriage who are more theoretical—such as Marjorie McElroy, Marilyn Manser, or Pierre-Andre Chiappori—seem to be less likely to interact professionally with demographers and sociologists. Economists who do macroeconomics of the household (covering topics such as national accounting with a household production sector), such as Australian Duncan Ironmonger, are also less visible at the PAA (see Ironmonger, forthcoming). The PAA being a less appropriate organization for the presentation of their ideas, these more theoretically inclined economists have fewer opportunities to present their ideas to sociologists and to learn from sociologists of marriage.

Within the study of the demographic aspects of marriage and fertility, the comparison between the economics and sociology of marriage and fertility should also be placed in the context of overall changes in demography. In recent years, the relative importance of fertility and population growth diminished within demography, and the relative importance of marriage, cohabitation, and divorce increased. In part this reflects the succession of a first demographic transition centered on decreased fertility by a second demographic transition, a term introduced by Lesthaeghe and Dirk van de Kaa (1986) to describe the changes in family formation, union dissolution, and patterns of family reconstruction in Western nations during the latter part of the twentieth century. As a result, because a clear majority of specialists on marriage are trained as sociologists, the overall ratio of economists to sociologists researching demography seems either to grow more slowly than it did in the late 1970s or to have fallen. This is reflected in less frequent use of the concepts of demand and supply at the PAA than was the case at the height of the influence of the economics of fertility. Even though within the field of marriage and within the field of fertility, the influence of economic models may actually be growing, there may be a diminished overall presence of economic models owing to a structural shift in the focus of research in demography. The relative penetration of economic theories such as supply and demand—(i.e., market analysis)—into the study of fertility and marriage has gone hand in hand with the penetration of economists into fields originated by sociologists.

It is there anything intrinsically wrong with the limited role that economists currently play in research on marriage? Yes, if you believe that mathematical models can be useful. In the polygamy example above, it is a theoretical analysis that led me to expect fewer co-wives in households where the first wife was more productive, given that in the case of a high-fertility society, women's productivity in the home is highly correlated with their fecundity. I therefore predicted that more co-wives would be found where the first wife was considered either below or above the optimal age for child-bearing, which led me to include a quadratic term of age in a regression of number of wives.

It is hoped that the value of an economic model will become even more apparent from the following comparison between an economic model and a sociological model, both of which address the question of household production in marriage.

Comparing Two Models of Intramarriage Division of Labor

This section compares a sociological and an economic theory that both deal with the question of in-marriage division of labor: an economic analysis of in-marriage household labor (see Grossbard 1976; Grossbard-Shechtman

1984) and an economic dependency model developed by sociologists Christine Delphy (1984), Sylvia Walby (1986), and Julie Brines (1994). Both theories take a rational choice perspective. In that sense, both theories follow Becker's theory of marriage and both consider exchanges between household labor and economic support. However, unlike the economic dependency model, the WIM model is based on standard microeconomics and this has a number of advantages.

Building on Becker's (1973) economic theory of marriage and the NHE concept of household production, Grossbard (1976) introduced the concept of a market for in-marriage household labor. This labor was called "wife services" in the context of a Nigerian polygamous society. Later, the concept was expanded to include "household labor" by either wife or husband (Grossbard-Shechtman 1984; Grossbard-Shechtman and Neuman 1988). This labor, which can also be called Work-in-Marriage (WIM), includes any activity that benefits a spouse, such as health care, counseling, child-care, or gardening. Taking a child to a piano lesson can also be considered household labor. "In-marriage" refers to work that benefits either a spouse or a cohabiting partner.

Not all household production is WIM. An activity enters the category "work" when people do things that they would not do for themselves, and they do it for others because they get "paid" to do so. In-marriage household labor has an opportunity cost: the value of leisure or home production that solely benefits the self. Driving a child to a piano lesson is WIM to the extent that the driver does this solely because his spouse wants the child to learn piano. Cleaning the floor is WIM only if she who mops the floor does it principally because her spouse wants the floor to shine.

Recent research on household work in the United States offers interesting insights on the nature of WIM. It has been shown that women engage in more household work when married or cohabiting than when unmarried, whereas the opposite is the case with men (Scott South and Glenna Spitze 1994). The extra loads of housework that women typically assume in cohabitation or marriage apparently benefit their husbands and allow husbands to reduce their hours of housework after formation of the union. Relative to men, American women who are married or cohabit thus appear to engage in more WIM. That does not mean that men do not work in marriage.

Rational choice implies that people will typically not engage in costly activities unless they personally benefit from them. Thus, WIM workers frequently get a material compensation, termed "quasi-wage" in Grossbard-Shechtman (1984). One example is that of a traditional division of labor in marriage where women are full-time housewives. This can be described as an exchange between a wife providing WIM and a husband providing income. The wife's access to her husband's income can be considered as quasi-wage earnings from that WIM. Recent research indicates that, whereas most married couples have access to each other's income, this is more likely to be the case when the wife is not in the labor force (Judith Treas 1993).[14]

Exchanges of women's WIM for men's income are not limited to marriages where women are full-time housewives. Individuals may be employed in WIM on a part-time basis, in addition to working at another job. Hence, WIM is then performed on a second shift. Not all in-marriage workers may be paid for their work. Some in-marriage work may be performed on a volunteer basis. Couples might exchange equal amounts of WIM, reducing the likelihood of one spouse receiving a material compensation from the other.

The WIM model assumes that WIM is portable in the sense that WIM can be valuable not only to the current beneficiary of such labor in a specific marriage, but also to other potential spouses. For instance, cooking skills may be appreciated by a number of potential spouses. Not only can married in-marriage workers have skills with a market value, but single individuals with WIM skills can be viewed as suppliers of WIM to potential spouses. The human capital embodied in an in-marriage worker is in part general human capital (as opposed to specific to a particular spouse), an adaptation of Becker's (1964) distinction between general and firm-specific human (labor) capital (see Chiswick and Lehrer 1990).

This portability/generality of the human capital of in-marriage workers (and potential in-marriage workers) opens the door to an analysis of markets for WIM.[15] In this analysis men and women are considered as participants in two markets: a market for female WIM supplied by women are on the supply side, and a market for male WIM supplied by men.

Supply of WIM

Standard microeconomics defines "supply" as a willingness to provide a service or product at different price levels. Likewise, an individual supply of WIM indicates an individual's willingness to provide WIM at various levels of quasi-wage for WIM. An individual supply is presented in Figure 8.1. Following the convention accepted in economics, quantity is plotted on the horizontal axis and price (quasi-wage) on the vertical axis. Supplies of WIM are upward-sloping for the same reasons that supplies of other forms of labor are generally upward-sloping.

As an individual supplies more and more hours of work, the opportunity cost (based on the value of other activities) of engaging in this activity increases while the marginal disutility of additional hours of work increases. Labor economists call this a "substitution effect," in the sense of individual substitution between alternative uses of time. Supply of work is also influ-

Figure 8.1 **Individual Supply of Work-in-Marriage**

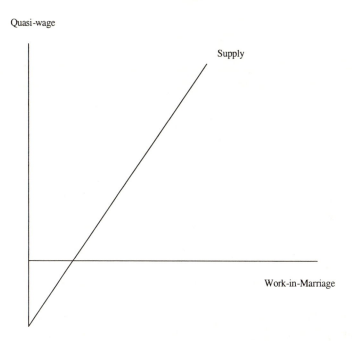

Quasi-wage

Supply

Work-in-Marriage

enced by an "income effect." The higher the compensation for work, the higher the income, and the less a person needs to work.[16] It is assumed in Figure 8.1 that the substitution effect dominates the income effect and that after a certain number of hours an individual reaches a limit beyond which he or she will not be capable of supplying more hours of WIM. Following Grossbard-Shechtman (1984), it is also assumed that the supply of WIM begins at a negative quasi-wage, implying that individuals start out by volunteering their WIM.

A Comparison with the Economic Dependency Model

The "WIM model" found in Grossbard (1976) and Grossbard-Shechtman (1984) and Delphy's and Walby's "economic dependency model" have much in common. According to the economic dependency model, household labor is provided in return for economic support. This corresponds to exchange of WIM for a material compensation. The correspondence between the two models can be highlighted by juxtaposing Figure 8.1 based on Grossbard-Shechtman (1984) with Figure 8.2, a reproduction of Figure 1 in the version of the economic dependency model developed by Brines (1994).

Figure 8.2 presents a relationship between economic dependency or

Figure 8.2 **Housework/Dependency Relationship**

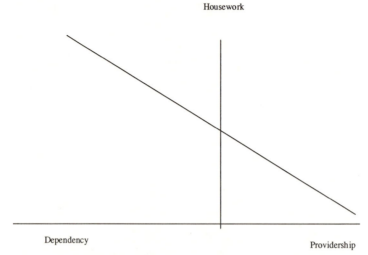

Housework

Dependency   Providership

Source: Brines (1994), Figure 1.

providership (on the horizontal axis) and participation in housework (on the vertical axis). Even though that relationship is not called "supply" in Brines (1994) it amounts to a supply of participation in housework. In fact, if one turns Brines's Figure 8.2 by fifteen minutes clockwise one can see the supply in Figure 8.1. The language is different: Brines' *dependency* corresponds to a positive quasi-wage in Grossbard-Shechtman, and Brines's *providership* corresponds to Grossbard-Shechtman's negative quasi-wage; what Grossbard-Shechtman calls a *supply* of WIM, Brines calls a *relationship between economic dependency or providership and participation in housework.*

If these two models are really equivalent, one may ask the following two questions: (1) Which model came first? and (2) Is one model preferable to the other? Time of publication settles the first question. The first version of the WIM model including a supply of WIM was published in 1976 (Grossbard 1976). That model, published in an anthropology journal, may have had limited influence among the sociologists who developed the economic dependency model. A similar model (Heer and Grossbard-Shechtman 1981), appeared in the *Journal of Marriage and the Family*, a journal widely read by sociologists. The first versions of the economic dependency model, by Delphy (1984) and Walby (1986), appeared about the time of publication of later versions of the WIM model in economics journals (Grossbard-Shechtman 1984), a general equilibrium model, and in the *Journal of Political Economy* (Grossbard-Shechtman and Neuman 1988), an application regarding compensating differentials in marriage and labor supply of married women.

Figure 8.3   **Individual Demand for Work-in-Marriage**

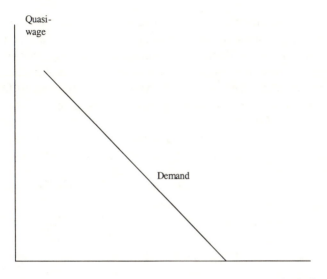

As for the second question above, there are at least two reasons why the WIM supply concept is preferable to the economic dependency concept: (a) it is compatible with other labor supply models; and (b) the concept of supply of WIM is more easily combined with other concepts from standard microeconomics; this facilitates additional insights that were not derived in the economic dependency models. Though the supply of household labor is similar in both models, Brines (1994) does not have a demand for household labor. In terms of the dependency model's terminology, the equivalent of a demand for WIM is a willingness to provide for the household worker. Brines's model does not analyze the willingness to provide. A related difference is that Brines's model does not have a market equilibrium. Ultimately, both these differences follow from Brines's assumption that household labor is not portable. Proponents of economic dependency view housework as nonportable and without market value (Brines 1994). In contrast, WIM can be portable, an assumption that opens the door to market analysis. This analysis is based not only on a supply, but also on a demand.

Demand for WIM

A positive quasi-wage (or a willingness to take on a dependent) implies that a spouse is willing to pay for another spouse's housework or WIM. Such willingness to pay for various quantities of a good or service is what economists call a "demand." Figure 8.3 depicts an individual demand for the labor of his or her spouse.

Demands are usually downward-sloping owing to diminishing marginal utility and/or diminishing marginal productivity. It is also expected that demands for WIM will be downward-sloping, as increasing hours of WIM become less and less valuable to the beneficiary. It is possible that the demand continues under the zero axis, to the extent that individuals have the option of benefiting from the work of a spouse subsidizing her own WIM. The quantity of WIM consumed is then associated with negative levels of (marginal) satisfaction. For instance, a husband may find it unpleasant to be overly attended by his wife. He longs for more freedom and privacy. He may consume what he considers excessive amounts of his wife's WIM to the extent that she subsidizes herself (e.g. in circumstances where her income exceeds his and they share their income).

Many factors influence demand and/or supply. Among the factors that are very important in the case of WIM, one can mention cultural values. Values that individuals absorb in their upbringing as part of a particular ethnic, national, or religious group will influence demand and supply of WIM. The more an individual is motivated to provide in-marriage services, the larger one's own supply (i.e., he is willing to provide more at given prices) and/or the larger the demand for a spouse's WIM (i.e., he is willing to acquire more at given prices.) Certain cultures encourage more of a traditional division of labor than do others. One expects more women brought up in a more traditional culture to have a larger supply of WIM than other women, and more traditional men to have a larger demand for WIM than less traditional men. Demand and supply of WIM will also be influenced by cultural rules regarding ethnic exogamy or age preference and by biological needs such as the need for procreation and genetic fitness.

Markets for WIM

Individual demands and supplies of people participating in the same market can be aggregated. This will establish an equilibrium in the particular market for WIM. Consider a market for WIM supplied by women. Many women can potentially substitute for each other's WIM, and the same can be said for men (in this case in their capacity of employers of WIM). Figure 8.4 presents such a market. It has an aggregate upward-sloping supply of WIM by women. The demand for this WIM by men is downward-sloping.

The market equilibrium obtained at the intersection of *demand* and *supply* in Figure 8.4 determines both how many people marry and how much time they spend working in marriage. Graphically, both these dimensions of

Figure 8.4   **Market for Work-in-Marriage**

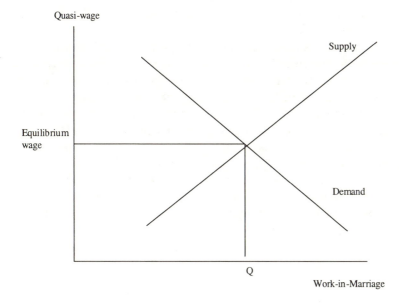

quantity supplied can be seen on the horizontal axis of Figure 8.4. As in labor supply theory, a point on the aggregate supply cannot specify simultaneously how many people work (in this case, enter marriage) and how much they work (in this case, how much they engage in WIM). As in other labor markets, average hours of work tend to be heavily influenced by institutional factors, including customs and cultural expectations.

As is the case with standard labor markets, markets for WIM also establish *equilibrium wages*, shown on the vertical axis of the WIM market depicted in Figure 8.4. The degree to which individuals are affected by conditions in markets for WIM depends on their position in the life-cycle. Markets for WIM are expected to be most influential when individuals prepare for marriage and before they find a partner. This is when many people are aware of the possibilities of substitution, which helps markets function. After people marry, they are still part of the market for WIM, to the extent that their current marriage may dissolve and they may actively participate in the market(s) again. A married in-marriage worker or employer of in-marriage work is part of a market for WIM in the same way that workers and employers who are not actively searching for jobs or workers are part of a market. A special interdependence between a particular wife and a particular husband may develop after marriage, similarly to the special interdependence between a worker and a firm. Investments can either be spouse-specific or can be transferable across marriages, similar to the concepts of general and specific capital in employees working for firms (see Grossbard-Shechtman 1986; Chiswick and Lehrer 1990).

By using the concepts of demand and supply, the WIM model obtains many more insights than does the economic dependency model. The WIM model has many advantages, including: the implication that sex ratios are likely to influence labor force participation, that husband's income influences wife's value of time regardless of whether a wife participates in the labor force or not (as opposed to an implication derived by Willis [1974] that husbands' income affects wives' value of time only if wives do not participate in the labor force; see Grossbard-Shechtman 1984); that labor supply is likely to be associated with compensating differentials in marriage (see Grossbard-Shechtman and Neuman 1988 for Israel; and Grossbard-Shechtman and Fu 2001 for Hawaii); and that in the United States, relative to white women, married black women are more likely to participate in the labor force (see Grossbard-Shechtman 1995) and less likely to work in home-based work (see Field-Hendry and Edwards, forthcoming).[17]

Conclusions

The economic analysis of marriage pioneered by Gary Becker has grown slowly at first. Since 1981, when Becker published his *Treatise on the Family*, and even more so since 1992, when he won the Nobel Prize in economics, Becker's economic models of marriage have gained in popularity among sociologists of marriage. Overall, however, the study of marriage remains overwhelmingly under the control of sociologists, and that is one reason why economic models—including models based on demand and supply— are not very commonly used in the study of marriage formation and decision making within marriages.

That economic models are not used more commonly in studies of marriage is regrettable. An example of a model that could be more useful than an alternative found in sociology is the model of Work-In-Marriage. It is hoped that this chapter will inspire some readers to look more into economic models of marriage, including those discussed here. The economics of marriage has an enormous growth potential. The range of questions to which it can be applied is wide, and as of now, there are few scholars—sociologists or economists—who apply economic models such as demand and supply to investigate the determinants and consequences of marriage and its alternatives.

Notes

1. Note that both these articles—as well as one of Michael Keeley's articles on the economics of marriage (Keeley 1979)—were published in the *International Economic Review*, then edited by Robert Pollak at the University of Pennsylvania.

2. It is when I heard the late sociologist William Hodge give a talk about sex ratio effects on cohort-specific marriage rates that I first started thinking of a wide range of consequences that historical variations in sex ratio may have caused in the United States. This led to cooperation between a sociologist and an economist: Heer and Grossbard-Shechtman (1981).

3. Early versions of Guttentag and Secord's book circulated before 1981, when David Heer and I published our article in *Journal of Marriage and the Family*, but we were unaware of their manuscript's existence (see Grossbard-Shechtman 1983b). More recent influential work by sociologists on these topics include Julius Wilson (1987) and work by Scott South (1988).

4. To some degree functionalism is about the rationality of institutions, and its viewpoint is similar to that of the New Institutional Economics (see the work of economic historian and Nobel Prize winner Douglas North 1981).

5. An exception is a brief note by Martin Bronfenbrenner (1971).

6. More on the history of the New Home Economics can be found in Grossbard-Shechtman (Forthcoming b).

7. More on those nonprice mechanisms can be found in Brien and Seran (Forthcoming).

8. Becker agrees with this assessment (personal communication, 1993).

9. Before writing her article with Horney, Marjorie McElroy was a postdoctorate candidate at Chicago, where she regularly attended Becker's workshop in the applications of economics.

10. A similar application of search theory was published by Dale Mortensen (1988) many years later.

11. Jim Heckman, who had recently arrived in Chicago, might have agreed to stay on my dissertation committee had I followed his advice and abandoned my research on the economics of polygamy in Nigeria. Becker, who was then writing his *Treatise on the Family*, was my principal adviser.

12. A recent exception is Brien et al. (1999).

13. Ironically, Becker's contribution to our understanding of marriage and family was not mentioned as one of the reasons why the White House selected him as one of the recipients.

14. Traditional marriages are often described as situations where the husband "supports" the wife, a term that ignores the quid pro quo of work for pay. This term bothers some contemporary women who engage in WIM and consider themselves paid rather than supported. The term "support" also raised protests among in-marriage workers earlier in the century, long before the onset of the feminist movement (Folbre 1994).

15. For a more detailed discussion, see Grossbard-Shechtman (1984, 1993, 1995).

16. To the extent that the income effect dominates the substitution effect, the supply bends backward.

17. See also Grossbard-Shechtman (2001).

References

Akerlof, George A., Janet L. Yellen, and Michael L. Katz. 1996. "An Analysis of Out-of-Wedlock Childbearing in the United States." *Quarterly Journal of Economics* 61: 277–317.

Becker, Gary S. 1960. "An Economic Analysis of Fertility." In *Demographic and Economic Change in Developed Countries*, a Conference of the Universities—National Bureau Committee for Economic Research. Princeton, NJ: Princeton University Press.

———. 1964. *Human Capital*. New York: Columbia University Press.

———. 1965. "A Theory of the Allocation of Time." *Economic Journal* 75: 493–515.

———. 1973. "A Theory of Marriage: Part I." *Journal of Political Economy* 81: 813–846.

———. 1981. *A Treatise on the Family*. Cambridge, MA: Harvard University Press.

Becker, Gary S., Elizabeth Landes, and Robert Michael. 1977. "An Economic Analysis of Marital Instability." *Journal of Political Economy* 85: 1141–1188.

Beller, Andrea H., and John W. Graham. 1993. *Small Change: The Economics of Child Support*. New Haven, CT: Yale University Press.

Bendix, Reinhard. 1962. *Max Weber, An Intellectual Portrait*. New York: Doubleday.

Bennett, Neil G., Ann Klimas Blanc, and David E. Bloom. 1988. "Commitment and the Modern Union: Assessing the Link Between Premarital Cohabitation and Subsequent Marital Stability." *American Sociological Review* 53: 127–138.

Bergstrom, Theodore C., and Mark Bagnoli. 1993. "Courtship as a Waiting Game." *Journal of Political Economy* 101: 185–202.

Blau, Peter M. 1964. *Exchange and Power in Social Life*. New York: Wiley.

Blood, Robert O., and Donald M. Wolfe. 1960. *Husbands and Wives*. New York: Free Press.

Bradbury, Katharine, Sheldon Danziger, Eugene Smolensky, and Paul Smolensky. 1979. "Public Assistance, Female Headship and Economic Well-Being." *Journal of Marriage and the Family* 41: 519–536.

Brien, Michael. 1997. "Racial Differences in Marriage and the Role of Marriage Markets." *Journal of Human Resources* 32: 741–778.

Brien, Michael, and Michelle Seran. Forthcoming. "The Economics of Marriage and Household Formation." In *Marriage and the Economy*, ed. Shoshana Grossbard-Shechtman. Cambridge and New York: Cambridge University Press.

Brien, Michael, Lee A. Lillard, and Linda J. Waite. 1999. "Interrelated Family Building Behaviors: Marriage, Cohabitation and Non-Marital Fertility." *Demography* 36: 535–551.

Brines, Julie. 1994. "Economic Dependency, Gender, and the Division of Labor at Home." *American Journal of Sociology* 100: 652–688.

Bronfenbrenner, Martin. 1971. "A Note on the Economics of the Marriage Market." *Journal of Political Economy* 79: 1424–1425.

Bumpass, Larry, and James Sweet. 1972. "Differentials in Marital Stability: 1970." *American Sociological Review* 37: 754–766.

Burr, Wesley R., Reuben Hill, F. Ivan Nye, and Ira L. Reiss, eds. 1979. *Contemporary Theories About the Family*, vol. 1. New York: Free Press.

Cherlin, Andrew. 1977. "The Effect of Children on Marital Dissolution and the Family." *Demography* 14: 265–272.

Chiappori, Pierre-Andre. 1992. "Collective Labor Supply and Welfare." *Journal of Political Economy* 100: 437–467.

Chiswick, Carmel, and Evelyn M. Lehrer. 1990. "On Marriage-Specific Human Capital: Its Role as a Determinant of Remarriage." *Journal of Population Economics* 3: 193–213.

Clignet, Remi, and Joyce Sween. 1977. "On Grossbard's Economic Analysis of Polygyny in Maiduguri." *Current Anthropology* 18: 100–102.

Cook, Karen S., and Richard M. Emerson. 1978. "Power, Equity and Commitment in Exchange Networks." *American Sociological Review* 43: 721–739.

Della Pergola, Sergio. 1976. "Demographic Perspectives on Mixed Marriage." *Encyclopedia Judaica Yearbook, 1975–1976*, pp. 198–210. Jerusalem.

Delphy, Christine. 1984. *Close to Home: A Materialist Analysis of Women's Oppression*. Amherst: University of Massachusetts Press.

Durkheim, Emile. 1949. *The Division of Labour in Society*, trans. by George Simpson. Glencoe, IL: Free Press.

Edlund, Lena. 1999. "Son Preference, Sex Ratios and Marriage Patterns." *Journal of Political Economy* 107: 1275–1304.

Field-Hendry, Elizabeth, and Linda Edwards. Forthcoming. "Marriage and Home-Based Work for Pay." In *Marriage and the Economy*, ed. Shoshana Grossbard-Shechtman. Cambridge and New York: Cambridge University Press.

Fisher, Wesley A. 1980. *The Soviet Marriage Market*. New York: Praeger.

Fitzgerald, John. Forthcoming. "Marriage Prospects and Welfare Use." In *Marriage and the Economy*, ed. Shoshana Grossbard-Shechtman. Cambridge and New York: Cambridge University Press.

Folbre, Nancy. 1994. *Who Pays for the Kids? Gender and the Structures of Constraint*. London: Routledge.

Gager, Constance, and Laura Sanchez. 1999. "Two as One? Couples' Perceptions of Time Spent Together, Marital Quality, and the Risk of Divorce." Paper presented at the Population Association of America, Washington, DC.

Glick, Paul C., John C. Beresford, and David M. Heer. 1963. "Family Formation and Family Composition: Trends and Prospects." In *Sourcebook in Marriage and the Family*, ed. Marvin B. Sussman. Boston: Houghton Mifflin.

Greenwell, Lisa, Arleen Leibowitz, and Jacob A. Klerman. 1998. "Welfare Backgkround, Attitudes, and Employment Among New Mothers." *Journal of Marriage and the Family* 60: 175–193.

Grossbard, Amyra. 1976. "An Economic Analysis of Polygamy: The Case of Maiduguri." *Current Anthropology* 17: 701–707.

Grossbard-Shechtman, Shoshana. 1981. "Gary Becker's Theory of the Family—Some Interdisciplinary Considerations." *Sociology and Social Research* 66: 1–11.

———. 1983a. "A Market Approach to Intermarriage." In *Papers in Jewish Demography, 1981*, ed. U.O. Schmelz, P. Gerson, and Sergio Della Pergola. Jerusalem: Hebrew University Institute of Contemporary Jewry.

———. 1983b. "Too Many Women: The Sex Ratio Question." *Sociology and Social Research* 68: 390–391.

———. 1984. "A Theory of Allocation of Time in Markets for Labor and Marriage." *Economic Journal* 94: 863–882.

———. 1986. "Marriage and Productivity: An Interdisciplinary Analysis." In *Handbook of Behavioral Economics*, vol. 4, eds. Benjamin Gilad and Stanley Kaish. Greenwich, CT: JAI Press.

———. 1993. *On the Economics of Marriage—A Theory of Marriage, Labor and Divorce*. Boulder, CO: Westview Press.

————. 1995. "Marriage Markets and Black/White Differences in Labor, Marriage and Welfare." Paper presented at the conference on Economics and Sociology in Honor of Gary Becker and James Coleman, San Diego, July.

————. 2001. "Models of Labor Supply and Marriage: Mincer, Becker, Gronau and Beyond." Paper presented at the Annual Meetings of the AEA, New Orleans, January.

————. Forthcoming a. *Marriage and the Economy.* Cambridge and New York: Cambridge University Press.

————. Forthcoming b. "The New Home Economics at Columbia and Chicago." *Feminist Economics.*

Grossbard-Shechtman, Shoshana, and Xuanning Fu. 2001. "Women's Labor Supply, Ethnicity and Compensating Differentials in Marriage." Paper presented at the meeting of the Population Association of America, March.

Grossbard-Shechtman, Shoshana, and Shoshana Neuman. 1988. "Labor Supply and Marital Choice." *Journal of Political Economy* 96: 1294–1302.

Guttentag, Marcia, and Paul F. Secord. 1983. *Too Many Women: The Sex Ratio Question.* Beverly Hills, CA: Sage.

Hannan, Michael T., Nancy Brandon Tuma, and Lyle P. Groeneveld. 1977. "Income and Marital Events: Evidence from an Income-Maintenance Experiment." *American Journal of Sociology* 82: 1186–1211.

Heer, David M. 1962. "The Trend of Interfaith Marriages in Canada: 1922–1957." *American Sociological Review* 27: 245–250.

————. 1963. "The Measurement and Bases of Family Power: An Overview." *Journal of Marriage and the Family* 25: 133–129.

Heer, David M., and Amyra Grossbard-Shechtman. 1981. "The Impact of the Female Marriage Squeeze and the Contraceptive Revolution on Sex Roles and the Women's Liberation Movement in the United States, 1960 to 1975." *Journal of Marriage and the Family* 43: 49–65.

Henry, Louis. 1966. "Perturbations de la Nuptialité Résultant de la Guerre 1914–1918." *Population* 21: 273–332 (in French).

————. 1975. "Schéma d' Evolution des Marriages après de Grandes Variations des Naissances." *Population* 30: 759–779 (in French).

Hersch, Joni. Forthcoming. "Marriage and Household Production." In *Marriage and the Economy*, ed. Shoshana Grossbard-Shechtman. Cambridge and New York: Cambridge University Press.

Hill, Reuben, A.M. Katz, and R.L. Simpson. 1957. "An Inventory of Research in Marriage and Family Behavior." *Marriage and Family Living* 19: 89–92.

Homans, George C. 1961. *Social Behavior: Its Elementary Forms.* New York: Harcourt, Brace & World.

————. 1964. "Bringing Men Back In." *American Sociological Review* 29: 809–818.

Ironmonger, Duncan. Forthcoming. "Married Households and Gross Household Product." In *Marriage and the Economy*, ed. Shoshana Grossbard-Shechtman. Cambridge and New York: Cambridge University Press.

Jacoby, Hanan G. 1995. "The Economics of Polygyny in Sub-Saharan Africa." *Journal of Political Economy* 103: 938–971.

Karmel, P. 1946. "The Relations Between Male and Female Nuptiality in a Stable Population." *Population Studies* 1: 353–387.

Keeley, Michael C. 1977. "The Economics of Family Formation: An Investigation of the Age at First Marriage." *Economic Inquiry* 15(2): 238–250.

―――. 1979. "An Analysis of the Age Pattern of First Marriage." *International Economic Review* 20: 527–544.

―――. 1981. *Labor Supply and Public Policy: A Critical Review*. New York: Academic Press.

Lancaster, Kelvin J. 1966. "A New Approach to Consumer Theory." *Journal of Political Economy* 74: 132–157.

Lee, Ronald D. 1977. "Target Fertility, Contraception and Aggregate Rates: Toward a Formal Synthesis." *Demography* 14 (4): 455–479.

―――. 1980. "Aiming at a Moving Target: Period Fertility and Changing Reproductive Goals." *Population Studies* 34(2): 205–226.

Lehrer, Evelyn M. 1995. "The Effects of Religion on the Labor Supply of Married Women." *Social Science Research* 24: 281–301.

―――. 1996. "Religion as a Determinant of Fertility." *Journal of Population Economics* 9: 173–196.

―――. Forthcoming. "The Economics of Divorce." In *Marriage and the Economy*, ed. Shoshana Grossbard-Shechtman. Cambridge and New York: Cambridge University Press.

Lehrer, Evelyn M., and Carmel Chiswick. 1993. "Religion as a Determinant of Marital Stability." *Demography* 30: 385–404.

Leibowitz, Arleen, Jacob A. Klerman, and Linda Waite. 1992. "Employment of New Mothers and Child Care Choice: Differences by Children's Age." *Journal of Human Resources* 27: 112–133.

Lesthaeghe, Ronald. 2001. "Family Formation Theory: The Complementarity of Economic And Social Explanations." In *International Encyclopedia of the Social and Behavioral Sciences*, eds. Neil J. Smelser and Paul B. Baltes. New York: Elsevier Science–Pergamon.

Lesthaeghe, Ronald, and Dirk van de Kaa. 1986. "Twee demographische transities." In *Bevolking—Groei en Krimp*, eds. R. Lesthaeghe and D. van de Kaa. Deventer: Van Loghum-Slaterus (in Dutch).

Levinger, George. 1965. "Marital Cohesiveness and Dissolution: An Integrative Review." *Journal of Marriage and the Family* 27: 19–28.

Lichter, Daniel T., Diane K. McLaughlin, George Kephart, and David J. Landry. 1992. "Race, Local Mate Availability, and Transitions to First Marriage Among Young Women." Paper Presented at the Population Association of America, Denver, March.

Lillard, Lee A., and Linda J. Waite. 1993. "A Joint Model of Marital Childbearing and Marital Disruption?" *Demography* 30: 653–683.

Lillard, Lee A., Michael J. Brien, and Linda J. Waite. 1995. "Pre-Marital Cohabitation and Subsequent Marital Dissolution: Is It Self-Selection?" *Demography* 32: 437–458.

Lundberg, Shelly, and Robert A. Pollak. 1993. "Separate Sphere Bargaining and the Marriage Market." *Journal of Political Economy* 101: 988–1010.

Manser, Marilyn, and Murray Brown. 1980. "Marriage and Household Decision-Making: A Bargaining Analysis." *International Economic Review* 21: 31–44.

McElroy, Marjorie B., and Mary Jane Horney. 1981. "Nash Bargained Household Decisions: Toward a Generalization of the Theory of Demand." *International Economic Review* 22: 333–349.

Merton, Robert K. 1941. "Intermarriage and the Social Structure: Fact and Theory." *Psychiatry* 4: 361–374.

Miller, Cynthia, Irwin Garfinkel, and Sara McLanahan. 1997. "Child Support in the U.S.: Can Fathers Afford to Pay More?" *Review of Income and Wealth* 43(3): 261–281.

Mincer, Jacob. 1962. "Labor Force Participation of Married Women: A Study of Labor Supply." In *Aspects of Labor Economics*, ed. H. Gregg Lewis, pp. 63–97. Princeton, N.J.: Princeton University Press.

———. 1963. "Market Prices, Opportunity Costs, and Income Effects." In *Measurement in Economics*, ed. C. Christ, pp. 67–82. Stanford, CA: Stanford University Press.

Mortensen, Dale T. 1988. "Property Rights and Efficiency in Mating, Racing, and Related Games." *American Journal of Sociology* 94: S215–S240.

North, Douglas C. 1981. *Structure and Change in Economic History*. New York: Norton.

Oppenheimer, Valerie K. 1970. *The Female Labor Force in the United States*. University of California, Berkeley: Population Monograph Series No. 5.

Parsons, Talcott. 1942. "Age and Sex in the Social Structure of the United States." *American Sociological Review* 7: 606–616.

Richardson, John. 1979. "Wife Occupational Superiority and Marital Troubles." *Journal of Marriage and the Family* 41: 63–73.

Rosenthal, Erich. 1970. "Divorce and Religious Intermarriage: The Effect of Previous Marital Status Upon Subsequent Marital Behavior." *Journal of Marriage and the Family* 32: 435–440.

South, Scott J. 1988. "Sex Ratios, Economic Power, and Women's Roles: A Theoretical Extension and Empirical Test." *Journal of Marriage and the Family* 50: 19–31.

South, Scott J., and Glenna Spitze. 1994. "Housework in Marital and Nonmarital Households." *American Sociological Review* 59: 327–351.

Spanier, Graham B., and Paul C. Glick. 1980. "Mate Selection Differentials Between Whites and Blacks in the United States." *Social Forces* 58: 707–725.

Thibaut, J.W., and H.H. Kelley. 1959. *The Social Psychology of Groups*. New York: Wiley.

Treas, Judith. 1993. "Money in the Bank: Transaction Costs and the Economic Organization of Marriage." *American Sociological Review* 58: 723–734.

Trent, Katherine, and Scott J. South. 1989. "Structural Determinants of the Divorce Rate: A Cross-Societal Analysis." *Journal of Marriage and the Family* 51: 391–404.

Waite, Linda J., and Arleen Leibowitz. 1988. "Child Care for Preschoolers: Differences by Child's Age." *Demography* 25: 205–220.

———. 1991. "What Parents Pay For: Child Care Characteristics, Quality and Costs." *Journal of Social Issues* 47: 33–48.

Waite, Linda J., and Lee A. Lillard. 1991. "Children and Marital Disruption." *American Journal of Sociology* 96: 930–953.

Walby, Silvia. 1986. "Gender, Class, and Stratification: Toward a New Approach." In *Gender and Stratification*, eds. R. Crompton and M. Mann. Cambridge, UK: Polity Press.

Waller, Willard. 1937. "The Rating-Dating Complex." *American Sociological Review* 2: 727–734.

Weiss, Yoram, and Robert T. Willis. 1985. "Children as Collective Goods and Divorce Settlements." *Journal of Labor Economics* 3: 268–292.

Whittington, Leslie, and James Alm. Forthcoming. "The Effects of Government Policies on Marriage and Divorce." In *Marriage and the Economy*, ed. Shoshana Grossbard-Shechtman. Cambridge and New York: Cambridge University Press.

Willis, Robert J. 1974. "A New Approach to the Economic Theory of Fertility Behavior." In *Economics of the Family*, ed. Theodore W. Schultz. Chicago: University of Chicago Press.

Wilson, W. Julius. 1987. *The Truly Disadvantaged*. Chicago: University of Chicago Press.

Wood, Robert G. 1995. "Marriage Rates and Marriageable Men: A Test of the Wilson Hypothesis." *Journal of Human Resources* 30: 163–193.

Woolley, Frances. 1988. "A Non-cooperative Model of Family Decision Making." Working paper no. 125. London: London School of Economics.

———. Forthcoming. "Marriage and Control Over Money." In *Marriage and the Economy*, ed. Shoshana Grossbard-Shechtman. Cambridge and New York: Cambridge University Press.

9

A Demographer on the Cusp Between Economics and Sociology: An Interview with David Heer

Shoshana Grossbard-Shechtman

Part I. On the History of Demography

Q. You have been a prominent demographer and sociologist for many years. What do you consider yourself first, a demographer or a sociologist?

A. I prefer to consider myself a demographer rather than a sociologist. That is because I and other demographers are interested in quantitative research, whereas many sociologists do only qualitative research.

Q. What is demography?

A. I would define demography as the study of populations, which would include the composition of existing populations and the study of the components of population change: natality, mortality, in-migration, and out-migration.

David M. Heer obtained his PhD in sociology at Harvard in 1958. He has studied many aspects of demography, including fertility, migration, and couple formation. He has taught at the University of California at Berkeley and the Harvard University School of Public Health. He recently retired from the University of Southern California, where he directed the Population Research Laboratory and was a professor of Sociology. He has written books on social demography and immigration and has published more than eighty articles in demography. He has collaborated on articles with scholars trained in economics, political economy, public health, sociology, and social work. We collaborated on "The Impact of the Female Marriage Squeeze and the Contraceptive Revolution on Sex Roles and the Women's Liberation Movement in the United States, 1960 to 1975," published in the *Journal of Marriage and the Family* (Heer and Grossbard-Shechtman 1981). These interviews were held in February 2001 in La Jolla, California. When editing the interview, Shoshana Grossbard-Shechtman benefited from comments by William J. Leasure.

Q. From the start, demography has been a multidisciplinary field. Can you tell me more about the origin of demography as a science?

A. There have been two principal founders of demography: John Graunt and Thomas Malthus. Graunt was a statistician in seventeenth century England. He invented the *life table*, a major tool in all demographic analysis. Malthus was an economist and an Anglican minister who became very concerned with the question of how population growth affected human well-being. The first prominent American demographer was Francis Walker. He was the first president of the American Economic Association, and was the first academic to be superintendent for the U.S. Census Bureau (for the 1880 Census). He later became president of M.I.T.

Q. When did demography become an academic discipline in modern universities?

A. The two founders of demography represented two different strands that have come together: formal demography, as represented by Graunt, and social demography, as represented by Malthus. Before World War I, we see the development of demographic methods, particularly by Alfred Lotka, who was born and trained in France and worked as a statistician for the Metropolitan Life Insurance Company in the United States. He developed the theory of the stable population, the most important theory in formal demography. Lotka showed that in the case of France, based on current fertility and mortality rates, the stable population would have a negative rate of population growth. This finding was a great concern to French political leaders, who were concerned about France's military power relative to Germany's.

In the early twentieth century in American academia, a leading figure was Walter Wilcox, who taught statistics at Cornell University. Frank Notestein, who in 1936 became the first director of the influential Office of Population Research at Princeton, was trained by Wilcox and had a Ph.D. in economics. Another influential demographer during this period was Joseph Spengler, who obtained a Ph.D. in economics from Ohio State University. He wrote one of the earliest books on U.S. fertility (Spengler 1930).

Another interesting influence on the evolution of demography as an academic specialty is the eugenics movement. Francis Galton in the United Kingdom and Henry Fairfield Osborn, Frederick Osborn, and Ellsworth Huntington in the United States were among the leaders of this movement. They argued that hereditary differences in intelligence and the higher reproduction rates of the less intelligent were highly detrimental to the future of society. Henry Fairfield Osborn, who was a leading biologist and head of the American Museum of Natural History in New York, was a proponent of the idea that there were racial differences in intelligence and wrote a preface to an influential book by Madison Grant (1921): *The Pass-*

ing of the Great Race, or the Racial Basis of European History.

Q. So eugenics and demography have been very closely related?

A. In the 1920s and the 1930s eugenicists and demographers were closely allied. Frederick Osborn, the author of a noted textbook on eugenics (Osborn 1940), and Frank Notestein worked together at the Millbank Memorial Fund. Osborn was instrumental in the founding of the Office of Population Research at Princeton in 1936 (Coale 2000). Racial eugenic theories were then used to justify immigration policies limiting the number of immigrants from Eastern and Southern Europe. Geography is another discipline that is related to demography and that also got heavily involved in eugenics during this period. Among the leading racial eugenicists was Ellsworth Huntington, a respected professor of geography at Yale (see Huntington 1924), who was also a founding member of the Population Association of America. Joseph Spengler openly opposed the very low quotas for Eastern and Southern Europe. He argued that immigration policy should be based on individual merit, not group merit (see Heer 1996).

Q. The Population Association of America (PAA) was founded in 1931. What academic disciplines and ideologies was it allied with?

A. The membership of the PAA typically represents the major disciplines active in demography at a particular time. The founders of the PAA were active in a variety of disciplines, including public health and biology, actuarial science, economics, statistics, and sociology. Margaret Sanger, the famous birth-control advocate, took a leading role. A predominating influence was an ideology that the poor and less intelligent had too many children, and the wealthy and more intelligent had too few. The first PAA president, Henry Pratt Fairchild, was devoted to two causes: (1) the promotion of birth control, and (2) severe restrictions on immigration to preserve ethnic homogeneity in the United States (Lorimer 1981). Given that not all PAA founders agreed on the same social policies, the original PAA constitution prohibited the organization from endorsing any recommendations concerning population policy (Notestein 1981).

Q. How did this change after World War II? Let us start with the change in composition of the demography profession in terms of academic affiliation.

A. After World War II the influence of sociologists in the PAA grew relatively to that of persons trained in public health or biology.

Q. Was this change associated with an ideological shift?

A. It obviously was associated with a de-emphasis on eugenics. This was to a large extent the result of the Holocaust and the denigration of Hitler's racial eugenic views.

Q. How fascinating! Who would have thought that the extermination of European Jewry would have an impact on the nature of demography. . . .

A. There is another Jewish connection in demography. Prior to World War II, there were very few Jewish demographers. Following World War II, a large number of prominent Jewish demographers made their mark. These include both economists and sociologists. In sociology, important contributions were made, for example, by Philip Hauser and Nathan Keyfitz at the University of Chicago, and Ronald Freedman at the University of Michigan. In economics, contributions were made by Simon Kuznets, Harvey Leibenstein, Jacob Mincer, Gary Becker, and Julian Simon. Understandably, none of these Jewish demographers espoused eugenic views. There is an interesting story linking the words of a Jewish rabbi to Julian Simon's conversion from a position favoring governmentally sponsored fertility reduction programs to opposition to such programs. In Simon (1981) he stated that his viewpoint was changed in 1969, when he was reminded of the words of a Jewish chaplain delivering a eulogy over the dead on the battlefield at Iwo Jima: "How many who would have been a Mozart or a Michelangelo or an Einstein have we buried here?"

Q. Let us get to the topic of the relative influence of economics and sociology on demography before and after World War II. It is clear from what you stated before that economists were extremely influential in demography prior to World War II.

A. In fact, I believe that economists became less influential in demography after World War II. In part, this was the result of the large-scale training of demographers by sociology departments at Chicago (by Philip Hauser and Donald Bogue), Wisconsin (by Samuel Stouffer), Michigan (by Ronald Freedman and Amos Hawley), and the University of North Carolina (by Howard Odum and Rupert Vance).

Q. How interesting that during this period the university housing the influential Office of Population Research at Princeton produced demographers trained in economics rather than sociology!

A. And many of these economists became prominent. For instance, Ansley Coale and Leibenstein got their Ph.Ds there. The University of Pennsylvania stands out in that it trained prominent demographers skilled in both economics and sociology. Simon Kuznets, who left Penn in 1954, had a major influence both directly through his own work, and indirectly through the work of his disciple, Richard Easterlin (Easterlin got his Ph.D. in 1953). An important demographer trained in sociology at Penn is Charles Westoff, who headed Princeton's Office of Population Research for many years.

Part II. On Economics and Sociology

Q. What are some of the differences between demographers trained as economists and those trained as sociologists?

A. Demographers who are sociologists have generally not been very much concerned with theory but rather with ascertaining the facts about population. It is a fair statement that most of the theory in social demography has been contributed by economists.

Q. Whom do you consider as the major contributors to this theory?

A. There are five economists who have been very important. First, Frank Notestein. He had obtained a Ph.D. in economics at Cornell University in 1927. He is credited for developing the concept of the *demographic transition*, although Kingsley Davis, who worked under Notestein, coined the term (see Coale 2000). Second, Ansley Coale. He developed a highly influential theory concerning how a reduction in fertility would enhance economic growth.[1] Third, Richard Easterlin. He contributed a very influential explanation of why the postwar baby-boom occurred.[2] Fourth, Gary Becker. Becker's models incorporate the opportunity cost of children and make the distinction between quantity and quality of children. Finally, Alfred Sauvy. This French economist made two important contributions: He showed that (1) the population size that maximized military power was always greater than the population size that maximized the standard of living, and (2) the economic value of a man was maximized at about age twenty, declined to zero at around age forty-five, and was negative at all ages after age forty-five.

Q. I certainly agree with your assessment that Becker's theories have been very influential in demography. However, I would like to point out that Jacob Mincer (1963) was the first economist who advanced the theoretical argument for the inclusion of household production time in estimating the cost of children.

A. Most people are aware of Becker's (1965) article on the allocation of time. I take credit for bringing Gary Becker into the membership of the PAA. When I was chair of the membership committee in 1982, I wrote Becker a letter inviting him to become a member. I told him "as you are no doubt aware, there are few if any demographers whose name is cited more frequently in the demographic literature than your own." He accepted and has been a member of the PAA ever since. He later received the Irene Taeuber award. I had forgotten about Mincer's work. Why do you think that Mincer's article has been ignored by most demographers?

Q. In fact, Mincer's (1963) article on opportunity costs has been overlooked not only by demographers, but also by economists. In part this has to do with the fact that Becker's article appeared in a major journal, whereas Mincer's appeared in a book read by relatively few people. This differential popularity can also be partially explained by economists' preferences for mathematical modeling. Becker's mathematical model is more sophisticated, in part owing to its inclusion of a household production function. Did the fact that economists like elegant mathematical models have anything to do with your decision to get a Ph.D. in sociology and not in economics?

A. When I was an undergraduate at Harvard in the late 1940s, my first major was economics. This was a natural choice for me, for my father, Clarence Heer, was a professor of economics at the University of North Carolina. My father considered himself an institutional economist and had received his Ph.D. at Columbia University under Wesley Clare Mitchell, the founder of the National Bureau of Economic Research. I took two semesters of the elementary economics course at Harvard during my sophomore year. Previously I had taken a course in sociology with George Homans. At the end of my sophomore year I decided to change my major from economics to a major in social relations, a combination of sociology, social psychology, and social anthropology. I switched because I mistrusted the deductive nature of economics, which seemed to be based on unrealistic assumptions such as perfect markets. I preferred sociology because it was more empirical and less deductive.

Q. How interesting that when you were at the margin between economics and sociology, it was Homans who helped you choose sociology rather than economics. Homans must have been very sympathetic to economics, was he not? His social exchange theories look very much like economic theories to me. What is Homans's background?

A. Homans had not been trained in sociology as an undergraduate at Harvard but had majored in English literature. As a graduate student at Harvard he was very influenced by the Harvard biologist L.J. Henderson, an expert on Vilfredo Pareto (Henderson 1935). Homans took Henderson's seminar on Pareto in the early 1930s.

Q. Pareto distinguished what he called "ophelimity" and "utility." While utility is totally subjective, Pareto believed that ophelimity can, in principle, be inferred by comparing different behaviors of the same person that have effects occurring in the economy (see Jurgen Backhaus 2001, 25). Is not there a clear connection between Homans's concept of social exchange and Pareto's concept of utility outside of ophelimity—that is, regarding effects that affect society outside the economy?

A. You seem to be right. Homans acknowledged his intellectual debt to Pareto by writing his first book about the Italian economist (Homans and Curtis 1934).

Q. How about Talcott Parsons? Vernon Ruttan, a prominent economist who has recently become interested in sociological contributions to the study of economic development, finds his work very interesting [see his chapter in this book]. Parsons was also one of your professors. Was he also influenced by economics?

A. He certainly was. In fact, Parsons was trained as an economist. His doctorate in economics was issued by the University of Heidelberg in Germany. Parsons began his career analyzing the theories of economic development pioneered by German economists/sociologists Werner Sombart, Max Weber, and Karl Marx.

Q. When did Parsons become a sociologist?

A. He gradually became a sociologist. He started at Harvard in 1927 as an instructor in economics. His first semester at Harvard coincided with the start of the Committee on Sociology and Social Ethics, an undergraduate program. Within a short time, Parsons, who soon made known his own interests in sociology, was appointed secretary to that committee. You have to realize that the sociology department at Harvard did not exist until the fall of 1931, when it absorbed the previous department of Social Ethics. Parsons then transferred to sociology (see Camic 1991).

Q. What about Simon Kuznets, the Nobel Prize–winning economist? Did he have an influence on you?

A. Kuznets was a friend of my father. They studied together at Columbia. However, Kuznets did not come to Harvard until 1958, after I had completed my Ph.D there. Kuznets is an important contributor to what we know about the relationship between economic growth and population growth. His first demographic work dealt with the impact of immigration on economic growth in the United States.

Q. In recent years, economists and sociologists have worked together on many research projects in demography, as I show in my chapter in this book. Do you welcome that trend?

A. Yes, I do. This collaboration between economists and sociologists active in demography was originally made possible by the small size of the PAA. Given that small size, at the annual meetings there were no concurrent sessions. Obviously, this enabled demographers from each academic discipline to hear the contributions from all other disciplines. Currently, there are many concurrent sessions at each annual meeting of the PAA. It is possible, therefore, for sociologists/demographers to ignore the contributions of economists/demographers, and vice versa. I think that the PAA should have more plenary panel sessions in which both economists and sociologists will be represented.

Q. Using your experience as a demographer, but extrapolating to other subject matters as well, what can you say about past and future relations between economics and sociology?

A. I think that quantitative sociologists have been very much attracted to the rational choice models of economics. James Coleman, who was one of the leading sociologists in the United States after World War II, became the leading spokesperson for rational choice theories. He and Gary Becker led a seminar on rational choice at the University of Chicago for many years. I am not happy to see quantitative sociologists under attack now. There currently is a trend for many postmodern sociologists to attack rational choice models, sometimes viciously. This helps explain why Lawrence Iannaccone, the author of the chapter on religion in your book, experienced a need to counterattack sociologists of religion. The postmodernist wave in sociology is mainly due to the generation that was in college during the Vietnam War. When this generation retires, there will be much more respect for quantitative sociology, and more sociologists may read Coleman's (1990) monumental work *Foundations of Social Theory*.

Q. Thank you for these fascinating insights.

Notes

1. Coale also made important contributions to the theory of a stable population and to the explanation of the historical decline in fertility.

2. Another important contribution of Richard Easterlin is his analysis of the effects of cohort size.

References

Backhaus, Jurgen G. 2001. "Fiscal Sociology: What For?" Public lecture presented at the University of Maastricht, the Netherlands, January 19.

Becker, Gary S. 1965. "A Theory of the Allocation of Time." *Economic Journal* 75: 493–515.

Camic, Charles. 1991. "Introduction." In *Talcott Parsons: The Early Essays*, ix–lxix. Chicago: University of Chicago Press.

Coale, Ansley J. 2000. *An Autobiography*. Philadelphia: American Philosophical Society.

Coleman, James S. 1990. *Foundations of Social Theory*. Cambridge, MA: Harvard University Press.

Grant, Madison. 1921. *The Passing of the Great Race, or the Racial Basis of European History*. New York: Scribner.

Heer, David M. 1996. *Immigration in America's Future: Social Science Findings and the Policy Debate*. Boulder, CO: Westview Press.

Heer, David M., and Amyra Grossbard-Shechtman. 1981. "The Impact of the Female Marriage Squeeze and the Contraceptive Revolution on Sex Roles and the Women's Liberation Movement in the United States, 1960 to 1975." *Journal of Marriage and the Family* 43: 49–65.

Henderson, Lawrence. 1935. *Pareto's General Sociology: A Physiologist's Interpretation*. Cambridge, MA: Harvard University Press.

Homans, George C., and Charles P. Curtis, Jr. 1934. *An Introduction to Pareto*. New York: Knopf.

Huntington, Ellsworth. 1924. *The Character of Races as Influenced by Physical Environment, Natural Selection, and Historical Development*. New York: Scribner.

Lorimer, Frank. 1981. "Memories of the Early Years of the Association." *Population Index* 47: 488–490.

Mincer, Jacob.1963. "Market Prices, Opportunity Costs, and Income Effects." In *Measurement in Economics*, ed. C. Christ, pp. 67–82. Stanford, CA: Stanford University Press.

Notestein, Frank. 1981. "Memories of the Early Years of the Association." *Population Index* 47: 484–488.

Osborn, Frederick. 1940. *Preface to Eugenics*. New York: Harper.

Simon, Julian. 1981. *The Ultimate Resource*. Princeton, NJ: Princeton University Press.

Spengler, Joseph. 1930. *The Fecundity of Native and Foreign-Born Women in New England*. Washington, DC: Brookings Institution.

10

A Marriage Made in Heaven? Economic Theory and Religious Studies

Laurence R. Iannaccone

Who in his right mind would invoke economic theory to explain religious behavior? Who but Adam Smith, the patron saint of economics and author of its most revered text. In *The Wealth of Nations*, Smith ([1776]1965, 740–766) analyzed religious activities as examples of rational choice rather than exceptions to it. He challenged his readers to recognize that self-interest motivates clergy just as it does secular producers; that market forces constrain churches just as they do secular firms; and that the benefits of competition, the burdens of monopoly, and the hazards of government regulation impact religious markets just as they do other sectors of the economy.

Although Smith laid the foundation for an economics of religion in 1776, two centuries would pass before academics built upon his insights. This was a double loss for the social sciences. The study of economics lost a provocative "nonmarket" application that broadens the field and encourages cross-disciplinary research. And the study of religion lost a critical perspective—one that complements, and sometimes contradicts, the theories of sociologists, anthropologists, religious historians, and others.

Inspired by Gary Becker's pioneering work on the family, economists finally returned to the study of religion in the 1970s and 1980s. The earliest

Direct all correspondence to Laurence R. Iannaccone, Department of Economics, Santa Clara University, Santa Clara, CA 95053. Portions of this chapter are based on an article published in the *Journal for the Scientific Study of Religion*: "Voodoo Economics? Defending the Rational Choice Approach to Religion" (Iannaccone 1995a). I thank David Bromley, Roger Finke, Daniel Olson, Stephen Warner, and Rodney Stark for their suggestions and criticisms.

papers modeled church attendance and contributions as examples of (Beckerian) "household production" (Azzi and Ehrenberg 1975; Ehrenberg 1977). Extensions to this work incorporated habit formation and human capital so as to address conversions, intermarriage, and the role of religion in marriage, fertility, and divorce (Iannaccone 1984, 1990; Neuman 1986; Lehrer and Chiswick 1993). By the late-1980s and early 1990s, the scope of inquiry had grown to include denominational growth, religious extremism, doctrinal innovation, religious risk, church market structure, and much more. And now—thanks to scores of published papers and a newly acquired *Journal of Economic Literature* code (Z12)—the study of religion can finally claim status as an "official" subfield of economics.

The economics of religion is not without detractors. As the field has grown, and especially as it has moved into the traditional domain of sociologists, its models, methods, and insights have come under fire. Despite the influential contributions of leading "rational-choice" sociologists (most notably Rodney Stark and Roger Finke), attacking the economic/rational-choice approach has become something of a cottage industry. See, for example, the publications of Steve Bruce (1993, 1995, 2000, 2001), Roland Robertson (1992), N.J. Demerath (1995), C. Kirk Hadaway and Penny Marler (1996), Gerald Marwell (1996), Mark Chaves (1995), Mary Jo Neitz and Peter R. Mueser (1997), Mark Chaves and Phillip Gorski (2001), and James Spickard (1998). It would be unfair to dismiss these critics as mere defenders of academic turf. Better to see them as advocates for an intellectual tradition that views religious activities and institutions as "less rational" than other aspects of culture—a sacred realm "set apart" from the profane and (at least partially) insulated from the "calculation of utility" (Wuthnow 1991, 273; Emile Durkheim 1915/1965, 62; Talcott Parsons 1968, 412).[1]

This chapter seeks to explain and defend the economic approach to the study of religion. It complements, but does not reiterate, a broader and more representative overview of the field (Iannaccone 1998). My arguments are frankly utilitarian. Above all, I commend the economic approach as one that has borne considerable fruit in the social sciences, is well suited to the task of modeling religious behavior, and has yet to receive sufficient attention among religious scholars.

The Basic Approach

Gary Becker (1976, 5) has characterized the essential features of the economic approach as the "combined assumptions of maximizing behavior, market equilibrium, and stable preferences, used relentlessly and unflinchingly." Although Becker's "relentlessly" utilitarian analysis of subjects like "the demand for children" provoked irritation in some and incredulity in others, I do believe his list goes to the heart of the matter, particularly for the study of religion.

Of the three assumptions, maximizing behavior is fundamental. It is, however, a simplifying *assumption* to be employed and assessed within the context of predictive models that are themselves simplified representations of reality. The assumption implies that people approach all actions in the same way, evaluating costs and benefits and acting so as to maximize their net benefits. Hence, people choose what religion, if any, they will accept and how extensively they will participate in it. Over time, most people modify their religious choices in significant ways, varying their rates of religious participation and modifying its character, or even switching religions altogether. Following assumption of stable preferences, economic theorists are almost never content to explain such changes with reference to changed tastes, norms, or beliefs. They seek instead to model changes as optimal responses to varying circumstances—different prices, incomes, skills, experiences, resource constraints, access to different technologies, and the like.

Similar simplifying assumptions apply to religion's supply side. Religious "producers" are also viewed as optimizers—maximizing members, net resources, government support, or some other basic determinant of institutional success. The actions of church and clergy are thus modeled as rational responses to the constraints and opportunities found in the religious marketplace.

The combined actions of religious consumers and religious producers form a religious market that, like other markets, tends toward a steady-state equilibrium. As in other markets, the consumers' freedom to choose constrains the producers of religion. A "seller" (whether of automobiles or absolution) cannot long survive without the steady support of "buyers" (whether money-paying customers, dues-paying members, contributors and coworkers, or governmental subsidizers). Consumer preferences thus shape the content of religious commodities and the structure of the institutions that provide them. These effects are felt more strongly where religion is less regulated and, as a consequence, competition among religious firms is more pronounced. In competitive environments, religions have little choice but to abandon inefficient modes of production and unpopular products in favor of more attractive and profitable alternatives.

For an overview of the large and rapidly growing literature oriented along these lines, the reader may wish to consult my introduction to "The Economics of Religion" in the *Journal of Economic Literature* (Iannaccone 1998). For book-length applications of the rational-choice perspective, one should read the recent works by Rodney Stark and Roger Finke—*The Churching of America* (Finke and Stark 1992), *The Rise of Christianity* (Stark 1996), and *Acts of Faith* (Stark and Finke 2000).

Integrated Explanations

Economic theory offers a new and comprehensive approach to the social scientific study of religion. For a field long on data but short on theory, this is no small thing. Prior to the economic invasion, leading sociologists of religion openly criticized their field's lack of coherence. Robert Wuthnow acknowledged that:

> The field has grown more rapidly in inductive empirical research and in subspecializations than it has in attempts to identify theoretically integrative concepts. . . . The problem is not one of lively disagreement over serious intellectual disputes but an absence of unifying constructs. (1988, 500)

Rodney Stark and William Bainbridge summarized the situation with characteristic force:

> [Despite] a major rebirth [leading to] an amazing variety of new and well-tested facts, . . . no sustained effort has gone into creating theories to give order and relevance to these facts. Indeed, there has been little theorizing about religion since the turn of the [twentieth] century. (1987, 11)

Economic theory thus provides the study of religion its first "new paradigm" in many years (Warner 1993)—a unified approach to numerous empirical regularities and dozens of (previously) distinct predictions. To summarize these contributions, it helps to distinguish three levels of analysis: the level of individuals and households; the level of congregations, denominations, and other groups; and the level of entire communities or societies.

At the individual level, "human capital" and "household production" models of religious participation explain observed patterns in denominational mobility, religious intermarriage and divorce, conversion ages, the relationship between church attendance and contributions, and the influence of upbringing and interfaith marriage on levels of religious participation (Iannaccone 1990, 1998—see also Grossbard-Shechtman and Neuman 1986; Lee 1992; Lehrer and Chiswick 1993; Sherkat and Wilson 1995; Chiswick 1999; and Stark and Finke 2000, among others).

At the level of religious groups, new models of church and sect account for the strength of strict churches, the dynamics of denominational change, and the empirical correlates of sectarianism: costly demands, definite conversions, high levels of religious participation, lower-class and minority appeal, and so forth (Iannaccone 1988, 1992, 1994; Stark and Finke 2000).

At the level of entire communities and societies, models of religious markets and religious regulation challenge the predictions of secularization theory, asserting instead the vitality of religion in pluralistic settings (Iannaccone 1991; Finke 1990, 1992; Iannaccone, Finke, and Stark 1997). For a summary of research at all three levels, see Iannaccone (1998).

Several sociologists of religion—most notably Bruce (1993, 2000, 2001), Chaves (1995), and Demerath (1995)—have criticized much of this work. Bruce, for example, has little use for theories of household production and human capital. He claims that data on denominational mobility can be explained "perfectly well without economic metaphors" if we instead suppose that "beliefs 'sediment' so as to shape our receptivity to future alternatives" (Bruce 1993, 198). Likewise, data on conversion ages are "compatible" with the explanation that "the plausibility of beliefs is a product of (a) social interaction with other like-minded believers, and (b) the extent to which those beliefs produce a satisfactory understanding of the world and one's place in it" (Bruce 1993, 199). Intermarriage patterns can be explained by noting that "churches provide an excellent venue for meeting young people who are similar not only in religion but also in social class, culture and ethnic background" (1993, 199). And the higher rates of church attendance that characterize shared-faith marriages fit the alternative hypothesis that "a significant other who reinforces [one's own] beliefs will have a profound impact on the strength of one's faith and hence on the enthusiasm with which one participates in collective expressions of such beliefs" (1993, 200).

I find this critique unconvincing, in that it neither undermines the logic of the production/capital model nor refutes its empirical success. Rather, it merely proposes other explanations for four of the model's predictions. This is tantamount to conceding that the model does indeed live up to its billing. Production and capital *do* integrate numerous predictions within a single conceptual framework and *do* fit that data. The noneconomic approach substitutes a distinct (and distinctly ad hoc) "alternative explanation" for each of the phenomena in question—first social sedimentation, then plausibility, then dating venues, and finally mutually reinforcing beliefs. These explanations do not sum to any overall model of religious participation, nor are they direct implications of any standard theory of behavior. By contrast, the full set of findings come together within a single, relatively simple model that posits rational choice and the formation of religious capital, thereby linking the analysis of religious participation to a large body of research on household behavior and capital accumulation.

New Questions and Hypotheses

The rational-choice approach also generates new questions, new methods, and new hypotheses.

For a small example, consider again the production/capital model. It predicts that people will not "produce" religion in just one way (involving, say, two hours of church attendance, twenty dollars of contributions, and thirty minutes of prayer each week), but will instead alter their "input ratios" as the value of their time changes (Iannaccone 1990, 310–312).[2] Just as businesses seek to conserve on labor when wage rates rise (turning perhaps to automated assembly lines), and just as parents seek to conserve on their household time when both work in the labor force (turning perhaps to more convenience foods and landscaping services), so also church members will shift to more "money-intensive" forms of religious activity when their value of time increases. In practice, this means that people with high wage rates will tend to contribute more money *relative* to their rates of church attendance, and people with low wage rates will tend to contribute fewer dollars per hour of church they attend. More importantly, congregations and denominations with higher average wage rates will tend to adopt more money-intensive (time-saving) styles of worship: shorter services, more reliance on professional staff, larger and more costly facilities, more reliance on purchased goods and services, and less reliance on volunteered labor. These predictions have no precedent within traditional models of religious participation, yet they receive both statistical and anecdotal support.

At the level of communities and countries, rational-choice models yield a series of hotly contested predictions concerning the vitality of competitive religious markets and the stultifying effects of state-sponsored religious regulation. Because the market model of religion and its challenge to traditional secularization theory has been the subject of so much attention (and debate) in recent years, I will not summarize the situation here. It suffices merely to acknowledge the model's capacity to invigorate old debates (about secularization, pluralism, and American exceptionalism) with a fresh perspective and new predictions. For an introduction to this literature, see Iannaccone (1991, 1998), Finke and Stark (1992), and Warner (1993).

Rational choice directs our attention to other issues, so obviously important that one wonders at their historic neglect. It is, for example, nearly impossible to speak of the costs and benefits of religion without inquiring into the money that people devote to it (Ehrenberg 1977, Sullivan 1985). It is equally impossible to observe or participate in organized religion, without recognizing the necessity to finance the enterprise. Yet, prior to the 1980s, virtually no surveys of religious behavior asked people about their contributions.[3] Indeed, even after Andrew Greeley and William McManus (1987) wrote a book on contributions and the National Opinion Research Center added a contributions question to its General Social Surveys, the subject received no attention at conference sessions of the Association for the Sociology of Religion, Religious Research Association, or Society for the Scientific Study of Religion or the pages of their respective journals. As if to illustrate economic principles, it finally began to generate interest in the 1990s, when the Lilly Foundation began offering substantial incentive to study the financing of American religion. For an overview of results from those studies, see Chaves and Miller (1999).

One is reminded of Kingsley Davis's (1937) pathbreaking sociological study of prostitution—the first, it seems, to emphasize that money changed hands. A student will search in vain through most texts in the sociology of religion (including those by McGuire 1987; Roberts 1990; Yinger 1970) for an extended discussion of the determinants of religious giving or the ways in which groups finance their activities. This omission may reflect a reluctance to deal with economic issues from a sociological perspective, a refusal to accept the importance of the subject, or simply a pervasive oversight. But whatever the cause, it highlights an obvious contribution of the rational choice approach.

Traditional research also neglects the *time* that people devote to religion. Countless studies of church attendance would appear to prove otherwise, but closer examination reveals that nearly every study treats attendance as just another "dimension" of religiosity or attribute of the individual. The field seems to have overlooked the critical difference between church attendance and a religious attitude. Attendance takes time, time that has an opportunity cost because it preempts other activities, and time that can be *measured* by researchers. It seems silly to have hundreds of surveys that ask people questions like "Did you, yourself, happen to attend church last week?" but scarcely any that ask them how many *hours* they devoted to religious activities last week or how those hours were divided among private worship, attendance at public worship services, and involvement in other group meetings and activities.

In contrast, rational choice all but requires the study of time and money and its consequences. Iannaccone, Olson, and Stark (1995) emphasize this point, and they show that contributed time and money "produce" membership growth at both congregational and denominational levels. They also show that different measures of a religion's resources (such as membership, attendance, weekday involvement, and money contributions) yield very different estimates of the relative size, strength, and "market share" of various denominations. Working within a very different religious tradition, Chiswick (1999) identifies the many ways in which time constraints and time-money trade-offs have influenced the development of twentieth century American Judaism.

Beneath the measure of time and money lie more fundamental questions about the costs and benefits of religious activities. Iannaccone (1992, 1994) provides a cost-benefit explanation for the strength of strict churches and the observed empirical regularities that came to be known as "church-sect theory."

Rather than argue the abstract merits of such explanations or debate the extent to which religious socialization alters perceptions of cost and benefit, I would draw attention to just one point. There are very few survey items (in the General Social Surveys [GSS], national polls, denominational surveys, or special studies designed and administered by scholars of religion) that even *try* to assess the perceived costs of religious practice; nor is there much attention to perceived benefits. Instead, we find scores of psychological batteries, attitude measures, belief inventories, affiliation items, and a few behavioral measures (Hill and Hood 1999). The value of cost-benefit models will remain hard to assess (but impossible to dismiss) until we begin asking people what they have sacrificed for the sake of their faith.

Similar observations apply to many other economic concepts—market equilibrium, the free-rider problem, the theory of monopoly, the concept of production, and more. But I will conclude this section with a single example of rational choice leading to insights that otherwise remain unthinkable or unthought.

While arguing that religion falls beyond the limits of economic rationality, Bruce (1993, 202) asserts that "one cannot hedge one's bets by buying only a small amount of a religion . . . ; we cannot regard religious promiscuity as a form of rational diversification of investment." This certainly sounds reasonable, and it accords with the standard sociological assumption that calculations are "off limits" when it comes to a great many areas of human behavior (Etzioni 1988). But by taking it for granted, one ignores a fascinating set of possibilities that I have labeled the theory of *religious portfolios* (Iannaccone 1995b).

The theory builds from the fact that religions are risky business. Their fundamental assertions lie within a realm of "radical uncertainty" beyond the range of empirical verification (Wuthnow 1988, 494; Stark and Bainbridge 1987, 39). Hence, subscribing to a religion is a bit like buying stock. A natural strategy for dealing with such risk is to hedge one's bets. "Pascal's wager" advocates one such hedge, trading finite losses in this life for the possibility of infinite rewards in the next. But other hedging strategies apply to the *content* of religiosity. "Religious investors" will be tempted to diversify their own religious portfolios, devoting their time and money to a variety of different religions, dabbling in, say, astrology, Methodism, meditation, and so forth.

As I have argued in Iannaccone (1995b, 1999), this unexpected prediction receives a great deal of empirical support when it is combined with the rational-choice theory of "strict churches." Together they yield an elegant typology, contrasting "collective" religions (which emphasize exclusive membership, employ sacrifice and stigma, maintain high levels of participation, and view all members as co-workers) and "private" religions (which obtain little or no brand loyalty, permit diversification, average low levels of participation, and focus on fee-for-service transactions). Western religions, particularly their more sectarian variants, exemplify the first type. Asian religions, New Age religion, and Greco-Roman paganism exemplify the second. I mention the theory of religious portfolios, not to suggest that one should accept its merits sight unseen, but rather to emphasize how a rational-choice perspective leads to hypotheses and data that otherwise are overlooked or rejected out of hand.

Resonance and Realism

Critics sometimes complain that rational-choice models house "unrealistic" assumptions. Bruce, for example, notes that a "very obvious criticism that can be made of the economic approach is that it has little resonance with the understandings of the people whose behavior it must explain" (Bruce 1993, 200; see also Etzioni 1988, 17; Feree 1992; Swedberg 1990). There is, of course, a long-standing philosophical debate over the importance of realism (Boland 1979). One is hard-pressed, for example, to defend relativistic or quantum-mechanical models of the universe as more intuitively plausible than their Newtonian predecessor. But for the sake of argument, let us accept the notion that, other things being equal, a social-scientific explanation is to be preferred if its underlying assumptions accord with perceived reality and/ or resonate with people's self-described behavior, motivations, and the like.

I would argue that from casual conversation to biblical commands, we find language that is compatible with, and often equivalent to, cost-benefit terminology. In this sense rational choice theory is at least as realistic and plausible as alternative interpretations. The basic issue, after all, is whether people attend to costs and benefits and act so as to maximize their net benefits. The principal alternative is unreflective action based on habit, norms, emotion, neurosis, socialization, cultural constraints, or the like—action that is largely unresponsive to changes in perceived costs, benefits, or probabilities of success.[4]

Consider the utilitarian admonitions that fill the Bible. "Honor your father and mother, that your days may be long in the land" (Exodus 20:12). "Behold, I set before you a blessing and a curse: the blessing if you obey . . . and the curse if you do not" (Deut. 11:26). "Take delight in the Lord, and he will give you the desires of your heart" (Psalms 37:4). Consider the investment-oriented appeals to faith: "Do not lay for yourself treasures on earth where moth and rust consume and where thieves break in and steal, but lay up for yourselves treasures in heaven" (Matt. 6:19). Consider the economic meta-

phors: Cast not your pearls before swine; the kingdom of heaven is like trea-
sure hidden in a field; the kingdom heaven is like a merchant in search of
fine pearls. Consider the crowds who followed Jesus, and who follow today,
in response to reports of miracles—an indication (insofar as they are believed) that the probability of divine presence is high and the possibility of
personal benefits is great.

Turning to ordinary speech and survey data, note that regular church
attenders are far more likely than others to view their religion as personally
beneficial and satisfying. They more often believe in other-worldly benefits
(heaven) and costs (hell). They impute higher probability to the existence of
God. They express more satisfaction with their denomination, congregation,
pastor, church-based friendships, and the like. Similar cost-benefit factors differentiate religious "dropouts" from those who remain active in their faith
(Hoge 1981). Some readers might discount these facts as obvious and unin-
formative, but they are obvious only to the extent that we adopt (or accept that
others adopt) a utilitarian perspective, persisting in behaviors perceived as
beneficial and avoiding those perceived as costly. Other readers might reject
people's own statements, arguing that they merely reveal the natural tendency
to rationalize actions that are, in fact, determined by norms, habit, social
pressures, and the like. But even if this were so, we are left with instrumental,
utilitarian language as a natural way people describe and defend their behavior.

The irony here is that many nonrational constructs resonate *less* well with
people's own statements. Ordinary people do not describe their religious
beliefs or behavior in terms of plausibility structures, status incongruity,
boundary maintenance, or their equivalents. They scarcely acknowledge the
possibility of doing what they do because they were socialized to do it. Rather,
they speak of the truth (i.e., the high probability) of their view, the blessings
(benefits) that accompany it, and the curses (costs) that accompany its alternative. They admit temptation (yearning for the benefits they sacrifice to
garner future blessings) and backsliding (when their degree of certainty falls
or the lure of worldly pleasures overwhelms the decision to wait for heav-
enly rewards). If we ask them to assess the dollar cost or utility gain of attending Sunday services, they will surely balk. But they readily concede that
people are drawn to faith and fellowship that "satisfy their spiritual needs."

Pervasive Principles

Utilitarian language may proliferate and yet utilitarian principles may fail to
account for religious behavior; people may say one thing and do another.
But here again, one finds strong prima facie evidence that people both talk
and act in accordance with rational principles.

Consider the short list of basic economic theorems given by Gary Becker (1976, 5–6) and quoted by Bruce (1993, 194–195; see also Robertson 1992, 154). They include the laws of demand and supply, the invisible hand theorem (asserting the superior efficiency of competitive markets), and the principle that taxing a commodity or activity reduces the amount that is produced. I would assert that it is nearly impossible to imagine these principles *not* applying to religious behavior. Moreover, even when they do (apparently) fail to apply, there is much to be gained from asking why.

The *law of demand* is by far the most basic economic principle, so basic that it applies to laboratory animals (Kagel et al. 1975). As Becker (1976, 151–168) has demonstrated, it is more a consequence of budget constraints than rationality, so that even those who act randomly or habitually tend to consume less when prices rise.

Does religious behavior violate this law? Consider church attendance. Consider a particular church member who averages two or three meetings a month, and consider an event that increases the "price" of attendance, other things remaining equal. Imagine, for example, a heavy snowstorm that makes the roads to and from church difficult to drive, thereby increasing the full cost of attendance. Without a doubt, this member will become less likely to attend. More importantly, we can aggregate this prediction and conclude that total attendance will be less than normal on such days. A similar phenomenon will arise on weekends with exceptionally good weather and three-day holiday weekends, because the "opportunity cost" of attendance rises with the increased availability of unusually attractive alternative activities (Iannaccone and Everton 2000). The argument extends to any event, attribute, or commitment that increases the opportunity cost of a person's time (and hence the cost of a morning spent in church)—project deadlines, special events, hectic stages in the life cycle. The same prediction applies to reduced benefits (the flip-side of costs)—a period of undistinguished stand-in preachers, the departure of many church friends, moving to a less pleasant facility, a cutback in child care and Sunday school services.

Again, the reader may object that these are obvious facts that require neither theory nor graphs to back them up. But that is just the point. The law of demand and that of most other fundamental economic theorems *are* obvious, and obviously correct. The power of rational choice lies in its having expressed these principles in verbal, graphical, and mathematical forms that allow us to apply, combine, and manipulate them *without* losing track of our own assumptions.[5] And even though this particular example does not yield an esoteric theory of church attendance, it does correctly identify most of the factors that prove significant in survey studies of attendance.

The *law of supply* is scarcely more debatable than the law of demand and may apply even to psychotics (Hirshleifer and Glazer 1992, 7). It predicts, among other things, that the charitable contributions "supplied" to a church will increase when the rewards for doing so increase (including, for example, more public recognition). It also predicts a reduction in entrants to the priesthood, when its pay, power, and prestige decline relative to that of other occupations. It further implies that the supply of new religions (and hence the growth of new religions) will rise when barriers to entry fall (decreasing startup costs, and thus effectively increasing the net price that religious suppliers receive for their services). Again, the predictions are obvious; but again that is the point.

The beauty, of course, is that these simple laws combine to produce a large body of insights and unexpected predictions regarding the effect of taxes, subsidies, quotas, rationing, and more. A subsidy to religious private schooling (via laws that ensure the deductibility of tuition) certainly will increase enrollments in Christian schools. A voucher system (which acts as an even larger subsidy) will increase it further still. Tax exemptions in the United States encourage groups to define themselves as religious rather than social or philosophical in nature, and, as Roger Finke (1990) has emphasized, the First Amendment functions like a vast subsidy to religious dissent and pluralism. Even small changes in the legal environment can have major consequences for religious groups, as is illustrated by a 1960 rule change permitting TV stations to *sell* the religious air time they had previously given away. Jeffrey Hadden (1993) documents the resulting massive decline in (previously subsidized) broadcasts by liberal "mainline" denominations and the corresponding increase in broadcasts by conservative "televangelists." The 1965 repeal of immigration quotas (which had limited the supply of Asian religious teachers) gave a major boost to new religions in America (Melton 1987, 52). David Martin (1990, 13) notes that the Protestant explosion in Latin America was contingent upon "the general deregulation of religion." And religious and political deregulation on the opposite end of the globe has inaugurated a comparable period of religious ferment in Eastern Europe and the former Soviet Union.

Historical Relevance

Some scholars turn the preceding claims on their head, arguing that the very evidence of religious "economization" proves its limited relevance (Robertson 1992, 150; see also Demerath 1995). According to this argument, religious traditions can only become "consumer commodities" (subject to individual choice and "the logic of market economics") within a modern, pluralistic society (Berger 1967, 138). The applicability of an economic perspective thus proves how far contemporary religion, especially American Protestant-ism, has strayed from its roots (Wilson 1966) and calls into question this economic perspective's capacity to illuminate any truly religious phenom-enon (Bruce 1993; Heelas 1993).

Insofar as this argument encourages historical sensitivity and global com-parisons, it certainly merits attention. A large body of social-scientific re-search traces the evolution of markets and capitalist institutions in medieval Europe and documents its immense political, social, and economic conse-quences. One might imagine a similar (and similarly illuminating) analysis of the emergence of "religious markets." Indeed, the most provocative re-cent histories of American religion do just that (Finke and Stark 1992; Hatch 1989; Moore 1994; see also Fogel 2000).

But it would be a serious mistake to conclude that economic explanations apply only to modern times. To do so understates past opportunities for choice while also overlooking long-standing theories of noncompetitive situations.

Stark and Bainbridge (1985, 111–122) have attacked "the illusion of a universal church," citing medieval Catholicism's continual and ultimately unsuccessful battles with heresy, schism, and dissent. Other state-supported churches, including the Church of England, had even more trouble main-taining a religious monopoly (Stark and Iannaccone 1994). I have already noted that choice, competition, and even "portfolio diversification" pervaded the Greco-Roman "religious economy." Competing religions filled the Ro-man Empire: civic worship of the old Greco-Roman gods, such as Zeus, Apollo, Artemis, Dionysus, and the like; Caesar worship; mystery religions of Isis, Mithras, Adonis, and others; magic and astrology; numerous schools of philosophy; and the intolerant faiths of Judaism and Christianity (Nock 1963). Japanese religious history reveals a complex mix of peaceful coexist-ence, spirited competition, and vigorous suppression. And Israel's sacred texts, from Genesis to Malachi, testify to the persistent lure and perennial presence of alternatives to the Jewish faith. Against the backdrop of the Old Testament prophets' condemnation of pervasive idolatry, apathy, material-ism, and unbelief, the contemporary situation looks less unique.

It is, of course, true that modern society, particularly late twentieth cen-tury America society, provides a far wider range of choices than were previ-ously available. Despite its many challenges, the Roman Catholic church *did* dominate medieval Europe's religious market, and the remnants of domi-nance still linger. But these facts hardly invalidate rational choice. Economic theory bristles with theories of imperfect competition—monopoly, cartels, monopolistic competition, oligopoly, and more. Insofar as historic religions kept their competitors at bay, these theories offer unique insights concerning market segmentation, price discrimination, collusion, and "economic rents."

Indeed, the first social scientific analysis of religion concerned the religious monopolies of medieval Catholicism and post-Reformation–established Protestantism (Smith [1776] 1965, 740–766).

Far from being restricted to Western capitalist settings, economic logic underpins many of the most provocative recent studies of religious history. This includes Stark's (1996) highly acclaimed *The Rise of Christianity*; a study of the medieval Catholic church by Robert Ekelund et al. (1996); a special (March 1997) volume of the *Journal of Institutional and Theoretical Economics*; and a wide range of articles on such diverse topics as the rise of monotheism in ancient Israel (Raskovich 1996); patterns of conversion to Islam in sub-Saharan Africa (Ensminger 1994); religious activity in Japan (Miller 1998); and the decline of Shaker communes (Murray 1995).

The Strength of Simplicity

In the end, most critics condemn rational choice for embracing too much and too little: too much, in that it assumes lightning powers of calculation, full information, and total self-control; too little, in that it fails to take account of preference formation, normative constraints, emotional impulses, social structures, and the like. Hence, it is said that more realistic models of human behavior must do more to acknowledge limitations of the human mind and the complexity of human culture (Etzioni 1988; Feree 1992; Robertson 1992; Wuthnow 1991, 273).

Fair enough. The rational-choice model *is* unrealistic in this sense (although it may be misleading to ignore the growing body of economic research that seeks to incorporate altruism, envy, cognitive biases, addiction, and limited self-control).[6] But while being realistic about society, let us be realistic about ourselves. Researchers possess the very limitations that they observe. Etzioni (1988, 117), quoting Herbert Simon, makes much of the fact that the human brain can accommodate only three to seven items in short-term memory. The "simple" assumptions of rational-choice theory, like the pieces of a chess game or the postulates of a mathematical system, more than suffice to tax most people's powers of deduction. How much harder is it therefore to develop, test, and extend models that incorporate cognitive limitations, preference formation, intrapersonal conflict, normative-affective constraints, and social interdependence?

Scholars rightly criticize economic arguments that border on tautology or lack testability, but they must turn the same criticisms back upon every proposed alternative. Religious researchers must work toward explanations that are well defined, consistent, and free of hidden leaps. Ordinary language jumps from X, to Y, to not-X, and never skips a beat. Formal modeling is about keeping one's notation straight, thereby avoiding the not-so-obvious contradictions and irrelevancies that creep into most verbal arguments, and simplifying assumptions help us grind through the logic that otherwise eludes us. One cannot but admire those who attempt to build rigorous verbal theories within a complex framework of realistic behavioral principles.[7] But recognizing the overwhelming difficulty of the task and the limited success to date, one must also sympathize with those who employ fewer assumptions and more formal analyses. In this respect, rational choice may well prove *more* realistic than its alternatives.

Conclusions

Social scientists have debated the merits of rational-choice theory for decades, and I make no claim to have resolved matters with this essay. Nevertheless, I have sought to clarify some issues and counter some criticisms that are of particular relevance when evaluating rational approaches to religion. The economic approach seeks to fill the theory gap within the study of religion, redressing an historic imbalance that has favored the accumulation of data over the discovery of unifying concepts. It integrates existing research on the religious behavior of individuals, groups, and societies. It also yields new questions, new methods, and new hypotheses to guide empirical research. Its utilitarian language parallels the stated promises of most religions and the explanations many people give for their own religious behavior. Its most basic principles and predictions prove relevant to religious markets, both present and past, competitive and monopolistic. Its relative simplicity greatly facilitates statements and tests of theory.

It goes without saying that I encourage attempts to construct comprehensive rational-choice models that unify existing insights, explain observed empirical regularities, and generate new research questions. Even so, it would be a mistake to interpret this position as "economic imperialism." One may harbor great hopes for one approach without denigrating every alternative.

Scholarly paradigms are subject to the same sort of diminishing returns that characterize other activities. Within the field of economics, which has been heavily mined with the tools of rational choice for more than a century, much of the most important recent work rests on insights from sociology and psychology. Consider, for example, the research on labor markets by Akerlof (1984), Frank (1985), Granovetter (1985), and Williamson (1985). Or consider studies of uncertainty and risk, for decades dominated by expected utility theory, but now revitalized by new results on cognitive limitations, stemming investigations of experimental psychologists and behavioral economists (Kahneman, Slovic, and Tversky 1982).

Within the field of religious research, the situation is exactly reversed. Economic theory now offers a high rate of return precisely because of its previous neglect. For decades, scholars have scrutinized religion from every angle *except* that of rational choice. Explanations of religious phenomena have stressed socialization, indoctrination, neurosis, cognitive dissonance, tradition, deviance, deprivation, functionalism, emotionalism, culture, and more. But rarely has anyone viewed religion as the product of cost-benefit decisions, and formal models of the religious behavior (rational or otherwise) scarcely exist. With so little previous work and so many potentially useful insights from microeconomics, exchange theory, and public choice, the marginal product of each additional project promises to be great.

If the recent past offers any guide, the economic approach will especially benefit those seeking to build and test models that explain broad categories of religious phenomena in terms of relatively simple principles. The human-capital approach to individual religious participation, the models of strict churches and religious portfolios, and the theory of religious markets are all cases in point. "Ideographic" research, which seeks to describe a single case or situation in all its fullness, may have less to gain. Likewise, questions concerning religious emotional states, moral imperatives, preference change, and self-control may prove difficult to explain within a rational-choice framework—though perhaps not impossible, as witness the work of Becker (1996) and others on addiction and the formation of tastes.

For my money (and time), I hesitate to concede any area of inquiry before the study of religion has accumulated more first-hand experience with the rational-choice approach. Browsing the standard sociology of religion textbooks, one finds few topics that are by their very nature off-limits. Current work has already begun to address the following: the underlying nature of religion; the determinants of individual religiosity and participation rates; conversion, commitment, and religious mobility; the emergence and viability of different types of religious institutions; secularization and its alternatives; deviant religions; the socioeconomic correlates of different types of religions; church-state issues; resource mobilization and the marketing of religion; plausibility problems; and more. The work is hardly definitive, but its future looks bright.

The genius of Adam Smith is thus again revealed (as if it needed further proof). Add "the economics of religion" to his list of seminal insights, great and small. And, while at it, chalk up a point for another great economist, George Stigler (1982, 4), who once observed that "if on first hearing a [Smith] passage you are inclined to disagree, you are reacting inefficiently; the correct response is to say to yourself: I wonder where I went amiss?"

Notes

1. Debate is further encouraged by an unfortunate but long-standing tradition distinguishing economics from sociology on the basis of rational versus nonrational action, to say nothing of other traditions that view religion as outright *ir*rationality, escapism, or psychopathology (Swedberg 1990, 11,13; Sigmund Freud [1927] 1961, 88).

2. This reference to the (monetary) value of time should not be viewed as an implicit assertion of the primacy of money. The predictions remain unchanged if we invert the model and value money in terms of its temporal (time-price) equivalent.

3. The principal exceptions are Charles Glock and Rodney Stark's 1963 Northern California Bay Area survey, the National Opinion Research Center's 1963 and 1974 surveys of American Catholics, and a 1969 National Jewish Population study.

4. Positing different types of rationality (economic, social, legal, political, communal, etc.) does not strike me as a meaningful alternative, although this distinction is advanced by some (Bruce 1993, 203; cf. Smelser 1976). Swedberg (1990, 241) quotes Jon Elster arguing for "one and the same notion of rationality . . . independent of what discipline you are in," and Etzioni (1988, 142) concludes that "none of [these alternatives] is in wide use, and hence one must assume they are not productive."

5. For a taste of this power, compare a verbal description of a change in market equilibrium to a far simpler graphical depiction of a supply-curve shift. Few college students can talk their way through the effects of an oil embargo, but once they recognize it as an inward shift of the supply curve, they are home free.

6. See, for example, Frank (1985, 1988). My own research on habit formation grew from the decision to model religious participation with reference to a person's past (Iannaccone 1984).

7. Etzioni (1988) outlines the general framework of one such model. The "prospect theory" of psychologists and behavioral economists may eventually coalesce into another alternative (Kahneman et al. 1982).

References

Akerlof, George A. 1984. *An Economic Theorist's Book of Tales.* Cambridge: Cambridge University Press.

Azzi, Corry, and Ronald Ehrenberg. 1975. "Household Allocation of Time and Church Attendance." *Journal of Political Economy* 84: 27–56.

Becker, Gary S. 1976. *The Economic Approach to Human Behavior.* Chicago: University of Chicago Press.

———. 1996. *Accounting for Tastes.* Cambridge, MA: Harvard University Press.

Berger, Peter L. 1967. *The Sacred Canopy.* Garden City, NY: Doubleday.

Boland, Lawrence A. 1979. "A Critique of Friedman's Critics." *Journal of Economic Literature* 17(2): 503–522.

Bruce, Steve. 1993. "Religion and Rational Choice: A Critique of Economic Explanations of Religious Behavior." *Sociology of Religion* 54(2): 193–205.

———. 1995. "The Truth About Religion in Britain." *Journal for the Scientific Study of Religion* 34(4): 417–430.

———. 2000. *Choice and Religion: A Critique of Rational Choice Theory.* Oxford: Oxford University Press.

———. 2001. "All Too Human." *First Things* 110 (February): 35–37.

Chaves, Mark. 1995. "On the Rational Choice Approach to Religion." *Journal for the Scientific Study of Religion* 34(1): 98–104.

Chaves, Mark, and Sharon L. Miller, eds. 1999. *Financing American Religion.* Walnut Creek, CA: Altamira Press.

Chaves, Mark, and Phillip S. Gorski. 2001. "Religious Pluralism and Religious Participation." *Annual Review of Sociology* 27: 261–281.

Chiswick, Carmel. 1999. "The Economics of Jewish Continuity." *Contemporary Jewry* 20: 30–56.

Davis, Kingsley. 1937. "The Sociology of Prostitution." *American Sociological Review* 2: 744–755.

Demerath, N. J. 1995. "Rational Paradigms, A-Rational Religion, and the Debate Over Secularization." *Journal for the Scientific Study of Religion* 34(1): 105–112.

Durkheim, Emile. [1915] 1965. *The Elementary Forms of Religious Life*, trans. by Joseph Ward Swain. New York: Free Press.

Ehrenberg, Ronald G. 1977. "Household Allocation of Time and Religiosity: Replication and Extension." *Journal of Political Economy* 85(2): 415–423.

Ekelund, Robert B., Robert F. Hébert, Robert D. Tollison, Gary M. Anderson, and Audrey B. Davidson. 1996. *Sacred Trust: The Medieval Church as an Economic Firm.* New York: Oxford University Press.

Ensminger, Jean. 1994. "The Political Economy of Religion: An Economic Anthropologist's Perspective." *Journal of Institutional and Theoretical Economics* 150(4): 745–754.

Etzioni, Amitai. 1988. *The Moral Dimension: Toward a New Economics.* New York: Free Press.

Feree, Myra Marx. 1992. "The Political Context of Rationality: Rational Choice Theory and Resource Mobilization." In *Frontiers in Social Movement Theory*, ed. Aldon D. Morris and Carol McClurg Mueller, pp. 29–52. New Haven, CT: Yale University Press.

Finke, Roger. 1990. "Religious Deregulation: Origins and Consequences." *Journal of Church and State* 32(3): 609–626.

———. 1992. "An Unsecular America." In *Religion and Modernization: Sociologists and Historians Debate the Secularization Thesis*, ed. Steve Bruce, pp. 145–169. Oxford: Clarendon Press.

Finke, Roger, and Rodney Stark. 1992. *The Churching of America.* New Brunswick, NJ: Rutgers University Press.

Fogel, Robert W. 2000. *The Fourth Great Awakening and the Future of Egalitarianism.* Chicago: University of Chicago Press.

Frank, Robert H. 1985. *Choosing the Right Pond: Human Behavior and the Quest for Status.* New York: Oxford University Press.

———. 1988. *Passions Within Reason: The Strategic Role of Emotions.* New York: Norton.

Freud, Sigmund. (1927) 1961. *The Future of an Illusion.* Garden City, NY: Doubleday.

Granovetter, Mark. 1985. "Economic Action and Social Structure: A Theory of Embeddedness." *American Journal of Sociology* 91: 481–510.

Greeley, Andrew M., and William E. McManus. 1987. *Catholic Contributions: Sociology and Policy.* Chicago: Thomas More Press.

Grossbard-Shechtman, Shoshana, and Shoshana Neuman. 1986. "Economic Behavior, Marriage and Religiosity." *Journal of Behavioral Economics* 15(1&2): 71–85.

Hadaway, C. Kirk, and Penny L. Marler. 1996. "Response to Iannaccone: Is There a Method to This Madness?" *Journal for the Scientific Study of Religion* 35(3): 217–222.

Hadden, Jeffrey K. 1993. "The Rise and Fall of American Televangelism." *The Annals of the American Academy of Political and Social Science* 527 (May): 113–130.

Hatch, Nathan O. 1989. *The Democratization of American Christianity.* New Haven, CT: Yale University Press.

Heelas, Paul. 1993. "The Limits of Consumption and the Post-Modern 'Religion' of the New Age." In *The Authority of the Consumer*, eds. N. Abercrombie, R. Keat, and N. Whiteley, pp. 102–115. London: Routledge.

Hill, Peter C., and Ralph W. Hood Jr., eds. 1999. *Measures of Religiosity.* Birmingham, AL: Religious Education Press.

Hirshleifer, Jack, and Amihai Glazer. 1992. *Price Theory and Applications*, 5th ed. Englewood Cliffs, NJ: Prentice-Hall.

Hoge, Dean R. 1981. *Converts, Dropouts, Returnees: A Study of Religious Change Among American Catholics.* Washington, DC: Pilgrim Press.

Iannaccone, Laurence R. 1984. "Consumption Capital and Habit Formation with an Application to Religious Participation." Doctoral dissertation, University of Chicago.

———. 1988. "A Formal Model of Church and Sect." *American Journal of Sociology* 94(supplement): S241–S268.

———. 1990. "Religious Participation: A Human Capital Approach." *Journal for the Scientific Study of Religion* 29(3): 297–314.

———. 1991. "The Consequences of Religious Market Structure: Adam Smith and the Economics of Religion." *Rationality and Society* 3(2): 156–177.

———. 1992. "Sacrifice and Stigma: Reducing Free-Riding in Cults, Communes, and Other Collectives." *Journal of Political Economy* 100(2): 271–291.

———. 1994. "Why Strict Churches Are Strong." *American Journal of Sociology* 99(5): 1180–1211.

———. 1995a. "Voodoo Economics? Defending the Rational Approach to Religion." *Journal for the Scientific Study of Religion* 34 (1): 76–88.

———. 1995b. "Risk, Rationality, and Religious Portfolios." *Economic Inquiry* 33(2): 285–295.

———. 1998. "The Economics of Religion: A Survey of Recent Work." *Journal of Economic Literature* 36(3): 1465–1496.

———. 1999. "Religious Extremism: Origins and Consequences." *Contemporary Jewry* 20: 8–29.

Iannaccone, Laurence R., Daniel V.A. Olson, and Rodney Stark. 1995. "Religious Resources and Church Growth." *Social Forces* 74(2): 705–731.

Iannaccone, Laurence R., Roger Finke, and Rodney Stark. 1997. "Deregulating Religion: The Economics of Church and State." *Economic Inquiry* 35(2): 350–364.

Iannaccone, Laurence R., and Sean Everton. 2000. "Never on Sun(ny) Days?" Conference paper, Society for the Scientific Study of Religion, Houston.

Kagel, J.H., H. Rachlin, L. Green, R.C. Battalio, R.L. Basman, and W.R. Klemm. 1975. "Experimental Studies of Consumer Demand Behavior Using Laboratory Animals." *Economic Inquiry* 13(1): 22–38.

Kahneman, Daniel, Paul Slovic, and Amos Tversky, eds. 1982. *Judgment Under Uncertainty: Heuristics and Biases.* New York: Cambridge University Press.

Lee, Richard R. 1992. "Religious Practice as Social Exchange." *Sociological Analysis* 53(10): 1–35.

Lehrer, Evelyn L., and Carmel U. Chiswick. 1993. "The Religious Composition of Unions: Its Role as a Determinant of Marital Stability." *Demography* 30(3): 385–404.

Martin, David. 1990. *Tongues of Fire: The Explosion of Protestantism in Latin America.* Oxford: Basil Blackwell.

Marwell, Gerald. 1996. "We Still Don't Know if Strict Churches Are Strong, Much Less Why: Comment on Iannaccone." *American Journal of Sociology* 101(4): 1097–1108.

McGuire, Meredith B. 1987. *Religion: The Social Context.* Belmont, CA: Wadsworth.

Melton, J. Gordon. 1987. "How New Is New? The Flowering of the 'New' Religious Consciousness Since 1965." In *The Future of New Religious Movements*, ed. David G. Bromley and Phillip E. Hammond, pp. 46–56. Macon, GA: Mercer University Press,

Miller, Alan S. 1998. "Why Japanese Religions Look Different: The Social Role of Religious Organizations in Japan." *Review of Religious Research* 39(4): 360–370.

Moore, R. Laurence. 1994. *Selling God: American Religion in the Marketplace of Culture.* New York: Oxford University Press.

Murray, John E. 1995. "Human Capital in Religious Communes: Literacy and Selection of Nineteenth Century Shakers." *Explorations in Economic History* 32(2): 217–235.

Neitz, Mary Jo, and Peter R. Mueser. 1997. "Economic Man and the Sociology of Religion." In *Rational Choice Theory and Religion*, ed. Lawerence A. Young, pp. 107–118. New York: Routledge.

Neuman, Shoshana. 1986. "Religious Observance Within a Human Capital Framework: Theory and Application." *Applied Economics* 18(11): 1193–1202.

Nock, Arthur Darby. 1963. *Conversion: The Old and the New in Religion from Alexander the Great to Augustine of Hippo.* London: Oxford University Press.

Parsons, Talcott. 1968. *The Structure of Social Action*, vol. 1. London: Collier-Macmillan.

Raskovich, Alexander. 1996. "You Shall Have No Other Gods Besides Me: A Legal-Economic Analysis of the Rise of Yahweh." *Journal of Institutional and Theoretical Economics* 152(3): 449–471.

Roberts, Keith A. 1990. *Religion in Sociological Perspective*, 2nd ed. Belmont, CA: Wadsworth.

Robertson, Roland. 1992. "The Economization of Religion? Reflections on the Promise and Limitations of the Economic Approach." *Social Compass* 39(1): 147–157.

Sherkat, Darren E., and John Wilson. 1995. "Preferences, Constraints, and Choices in Religious Markets: An Examination of Religious Switching and Apostasy." *Social Forces* 73: 993–1026.

Smelser, Neil J. 1976. "On the Relevance of Economic Sociology for Economics." In *Economics and Sociology: Towards an Integration*, ed. Tjerk Huppes, pp. 1–20. Leiden: Martinus Nijhoff.

Smith, Adam. [1776] 1965. *An Inquiry into Nature and Causes of the Wealth of Nations.* New York: Modern Library.

Spickard, James V. 1998. "Rethinking Religious Social Action: What Is 'Rational' About Rational-Choice Theory?" *Sociology of Religion* 59(2): 99–115.

Stark, Rodney. 1996. *The Rise of Christianity: A Sociologist Reconsiders History.* Princeton, NJ: Princeton University Press.

Stark, Rodney, and Laurence R. Iannaccone. 1994. "A Supply-Side Reinterpretation of the 'Secularization' of Europe." *Journal for the Scientific Study of Religion* 33(3): 230–252.

Stark, Rodney, and Roger Finke. 2000. *Acts of Faith: Explaining the Human Side of Religion.* Berkeley: University of California Press.

Stark, Rodney, and William S. Bainbridge. 1985. *The Future of Religion.* Berkeley: University of California Press.

———. 1987. *A Theory of Religion.* New York: Peter Lang.

Stigler, George. 1982. *The Economist as Preacher and Other Essays.* Chicago: University of Chicago Press.

Sullivan, Dennis H. 1985. "Simultaneous Determination of Church Contributions and Church Attendance." *Economic Inquiry* 23(2): 309–320.

Swedberg, Richard. 1990. *Economics and Sociology. Redefining Their Boundaries: Conversations with Economists and Sociologists.* Princeton, NJ: Princeton University Press.

Warner, R. Stephen. 1993. "Work in Progress Toward a New Paradigm in the Sociology of Religion." *American Journal of Sociology* 98(5): 1044–1093.

Williamson, Oliver E. 1985. *The Economic Institutions of Capitalism: Firms, Markets, Relational Contracting.* New York: Free Press.

Wilson, Bryan. 1966. *Religion ini Sociological Perspective.* Oxford, UK: Oxford University Press.

Wuthnow, Robert J. 1988. "Sociology of Religion." In *Handbook of Sociology,* ed. Neil J. Smelser. Newbury Park, CA: Sage.

———. 1991. "Religion as Culture." In *Religion and the Social Order,* vol. 1, ed. David G. Bromley. Greenwich, CT: JAI Press.

Yinger, J. Milton. 1970. *The Scientific Study of Religion.* New York: Macmillan.

Part V

Comparing Ideas on Individual and Collective Behavior

11

On the Rationality of Cognitive Dissonance

Louis Lévy-Garboua and Serge Blondel

Introduction: Rationality in Economics and Cognitive Psychology

Modern economics describes rational behavior by a small set of axioms that ensure the *logical consistency* of choices. Von Neumann and Morgenstern (1947) pioneered this approach for choices under risk, with objective probabilities, and Savage (1954) extended it to choices under uncertainty, with subjective probabilities. The main achievement of the axiomatic approach is to allow the derivation, for each individual, of a unique ordered set of preferences, the *expected utility* (EU), which can be defined *prior* to knowing each particular choice set. Consequently, the decision-making process is seen by economists as irrelevant for determining rational choices.

By contrast, cognitive psychology has focused on decision-making procedures, information processing, and limitations of the human mind. The definition of *cognitive consistency* that is most often mentioned is that an individual suffers from holding two opposite cognitions and will thus seek ways of reducing his or her *cognitive dissonance*. For instance, Festinger's (1957) famous theory of cognitive dissonance states that people confronted with a bad experience after having made a choice will be looking for justifications of their past decision and will tend to ignore the dissonant information.

One consequence of economics and cognitive psychology having taken divergent paths is that, while these approaches have been contrasted many times (see, for instance, Hogarth and Reder 1986; Smith 1991), few serious attempts have been made to bring them together into a common framework. In light of the greater mathematical rigor of economic analysis, the emerging consensus among researchers from various fields has been that normative rationality defines an ideal goal for rational behavior that will sometimes be beyond human reach for a number of benign reasons summarized by the concept of *bounded rationality* (small decision costs, use of approximate heuristics).

Perhaps the most impenetrable line between economics and psychology lies in the economic postulate of given and known preferences to which psychology does not adhere. This has to do with what Simon (1976) labeled *procedural rationality.* We reformulate cognitive dissonance theory in this paper and show that it is inconsistent with normative rationality and implies dynamic uncertainty for the decision-maker. Because this dynamic uncertainty is invisible to the normative eye, it is wrongly inferred that cognitive dissonance implies irrational behavior. Instead, we argue that cognitive consistency is the adequate rationality concept under dynamic uncertainty because, with an appropriate definition of cognition, it reduces to the use of all available information. If we are prepared to take these steps, it is possible to bring economics and cognitive psychology into a common framework for the purpose of decision theory.

Normative rationality and cognitive dissonance are first presented in the next two sections. The theoretical implications of cognitive dissonance for rational behavior are then analyzed in the section following those.

Normative Rationality

The most comprehensive view of rationality is probably that a choice is rational if it is justified by a consistent set of reasons. At first sight, this broad definition of rationality is alien to the mathematical precision required by modern economics. But it turns out to be a surprisingly fertile exercise, because axioms of logical consistency obviously form a consistent set of reasons for justifying one's choice. A long time ago, Ramsey [1926] 1964 justified the *transitivity* of preferences by the immunization that it provides against the money pump danger. More recently, Sugden (1991) has provided a nice interpretation for the *completeness* of preferences by saying that it ensures that no choice will be made without having reasons for it. For choices under uncertainty, the *reduction of probabilities axiom, the independence axiom,* or the *sure-thing principle* may be viewed as elementary expressions of *description and procedure invariance.* The latter property is obviously a consistent reason for justifying one's choice without prior knowledge of the choice set. Under the veil of ignorance, rational individuals should consider the context of their future decisions and the presentation of their future objects of choice as irrelevant, by the principle of insufficient reason. We believe that this is what makes the EU axioms of Von Neumann and Morgenstern (1947) and Savage (1954) so intuitive and appealing.

But our analysis also demonstrates that the axioms defining description and procedure invariance essentially identify an individual's prior preference—that is, the preference judgment that can be made by a person prior to being aware of the particular problems and alternatives that he or she will face. Abstraction from the singularity of each decision characterizes the normative perspective, whether it applies to individual or to social choices. It is thus more accurate to speak of the individual preferences deriving from a set of axioms as *normative preferences*, and Savage (1954) himself recognized the normative character of his theory after his controversy with Allais (1953).

As a descriptive theory, the economic theory of choice maintains that the preferences revealed by observed choices and judgments always coincide with (or are closely approximated by) the normative preference. But, having described axioms of logical consistency as context or choice-set–independent reasons for justifying one's choices, it becomes clear that axioms cannot describe *all* the potential reasons that can be invoked to justify any single decision.[1] Therefore, it is far from obvious that rational choices always coincide with normative preferences. One good reason for complying with one's normative preference is that the latter constitutes an individual norm, in the sense of being a prescription of behavior, which is given to the individual because all the information needed is gathered prior to the choice, and known to the person because it is merely his or her own preference in a specific state of information. Although individual norms cannot be accompanied by social sanctions, their consistency requirement acts as a built-in sanction that a rational agent wishes to impose on oneself. This was exactly Ramsey's (1964) plea for transitivity. However, this is not a full-proof argument in favor of the normative preference in the presence of uncertainty because the consistency requirement is then constrained by a strong additional informational requirement. Cases exist where it may be better to use more information (drawn from the context or the choice set) and give up some logical consistency.

By postulating that rational choice always coincides with normative preference, normative rationality implies that normative preference summarizes all available information, not only before proceeding to the choice, but also at the very time of choosing and revealing one's preference. Recent advances in the cognitive sciences (e.g., Dennett 1991) make it clear that this is in fact a strong assumption that overlooks the sequence of information in the brain and how individuals reason and treat such information.

Cognitive Dissonance

Cognitive dissonance theory is a theory of attitude change or, to speak like an economist, of preference change. The mere fact of being committed to one decision seems to trigger off a positive reevaluation of the chosen object and a negative reevaluation of unchosen objects. To get a flavor of the theory, let us borrow a nice example of this phenomenon from an early experiment (1956) of Jack Brehm reported by Aronson:

> Brehm showed each of several women eight different appliances (a toaster, an electric coffee maker, a sandwich grill, and the like) and asked that she rate them in terms of how attractive each appliance was to her. As a reward, each woman was told she could have one of the appliances as a gift and she was given a choice between two of the products she had rated as being equally attractive. After she chose one, it was wrapped up and given to her. Several minutes later, she was asked to rate the products again. It was found that after receiving the product of her choice, each woman rated the attractiveness of that appliance somewhat higher and decreased the rating of the appliance she had a chance to own but rejected. (1991, 186)

Immediately after reporting this experiment, Aronson provides the following explanation:

> Again, making a decision produces dissonance: Cognitions about any negative aspects of the preferred object are dissonant with having chosen it, and cognitions about the positive aspect of the unchosen object are dissonant with not having chosen it. To reduce dissonance, people cognitively spread apart the alternatives. That is, after the decision, the women in Brehm's study emphasized the positive attributes of the appliance they decided to own, while de-emphasizing its negative attributes; for the appliance they decided not to own, they emphasized its negative attributes and de-emphasized its positive attributes. (1991, 186)

From this account, we see that the psychologists who adopt cognitive dissonance theory tell a wholly different story about decision making than economists do. Economists like to describe decisions as originating from a stable normative preference

$$\text{normative preference} \rightarrow \text{decision}$$

whereas psychologists stress the influence of decision making, including one's past decision of a similar kind, on revealed preference (attitude)

$$\text{decision} \rightarrow \text{revealed preference.}$$

The psychological view essentially recognizes that individual preferences may change over a very short time span. Because the preference changes that have been observed experimentally normally took place shortly after a decision was made, as in the Brehm study, or even immediately after as in some other experiments, it is natural to believe that, at the limit, we are just observing the revealed preference at the time of decision. What cognitive dissonance theory then implies is that decision-makers may shift from their prior preference to a different revealed preference at the time of decision. If we take the normative preference as the individual's prior preference, we come up with a simple interpretation of the psychological view: After feeling cognitive dissonance, individuals may deviate from their normative preference by the end of the decision process in an attempt to reduce such unpleasant feeling.

This is plainly inconsistent with the economic view, as no changing revealed preference can maximize any one stable normative preference function. However, as pointed out by Akerlof and Dickens (1982), it cannot be simply dismissed by the economic profession because it is based on a lot of careful evidence. Furthermore, the revelation of many paradoxes to the conventional economic wisdom about rational behavior under uncertainty (Machina 1987) and in seemingly riskless situations (Tversky and Kahneman 1991; Lévy-Garboua and Montmarquette 1996) brings a proof, or at least a very strong presumption, that normative rationality fails to provide a fair account of all observed behavior. In the sequel to this chapter, we propose to take the evidence about cognitive dissonance seriously and to have a closer look at the theoretical implications of this phenomenon for rational behavior.

Cognitive Dissonance and Rational Behavior

We hope that our brief account of cognitive dissonance theory will convince economists that the latter brings an original contribution to the analysis of decision; but we are conscious that it first needs to be explained in words that any economist will understand. This effort will turn out to be rewarding as it yields a radically new vision of cognitive dissonance and decision theory, which is implied not by normative rationality but by a more general form of rationality, cognitive consistency or informational efficiency.

Let us begin this task by mentioning that psychology describes people, either making a new decision or considering to repeat a past decision, as capable of holding *two cognitions*, like two preferences or two probabilistic beliefs, that *contradict* each other. In this last sentence, the three words needing an explanation have been italicized. Cognitions are information states about the determinants of choice (prices, wealth, preferences, beliefs) that can best be summarized, for the need of exposition, by the individual's choices given this information. For instance, the normative preference is a potential cognition because it relates to an information state that is perfectly conceivable prior to the decision. The evidence mentally represented by one cognition can either take the form of a sure outcome (pure cognition) or a lottery (mixed cognition); and it may either take the form of simple evidence (e.g., one particular outcome has just been observed) or complex evidence, which needs to be aggregated. It is further contended that several different cognitions can be held during the decision process.

People who feel cognitive dissonance go through at least two information states and perceive two preferences, conditional on different informational states, which contradict each other. Although these two cognitions are supposed to be simultaneous in standard accounts of the theory, it is certainly more realistic to describe them sequentially as in search theory, with both perceptions probably following one another by milliseconds. This provides a natural method for aggregating all the evidence accumulated in the past into one prior cognition. Thus, we are led to the view that decision-makers comparing two objects A and B generally perceive one preference first, say for A, *then* perceive whatever objections they may find to their prior preference and in favor of B. But it is impossible that the first cognition "I choose A" and the second cognition "I reject A" both describe the true preference, if the latter is assumed to exist. Cognitive dissonance theory *must* imply that individuals in general *do not know* their true preferences and may change their decision or judgment over time after being exposed to dissonant cognitions. They must feel that they behave under *dynamic uncertainty*, with each simple cognition representing a random draw from one stable distribution. Consequently, they will be very sensitive to what they perceived, and will consistently weigh contradictory evidence in order to update their beliefs and resulting choices. They will have unambiguous temporary preferences at any time but will never know their true preferences with certainty (an early assessment of this view can be found in Lévy-Garboua 1979).

In trying to derive the theoretical implications of cognitive dissonance theory, we have come up with the sketch of an alternative to the normative theory of choice. The only assumption that we added reflects the emerging consensus within the cognitive sciences that people do not make one grand decision at some fixed place in the brain, but keep reassessing their immediate environment and their temporary preferences in search for valuable information that keeps arriving at various points in the brain (see Dennett 1991; Damasio 1999, among others). This is a sequential and uninterrupted process.

For the purpose of decision theory, situations of cognitive dissonance are especially interesting because they are necessary for causing preference reversals. If the two dissonant cognitions were perceived simultaneously, decision would appear to be a case of conflict resolution between two selves having systematically opposite preferences, like a good self and a bad self (Aronson 1991). Instead, when cognitions arrive sequentially in the brain, decision becomes the output of learning and information acquisition by one single self. In this new framework, cognitive dissonance will be reduced essentially by the sequential use of all available information.

One claim of this chapter is that, when properly interpreted, cognitive dissonance theory is, or should be extended into, a descriptive theory of decision. But this was not originally the case. Festinger's (1957) seminal work was concerned with the reactions of one person confronted by a bad experience after having made a choice. Aronson's account of the theory (quoted on p. 230) kept the same track. Both argued that cognitive dissonance was aroused by the contradiction between having made a choice—which ought to be good—and experiencing a bad outcome, and that it was typically resolved by ignoring the dissonant information and adjusting one's preference to one's past decision.

To examine the welfare implications of cognitive dissonance–reducing behavior, Akerlof and Dickens (1982) incorporated this psychological theory into the standard economic model. They assumed that individuals had the power to control their beliefs and to choose the "best" one. Workers employed in dangerous jobs, for instance, were relieved from fear by underestimating the risk of accident. With a sufficiently low estimate for the latter (below the true risk, anyway), they would both reduce the unpleasantness of cognitive dissonance ("fear") and save the cost of purchasing safety equipment over and above the expected cost of making more mistakes through their intended departure from rational behavior.

Can our personal account of cognitive dissonance also explain the influence of past decisions on currently revealed preferences? The answer is yes for a basic reason overlooked by previous models: dynamic uncertainty. If preferences are drawn from a given stable stochastic process, the latter naturally relates current preferences with past preferences that summarize prior information. The greater the precision of the prior information relative to the news received after the choice was made, the more it is likely that individuals will stick to their past decisions. It takes a sufficiently bad surprise to reverse a person's prior decision (for a formal treatment of preference reversal in this framework, see Lévy-Garboua and Montmarquette 1996). In addition to providing a rational explanation for the cognitive dissonance phenomenon studied by Festinger (1957) and others, dynamic uncertainty radically alters the welfare implications of that phenomenon. If individuals are Bayesians, the inefficiency related to cognitive dissonance does not stem from the inertia of beliefs and preferences but from the inevitable presence of a background uncertainty.

Table 11.1

The Payoff Matrix

State	1	2
Probability	.80	.20
S_1	$3,000	$3,000
R_1	$4,000	$0

The sequence of two opposite cognitions is clearly visible in some applications, like the bad surprise experienced after one choice. Unfortunately, it is less clear in many other examples found in the psychological literature, including the Brehm experiment quoted here. We shall attempt to make it clear in the canonical context of a comparison between two uncertain objects of choice. A sound example is provided by the comparison between two risky actions sharing common states of the world, each of which occurs with a given probability, because the two dissonant cognitions can then be characterized objectively. The simplest case, inspired by a well-known problem of Kahneman and Tversky (1979), compares one sure money gain S_1 (e.g., win $3,000) with a bet like R_1 (win $4,000 with probability .80, and nothing with probability .20). The payoff matrix is shown in Table 11.1.

Consider this problem. According to the "certainty effect" (Kahneman and Tversky 1979), which has received a lot of experimental support, a large majority of subjects would choose the sure outcome S_1, although the risky bet R_1 has a greater expected value ($3,200) than does S_1 ($3,000). This behavior is inconsistent with the expected value criterion, but it can be described by EU theory, taking risk aversion into account. According to the EU rule, S_1 will be chosen if the utility of winning $3,000 is greater than 80 percent of the utility of winning $4,000 (the utility of winning nothing is always set to 0). Otherwise, R_1 will be chosen. Because cognitive dissonance should be able to explain why the choice deviates from the normative preference according to our interpretation, let us suppose that the utility is linear: a gain of $X has a utility X. In this case, which makes computations easy, EU is equal to 3,000 for S_1 and to 3,200 for R_1. The risky bet R_1 is selected by the normative preference. How can cognitive dissonance arise and possibly reverse the choice in favor of the sure outcome?

The answer is that having a normative preference does not suppress the risk of decision here because no option dominates the other. Consequently, the decision-maker is seeking more information. He wishes that some genie could tell him the gamble's outcome a few seconds before playing so that he always is able to choose the winning option. If he really had this opportunity, his expected gain would be .80 (4,000) + .20 (3,000) = 3,800 instead of 3,200. Therefore, he would be ready to pay the compensating variation 3,800 – 3,200 = 600 to the genie, if the latter ever existed. This sum[2] represents the value of perfect information and, equivalently (e.g., see Raiffa 1968), the expected opportunity loss of choosing according to the normative preference R_1, : .20 (3,000 – 0) = 600. The latter is obviously related to cognitive dissonance: it describes the dissonant cognition that, if one chooses R_1, one faces the risk (with probability .20) of winning nothing and losing the opportunity to win 3,000.

In everyday language, a dissonant cognition aroused before the choice is made is termed an *objection to the prior preference. Doubt* is the feeling of an objection to one's prior judgment, and it is unpleasant because it manifests a latent demand for information. It is experienced each time no option dominates the other. Thus, after perceiving his own normative preference, the decision-maker in doubt will be looking for information and, in the process, automatically perceive the objection to the former. The objection is treated by the brain as an available message, which is obviously context or choice-set–dependent so that the normative observer and the decision-maker are in a state of asymmetric information: The former cannot perceive what the latter does. What matters to a descriptive theory of choice is the decision-maker's perspective. An individual doubting his or her normative preference reduces doubt (cognitive dissonance) by making use of all available information and legitimately treats the perceived objection as information. Whenever one finds this information valuable, he or she will make a choice that deviates from the person's normative preference; otherwise, the individual will discard the information and confirm the latter. A formal theory of cognitive consistency under risk and uncertainty explaining many well-known paradoxes and anomalies of EU theory can be found in Lévy-Garboua (1999) and it will not be pursued here.

The above discussion has suggested how, in order to reduce cognitive dissonance, a risk-neutral agent might prefer a sure gain to a great possibility of winning more money offering a higher expected gain. Kahneman and Tversky (1979) have shown that, although many people were attracted by the certainty of a gain, quite as many were attracted by a great possibility of losing more money, offering a greater expected loss but a small chance to escape as well. For example, consider that most people would prefer the bet R_2 (lose $4,000 with probability .80, and nothing with probability .20) to the sure loss S_2 (lose $3,000). These two options were obtained by mere "reflection" of R_1 and S_1, converting gains into losses of an equal amount with the same probabilities. It is interesting to see how a risk-neutral agent attracted by a sure gain out of cognitive dissonance might as well wish to avoid a sure loss for the same reason. By reflection, the normative preference for R_1 converts into one for S_2, which minimizes the expected loss. However, doubt drives the individual, in his or her quest for information, to perceive the dissonant cognition that, if he or she chose S_2, the person would bear the risk (with probability .20) of losing \$3,000 and missing the opportunity to lose nothing. With cognitive consistency theory, risk-neutral agents exhibiting the "certainty effect" would always exhibit the "reflection effect" as well.[3] We believe that cognitive dissonance is a powerful tool for explaining anomalous behavior of this kind with simple and well-behaved utility functions (e.g., Blondel 1997).

It is time to explain the finding of Brehm's experiment quoted earlier. Here again, the women were in a state of dynamic uncertainty because they were exposed to surprises in the course of the experiment. After she was asked to rate several appliances, each woman was given a choice between two equally rated appliances as a reward for her participation and received the appliance she had chosen as a gift. As a matter of fact, when she was asked again, a few minutes later, to rate the two appliances among which she had to choose, she had been exposed sequentially to two cognitions: the prior rating (before knowing that she would receive her preferred appliance as a gift), and the later cognition that she had previously chosen or rejected the option. These two cognitions were consonant in the case of the chosen appliance, but they were dissonant in the case of the unchosen one as the two appliances initially had an equal rating. Because the final rating is a consistent estimate based on a sample of two observations (cognitions), the chosen appliance logically ended up with a higher value and the rejected appliance with a lower value. It is worth noting that this outcome is somewhat similar to the "endowment effect" exhibited by Thaler (1980) and others, the difference being that the gift received by subjects is exogenous in one case and endogenous in the other (Lévy-Garboua and Montmarquette [1996] explain the endowment effect in the same spirit).

The comparison of Brehm's experiment with the choice among two risky actions examined before brings two important lessons. First, it shows how dynamic uncertainty lies, invisibly to the normative eye, both behind a host of seemingly riskless situations and all situations of "static" risk without dominance. Second, we have found a case of cognitive consonance in Brehm's experiment, so that cognitive dissonance is too restrictive as a theory of decision and we are aiming at a more general theory of cognitive consistency rather than just cognitive dissonance.

Conclusion

One consequence of economics and cognitive psychology having taken so divergent paths is that, whereas these approaches have been opposed many times, few serious attempts have been made to bring them together into a common framework. This is rather unfortunate, for the tremendous growth of anomalies, paradoxes, and puzzles to the conventional theory of choice discovered in the last two decades (Machina 1987; Thaler 1980; and Rabin 1998 provide many examples) has led many researchers to introduce psychological assumptions into economic models with no check that the two approaches were behaviorally consistent. We demonstrate in this chapter that it is possible to bring economics and cognitive psychology into a common framework.

Cognitive dissonance or cognitive consistency theory, as we understand it, does not presume irrational behavior, although it is inconsistent with normative rationality. Previous discussions have overlooked that cognitive dissonance implied dynamic uncertainty. Once this dimension of choice is restored, it becomes obvious why normative rationality does not properly describe fully rational behavior. Aiming at cognitive consistency is then the optimal way to behave.

Notes

1. Shafir, Simonson, and Tversky (1993, 34) have made a similar comment by suggesting that "the axioms of rational choice act as compelling arguments, or reasons, for making decisions when their applicability has been detected, not as universal laws that constrain people's choices."

2. The value of perfect information is directly expressed in money terms thanks to the assumption of risk neutrality.

3. Lévy-Garboua (1999) obtains perfect reflection under the risk-neutrality assumption. Nonlinearity of the utility function would mitigate the "reflection effect."

References

Akerlof, George A., and Williams T. Dickens. 1982. "The Economic Consequences of Cognitive Dissonance." *American Economic Review* 72: 307–319.

Allais, Maurice. 1953. "Le Comportement de l'Homme Rationnel Devant le Risque: Critique des Postulats de l'École Américaine." *Econometrica* 21: 503–546.

Aronson, Elliot. 1991. *The Social Animal*. New York: Freeman.

Blondel, Serge. 1997. "Testing Theories of Choice Under Risk: From Normative Rationality to Cognitive Rationality." Unpublished PhD dissertation, University Paris 1 Panthéon-Sorbonne.

Damasio, Antonio R. 1999. *The Feeling of What Happens. Body and Emotion in the Making of Consciousness*. New York: Harcourt Brace.

Dennett, Daniel C. 1991. *Consciousness Explained*. Boston: Little, Brown.

Festinger, Leon. 1957. *A Theory of Cognitive Dissonance*. Stanford, CA: Stanford University Press.

Hogarth, Robin M., and Melvin W. Reder. 1986. *Rational Choice: The Contrast Between Economics and Psychology*. Chicago: University of Chicago Press.

Kahneman, Daniel, and Amos Tversky. 1979. "Prospect Theory: An Analysis of Decisions under Risk." *Econometrica* 47: 263–291.

Lévy-Garboua, Louis. 1979. "Perception and the Formation of Choice." In Lévy-Garboua, ed., *Sociological Economics*, pp. 97–121. London: Sage.

———. 1999. "Expected Utility and Cognitive Consistency." TEAM Working Paper 1999.104, University Paris 1 Panthéon-Sorbonne. The paper is available on http://www.univ-paris1.fr/MSE/CahiersMSE.

Lévy-Garboua, Louis, and Claude Montmarquette. 1996. "Cognition in Seemingly Riskless Choices and Judgments." *Rationality and Society* 8: 167–185.

Machina, Mark J. 1987. "Choice Under Uncertainty: Problems Solved and Unsolved." *Journal of Economic Perspectives* 1: 121–154.

Rabin, Matthew. 1998. "Psychology and Economics." *Journal of Economic Literature* 36: 11–46.

Raiffa, Howard. 1968. *Decision Analysis*. Reading, MA: Addison-Wesley.

Ramsey, Frank. [1926] 1964. "Truth and Probability." Reprinted in *Studies in Subjective Probability*, H.E. Kyberg and H.E. Smokler, eds., 61–92. New York: Wiley.

Savage, Leonard J. 1954. *The Foundations of Statistics*. New York: Wiley.

Shafir, Eldar, Itamar Simonson, and Amos Tversky. 1993. "Reason-Based Choice." *Cognition* 49: 11–36.

Simon, Herbert A. 1976. "From Substantive to Procedural Rationality." In J.L. Spiro, ed., *Method and Appraisal in Economics*. Cambridge: Cambridge University Press.

Smith, Vernon. 1991. "Rational Choice: The Contrast Between Economics and Psychology." *Journal of Political Economy* 99: 877–897.

Sugden, Robert. 1991. "Rational Choice: A Survey of Contributions from Economics and Philosophy." *Economic Journal* 101: 751–785.

Thaler, Richard H. 1980. "Toward a Positive Theory of Consumer Choice." *Journal of Economic Behavior and Organization* 1: 39–60.

Tversky, Amos, and Daniel Kahneman. 1991. "Loss Aversion in Riskless Choice: A Reference-Dependent Model." *Quarterly Journal of Economics* 95: 1039–1061.

Von Neumann, John, and Oskar Morgenstern. 1947. *Theory of Games and Economic Behavior*. Princeton, NJ: Princeton University Press.

12

Economics and Collective Identity: Explaining Collective Action

Dipak K. Gupta

As social animals, all of us, on numerous occasions during our everyday lives, take part in collective actions based on the welfare of our family, clan, the nation, or our specie that come directly in conflict with our short-term self-interest. Yet, unfortunately, despite its impressive performance as an analytical tool for many market and nonmarket actions, the tools of neoclassical economics and the public-choice school of political science and sociology offer but inadequate explanations of an individual's decision to participate in a collective action. Because much of the preoccupation of political science and sociology revolves around people's collective actions, this is an important question. I argue that the history of epistemological evolution of economics is rooted deeply in the demand and supply of physical commodities. Because collective actions are often about benefits that have to be shared with the community regardless of the contributions of individual members, standard theories of neoclassical economics, in the final analysis, succumb to the logical quagmire of Olson's paradox. Facing the "free-rider problem," it fails to provide us with a satisfactory explanation for the demand for public goods. In this chapter, I have sought a fuller explanation for a rational actor's motivation for joining a collective action by combining the elegance of economic analyses with the insights on group behavior drawn from the advances in social psychology.

Toward this goal, in the first section I briefly discuss the various attempts to circumvent Olson's paradox within the paradigm of neoclassical econom-

I am extremely grateful to Shoshana Grossbard-Shechtman, Taradas Bandyopadhyay, and Radmila Prislin for their help. The remaining errors reflect my own shortcomings.

ics. The second part of the chapter presents the arguments of social psychology as explanation of group behavior. In the third section, I attempt to provide an integrated framework for explaining an actor's decisions to allocate resources between private and collective goods.

Offering Partial Solutions to Olson's Paradox

Thanks to the pioneering work of Gary Becker and others, rational-choice theories have found applications in wide-ranging areas of social science, history, psychology, law, and philosophy. There are two main reasons for this popularity. First, rational-choice theory provides testable hypotheses based on microlevel explanations. Second, the rationality hypotheses allow researchers to interpret an action from an internal or actor-centered viewpoint, explaining how a choice should be made *given* the actor's beliefs and desires. In other words, rational-choice theory provides both external or scientific explanation as well as an internal (behavioral) understanding of the process of choice. Yet, this advantage, to a large extent, seems to break down when it comes to participation in a collective action, particularly when such action is contrary to the actors' short-run personal welfare. Economic actors choose among alternatives that maximize their preference satisfaction. However, there is a wide schism among economists whether preferences and beliefs either exist as mental states or play an important role in the choice process (Satz and Ferejohn 1994). Although most economists would prefer to remain agnostic regarding the origins of beliefs and preferences, it is fair to state that a minimal independence between preferences and choices must be maintained to save our theories from tautological reasoning.

The problem of the so-called Olson's paradox or the "Social Dilemma" in the explanation of an individual's decision to join a collective action to procure collective goods arises because of a simple lapse in logical reasoning. Collective goods are separated from private goods by the fact that they are nonrivalrous in consumption and are to be shared with everyone in the community regardless of individual contribution. That is, in contrast to a private good, the utility derived from the consumption of a collective or a public good does not go down when an additional consumer is introduced. Further, the distribution of a collective good cannot be restricted only to those who have chosen to contribute toward its procurement. Take, for instance, the public good of protection from external threats provided by the national defense forces. This public good is qualitatively different from a private good, such as owning a firearm for personal protection. If I have to share my personal weapon with another individual, my utility from this particular good will diminish. In contrast, the birth of an infant should not concern us about too many people under the protective umbrella of the military. Second, I can deny anyone the use of my gun, but if there is an external threat, the armed forces cannot exclude those who did not pay enough taxes for military expenditure. Given this definition of a collective good, Olson's (1965) arguments regarding the decision facing a rational actor considering a contribution to a collective cause may be presented as follows:

$$\text{Contribute} = p\ (B) - (1-p)\ (C) \tag{1}$$

$$\text{Don't contribute} = p\ (B) \tag{2}$$

where,

p = probability of success; B = individual benefits derived from the collective good; and C = individual costs of contribution to the collective action.

The basic nature of Olson's paradox can be easily understood by looking at the above decision matrix open to each prospective contributor to a collective action. Because benefits of a collective goods cannot be restricted to those who have chosen to contribute, every rational actor, by the dictum of short-run self-utility maximization, *should* attempt to free-ride (get the benefits of a public good without paying for it) by choosing not to contribute. This logical imperative inevitably leads us to conclusion that—particularly when it comes to large groups—no collective action would ever take place. Facing the intractable Social Dilemma, scholars have attempted to circumvent the problem in several ways. In this section I demonstrate that such attempts have largely been ineffective.

Political scientist Mark Lichbach (1995, 19–21) has attempted to offer one of the most comprehensive set of arguments regarding the solution to Olson's paradox. He argues that Olson's paradox can be "partially" addressed through, what he calls, *market, community, contract,* and *hierarchy.* Market solutions refer to the changing of a potential participant's perception of benefits and costs of joining a collective action. Community solutions are based on developing *Gemeinschaft*—a communal existence based on a shared belief system. Contract solutions depend upon *Gesselschaft*—the portrayal of an enemy image, where neighbors keep an eye on the neighbors for possible defection; and hierarchy solutions are predicated upon the formation of organizational hierarchy for implementing a collective action. Lichbach contends that market and community solutions take place in a largely unplanned way, whereas contract and hierarchy require conscious planning.

According to Lichbach, a market solution to Olson's paradox is reached when, for an individual actor, one or more components of the decision-making scheme is altered either by the actions of the leadership or as a result of a change in the objective conditions within the society. In such cases, an individual overcomes the dictates of economic rationality and joins the forces of collective rebellion. Thus, the argument would go as follows: If an individual is convinced of higher levels of benefits and/or the probability of their attainment, or lower levels of costs and/or the probability of their incurring, he or she will decide to participate in a collective action.

There are, however, several problems with finding a market solution to Olson's paradox. Microeconomic analyses can produce brilliant results when we consider a trade-off between two private goods, such as apples and oranges. They also provide invaluable insight into allocation of resources between present and future consumption. However, when the choice is between participation in a collective action or the pursuit of private utility there is hardly a simple solution.[1] This is because the benefits of public goods may be difficult to define.

Consider, for instance, the case of increased benefits. If I have to choose between two baskets of goods, with one offering a greater quantity than the other, then I will take the one offering a higher level of benefit. When the size of the prize goes up in a state lottery, people line up to buy tickets. However, when it comes to collective actions, such assumptions may not work. This is primarily because of two reasons. First, most outcomes (benefits) of collective action happen in the long run, yet the costs have to be paid immediately. Any "rational" actor engaged in the present value analysis of the net benefit of participation will soon find out the "irrationality" of participation in most collective movements.

Second, even if the problem of intertemporal choice were overcome with the choice of an appropriate discount rate, the exact nature of benefits of collective action—the necessary mortar that binds quantity demanded to its price—would remain difficult to define. For instance, if I am involved in a movement aimed at closing down an adult entertainment facility in my neighborhood, will I necessarily put forward a greater effort if offered to work on a national morality campaign? The answer to this question becomes more complicated as the group size increases, as it makes free-riding even more attractive.

For public goods, the fundamental problem of Olson's paradox remains intractable; the argument of increased benefits fails to overcome Social Dilemma if the benefit gets distributed universally in the group and the costs fall only on the participants. If the paradox is not solved by increasing the amount of benefit, then how about the case when the increase in benefit is restricted to only those who participate? That is, if the revolution is successful, those who decided to participate are going to be the "first among the equals" for the spoils of the war. Would not the prospect of a larger personal reward overcome the obstacles of social dilemma? Tarrow (1994) attempts to show that selected benefits may prompt some to participate in collective action. However, if we accept the proposition of differential individual benefit based on participation, the outcome no longer remains a pure public good, for by definition, public good precludes restricted benefits to a selected group of individuals within a larger amalgam of beneficiaries. Therefore, based on a rational-choice hypothesis, we are able to explain the allocation of quasi-public goods (Ostrom 1998) but not of pure public goods.

If not benefit, how about considering a change in cost? The standard economic argument is that a change in cost inevitably reduces people's appetite for extralegal activities (Becker 1965, 1976, 1981, 1996; Becker and Landes 1974). Before, examining this argument closely, let us define "costs" of participation in a collective action.

The costs of participation have two components, which we can alternately call *market* and *nonmarket,* or *economic* and *noneconomic* costs. Market costs involve the loss of time and the consequent forgone income (the opportunity cost), whereas physical punishments (from beatings and imprisonment to death) imposed by the regime or the opposition group are classified as nonmarket costs of participation.

The case of opportunity cost is relatively clear-cut. By looking at any picture coming from an area plagued by mass rebellion, we can see that an overwhelming proportion of the participants is young, unattached males. For most guerrilla groups, from the Shining Path to the various rebel forces in Africa, it is the youth that carries the torch of rebellion. The reason for this overwhelming proportion of youth participation rests with their low opportunity costs. Yet to enter the job market, often assured of free room and board from their families, young men and, in lesser numbers, women fill the ranks of the active revolutionaries.[2] Some scholars have pointed out that women are often constrained by the demands of their reproductive activities and their domestic duties (Reif 1986, 148), which explains this apparent disparity in the levels of participation. However, the argument of a lower opportunity cost for women is not particularly clear. Evidence shows that all over the world, young women also join terrorist organizations in significant numbers (Jenkins 1982, 15). Because women often do not take employment in the formal sector, they may have the time to join protest movements, particularly working behind the scene, providing logistical support for the men at the front. Women have historically been active in almost every collective movement. They have joined in large numbers in the French (Rud 1964, 220) and the Russian revolutions (Chamberlain [1937] 1987, 28). Under the leadership of M.K. Gandhi, women overwhelmingly supported the anticolonial movement in British India (Juergensmeyer 1984, 17). The "mothers of lost children" in many parts of Latin America have carried out their long-drawn protests (Navarro 1989, 257).

Just as low opportunity costs may prompt the young to participate in collective movements, high market costs of participation can prevent other groups from joining the rebel forces. These are typically the peasants and the poorest of the poor—the *Lumpenproletariat*. The peasants are difficult to recruit into the causes of revolution because they face extremely high opportunity costs of time. If they miss the planting season, they may have to starve for the rest of the year.[3] Thus, in his political rhetoric, like all other practicing revolutionaries, Ho Chi Minh had claimed: "One becomes revolutionary because one is oppressed. The more oppressed one is, the more unshakably resolved one is to carry out the revolution."[4] Yet at the same time, like Mao and Lenin, Ho was careful to point out that, for peasants to take part in a collective movement, they must first be carefully indoctrinated (Lacouture 1968, 49).

The nonmarket or the physical side of cost is what the authorities impose on a participant in a collective action. Naturally, the certainty (the probability of getting apprehended) and severity of punishment vary across nations. Thus, in a totalitarian nation, such as in today's China, the dissidents risk a far greater chance of being apprehended than in a less coercive society such as in Britain.[5] Also, once a person is apprehended, the severity of punishment is likely to be heavier in Communist China than in democratic Britain.

However, the real puzzle is to formulate a rule as to how people are likely to alter their behavior in face of an increased level of coercion. Economic theory predicts that as cost would increase, an individual's desire to participate would correspondingly decrease.[6] If the price of beef goes up, we consume less beef, yet the link between participation and punishment is anything but clear, particularly when it comes to collective actions (Lichbach 1987). For instance, alongside the argument of fear as deterrence, we can also argue that to resist force with counterforce is part and parcel of human nature. Therefore, as repression rises, so does the urge to apply counterforce.[7]

According to this line of reasoning, an increase in the costs of participation would lead to more, rather than less, dissident activities. For instance, the tactics of open repression by Sheriff Bull Connors only helped solidify the opposition among Civil Rights activists in the American South. Facing these two opposite views, even empirical studies fail to provide a definitive answer. There is empirical evidence that when a regime applies coercive force, dissident activities go up in the democratic regimes; in the nondemocratic nations, they go up but, after a threshold of high protest and high repression, antigovernment movements are squashed into silence (Gupta, Singh, and Sprague 1993). Others have hypothesized that although coercion brings down rebellion, it is only a short-run solution. In the long run, past repression helps escalate dissent (Rasler 1996). Some others argue that coercion causes the rebel groups to change their tactics; in response to the government's tactics, the dissident groups switch between violent and nonviolent forms of protest (Lichbach 1987; Moore 1998). In sum, the myriad empirical studies fail to find a strong negative relationship between participation in dissident activities and their cost.

It stands to reason to hypothesize that an increase in the probability of success would encourage a prospective participant to plunge into a collective action.[8] Thus, if my perceived chances of winning a contract improve, I will be more willing to make a bid (by expending a resource-consuming activity) for it. However, even this simple logic of economic rationality does not always hold water for collective action. The perception of probability of success in attaining a collective goal is a product of a number of determining factors. For instance, the political or ideological leadership can take certain strategic actions that might cause an increase in the perception of probability of success to the potential participant. These actions can span an entire spectrum of collective actions, from nonviolent protests to acts of terrorism.[9] In fact, all of these actions are designed to communicate with a certain audience. Through its political actions, a dissident organization sends messages of its strength and/or its moral, ideological stance to the potential participants, the enemy camp, or to its benefactors (Schmid and de Graaf 1982).

Individual inertia of joining a collective action can also be successfully overcome by blocking all sources of information but for those coming from the group leaders. All enforcers of collective will—from Mao Tse-tung and Ayatollah Khomeini to Jim Jones—have succeeded in mobilizing participants by creating a basic asymmetry of information between the leaders and the followers (Lichbach 1995, 86–96). Authorities in power attempt to maintain this asymmetry of information by making information favorable to the group cheap, and/or receiving information critical to the group expensive. The former is accomplished through ample propaganda; the latter is imposed through punishment.

However, the increase in the probability of winning may not be sufficient in inducing a prospective participant to voluntarily join the forces of rebellion. Unfortunately, as the probability of success increases, Olson's paradox once again rears its ugly head. With the goals increasingly at hand, a "rational" human being is apt to argue for less participation, as no one wants to be the last casualty of the war. With every potential participant deciding according to the precept of economic rationality, no war will ever be won, no revolution will be complete, no collective good will be attained.[10]

If the "market solution" offers precious little toward solving the Social Dilemma, so do the others suggested by Lichbach. The *community solution* or the development of a common belief system comes closest to the notion of collective identity that I am offering here. However, Lichbach does not explain the process by which these common belief systems may develop and the way they may be inculcated on a group. In an argument close to the community solution, Akerlof and Kranton (2000) offer a thoughtful perspective on the impact of identity on economic choice. In their formulation, they expand the horizon of traditional microeconomics by suggesting that the utility that an individual derives depends not only on her actions and the actions of the others in the economy, but also on her identity or self-image. However, Akerlof and Kranton define identity as solely the way an individual perceives herself. As a result, despite many interesting examples of noneconomic choices of occupation and avocation based on an actor's self-image, the investigators fail to explain collective action. Thus, while attempting to explain the act of alumni giving, Akerlof and Kranton (2000, 722) correctly point out that their explanation "suffers from collective action problem."

Similarly, Lichbach's solutions of contract and hierarchy simply emphasize the increasing costs of defection. As an example of contract, where the society uses a network of informers to enforce collective action, we can cite the so-called Chinese Granny Patrol. The Chinese authorities used old ladies with access to knowledge of pregnancy among neighborhood women to enforce the nation's single-child law. The hierarchy solution refers to the organized society's ability to impose sanctions on the dissenters. However, as we know from our everyday experience, these nonmarket costs often fail to dissuade a potential dissenter from acting in conformity with the will of the collective. Young men avoid military conscription even in the face of an organized effort to enforce the draft, people free ride despite overriding moral imperatives.

Therefore, I conclude that despite claims of "partial solutions," Lichbach's solutions are either not applicable to the cases of pure public goods or they offer no overall solution to the conceptual problem of Social Dilemma. In fact, the problem with Olson's paradox is that it is a conceptual problem arising out of a narrow definition of self-utility. The truth of the matter is that if we accept the behavioral assumption of the *homo economicus*, then there is no conceptual solution to the Olsonian paradox whatsoever, total or partial. In fact, Olson (1965, 161–162) himself acknowledged that "It is not clear that this is the best way of theorizing about either utopian or religious groups. . . . Where non-rational or irrational is the basis for a lobby, it would perhaps be better to turn to psychology or social psychology than to economics for a relevant theory."

Although no conceptual solution exists to the conceptual problem, in reality, activists of every sort overcome Olson's paradox with as much ease as taking any other market decision. Thus, Elinor Ostrom (1998) says it best in her presidential address to the American Political Science Association:

> Let me start with a provocative statement. You would not be reading this article if it were not for some our ancestors learning how to undertake collective action to solve social dilemmas. Successive generations have added to the stock of everyday knowledge about how to instill productive norms of behavior in their children and to craft rules to support collective action that produces public goods and avoids "tragedies of commons."[11] What our ancestors and contemporaries have learned about engaging in collective action for mutual defense, child rearing, and survival is not, however, understood or explained by the extant theory of collective action. (1998, 1)

The adherents of the self-interest assumption have essentially dealt with the dissonance between theory and reality in several ways. Some have argued (Ostrom 1998, 9) that the models based on economic rationality have been incorrectly confused as "a general theory of human behavior." Therefore, do not expect these models to provide answers for every kind of human behavior. In other words, we should be satisfied with a partial explanation of human behavior, even when the "anomalous" behavior forms the core of our social interaction. The behavior we can explain should be considered "rational," whereas the rest, we are assured, can be relegated to the realm of irrationality or, more kindly, a-rationality.

To some others, this truncated assumption of human behavior is a reflection of practicality. In a complex world, the monolithic explanation provides the anchor for an ever-drifting ship. If we cloud our explanation by bringing in other factors, they would only muddy the water. Hence, they have argued that in the final analysis, models based on self-interest are in fact superior to those based on psychology and biology. Thus, Becker (1996, 7) states that "[O]ur assumption of stable preferences (based on self-utility alone) was intended not as a philosophical or methodological 'law,' but as a productive way to analyze and explain behavior. We are impressed by how little has been achieved by the many discussions in economics, sociology, history, and other fields that postulate almost arbitrary variations in preferences and values when confronted by puzzling behavior." However, even if we do not question the futility of a multidisciplinary approach, we do wonder about characterizing much of our collective behavior as "puzzling." To be sure, Becker's many-faceted work has provided the necessary groundwork for analyzing individual actions from marriage to crime, but the extension of economic logic cannot solve the mystery of participation in collective action to procure public goods.

In support of this reductionistic assumption of human nature, some have found solace in another curious fact. Lichbach (1997, 95), for instance, points out that, although most people and groups have serious grievances, "at least ninety-five percent of the time, in at least ninety five percent of the places," they do not rebel. Therefore, if we accept the aim of the theory to explain both action and inaction, the self-interest-based theory does work very well at least 95 percent of the time. This is an extraordinary claim coming from someone attempting to explore the root causes of mass revolt. It is analogous to geologists finding comfort in the fact that their theory is right (at least 95 percent of the times, no less) in explaining terrestrial stability, or someone interested in violent weather patterns taking pride in developing a model that predicts calm weather but fails to predict a tornado.

The final argument for continuing to use the assumption of self-interest is that to do otherwise would result in tautological explanations. This claim leads to the argument that theories of the real world have to offer only a partial explanation. The reality is too complex to fit in any theory. Therefore, any theory that offers to explain everything becomes "vague and an unfalsifiable sponge" (Lichbach 1995, 12). To me, this is the most confounding of all the arguments against expanding the fundamental assumption of human rationality. It is indeed true that a theory must follow Karl Popper's (1968) dictum of falsifiability. That is, to be scientific, a theory must offer hypotheses that will allow empirical testing for proving and disproving it. Metaphysical queries such as the existence of God and soul cannot be held as scientific, because we cannot collect verifiable empirical data to test our hypotheses. The problem with using this criterion in the social sciences is that if we use self-interest in the narrow sense of "selfish-utility," it becomes falsifiable and is readily falsified by our everyday experience of myriad acts of pure altruism, where people donate in complete anonymity, or even put themselves in eminent danger to protect even a complete stranger. In contrast, if we broaden self-interest to include every human action by arguing that even the most generous feat of self-sacrifice is a reflection of maximization of selfish-utility—because it may accord the actor immense respect in history, may assure a place in heaven, or may preserve the actor's gene pool—such a definition becomes patently unfalsifiable.

The strongest argument, however, for holding onto an inadequate theory for the explanation of collective action is to hold there is no other alternative to the narrowly defined "rational actor" hypothesis. No established theory is discarded or significantly altered without another one replacing it. Thus, with no other alternative in sight, Ostrom (1998, 9) could assert that: "While incorrectly confused with a general theory of human behavior, complete rationality models will be continued to be used productively by social scientists, including the author." Hence, with considerable justification, Ostrom (1998, 9) found solace in the assumption of self-interest: "I therefore find assumptions about rational dissidents to be neither always true nor always good, merely almost always useful."

However, in this chapter, I argue that such a narrow definition of human action, classified into "rational" and "nonrational" or "economic" and "noneconomic," creates a barrier to understanding human motivation within a society. Therefore, in the following section, I attempt to demonstrate how we can incorporate the insights of social psychology within a generalized framework of standard microeconomic analysis. In effect, I posit that the assumption of "rationality" needs to be broadened to include the motivations of the group if we are to understand human beings as social animals.

Group Motivations: The Contributions of Social Psychology

Whereas the primary contribution of neoclassical economics is to point out the importance of self-utility, the contribution of social psychology is to underscore the significance of group-motivations in our everyday decision-making process.

The rapidly enlarging field of experimental social psychology has demonstrated that:

- Group formation is almost instinctive.
- When a group is formed, an actor develops set perceptions of those who are "in" (favorable) and "out" (unfavorable) of the group.
- An actor may often sacrifice his own interest in favor of the interest of his group.
- An actor's decisions, in general, are significantly influenced by the authority figures who "frame" an issue to elicit a certain response from their audiences.

Forming groups is rooted deep in the human psyche. In the post–World War II period, advancements in social psychology have established our primordial desire to belong to a group and, often, to hate those who are perceived to be outside of the group. In their many experiments, social psychologists have demonstrated that people form groups almost instinctively. And once a group is formed and the members of the "in" and the "out" groups (or alternately, "us" and "them") are identified, the subjects develop ethnocentric pride (favoring members of the "in" group) and prejudice (unfavorable attitudes) toward the "out" group. In a famous experiment, Sherif and Hovland (1961) demonstrated the ease with which two competing groups of boys, during a period of only three weeks in a summer camp, could develop pride in their group and, at the same time, learn to look down upon the members of the other group.

Social psychologists have often found experimental results that contradict the precepts of "economic rationality."[12] For instance, Tajfel and his associates (Tajfel 1981, 1982; Tajfel and Turner 1986) took a direct aim at this mythical *homo economicus*. In their experiment, they offered the subjects two separate strategies. By following the first strategy, the subjects would maximize the total return of the "in" and "out" groups. The alternate strategy, however, allows them to maximize their own "in" group returns relative to those of the "out" group. By following the first strategy, both groups receive the same amount of return, which is greater than what one group would receive by trying to beat out the other group. For instance, the first strategy may yield $5 for each group but the second would give $4 to the "in" and $1 to the "out" group. By the laws of economic utility maximization, a "rational" actor would choose strategy 1 as it gives his group the maximum benefit, yet in a telling testimony to human group behavior, most subjects chose the second strategy.

Therefore, advances in social psychology have shown the fundamental allure of group formation in the human psyche (Volkan 1990). Given the strength of this proclivity, it is inconceivable that we will be able to understand our social behavior with the help of self-utility alone. Human beings came out of their simian past having formed groups. Chances are, we will continue to form groups until we are no longer in existence. Whether it is our need for collective survival, need for reciprocal reassurance, selective group benefits of nepotism or our insatiable need for social identification, formation of groups is as fundamental as (and, in fact, conceptually inseparable from) the maximization of self-utility.

Another important aspect of our group identity is our proclivity for suspending our own values and judgment facing the possibility of peer pressure or in the presence of an authority figure. In 1974, Stanley Milgram reported the results of an extraordinary series of experiments in which he demonstrated the willingness of people to go to extraordinary lengths to obey orders from authority figures.

The other important finding of social psychology relates to "framing." Every society carries in it collective memories relating tales of heroes and villains, past deeds of right and wrong. Digging deep into the reservoir of hopes and aspiration, despair and nightmares, *political entrepreneurs* develop their own political platforms. In terms of social psychology, they "frame" an issue. "Framing" is extremely important in how we view a complex reality.

For instance, if a patient is told that he has a 95 percent chance of survival, then we can get one kind of answer. However, if he or she is told that there is a 5 percent chance of death, the answer is likely to be significantly different. The mastery of political entrepreneurs lies in their ability to frame issues for their audience. Although the importance of "framing" in our decision-making process has been recognized for some time, perhaps its best proof through experimental design can be found in the works of Kahneman and his associates (Kahneman 1973; Kahneman, Slovic, and Tversky 1982). In their work, they demonstrated that individuals tend to make distinct choices depending on whether the outcomes are "framed" in terms of gains (e.g., survival) or losses (death). Ever since their ground-breaking studies, the effects of framing have been examined in the diverse fields of cognitive science, communications studies, law, political science, psychology, and economics.[13]

Collective: The Contextual Identity

One of the most significant problems of considering group identity as a part of the fundamental behavioral assumption is that our group identity is fickle. Collective identity, in the ultimate analysis, makes us members of an imagined community, which at any one point can include or exclude anyone else in the world (Anderson 1983). However, this weakness can also be the source of its analytical strength. Because group identity is not invariant, its inclusion cannot be regarded as leading to a tautological argument. That is, if we were born with our group identities, we could have explained away everything and, in the process, explained nothing. If social science makes any claim to be recognized as a "science," its assumptions must pass the test of "falsifiability." Because group identity is not imprinted in the genetic map of an individual, and is developed through the external world, both its existence and its relative strength are amenable to empirical testing (Gupta, Hofstetter, and Buss 1997). We can hypothesize that an individual's group identity and its strength will depend upon a number of *passive* factors, of which, perhaps the most important are economic, cultural, religious, and linguistic factors. We call them "passive" because they provide the basis on which people draw boundaries around each other. The divisions along these passive variables are reinforced and shaped into forces of collective action by the *catalytic* influence of political entrepreneurs and by a changing social, political, and economic environment.

Accounting for the Social Man: A Generalized Framework

Based on the above discussion, we may attempt to build a basic model that can incorporate factors of individual and collective identity. The arguments can be presented with the help of the standard methodological tools of microeconomics. By combining the two motivations of the self and of the collectivity, we can posit that an individual's actions are motivated not only by self-interest, but also from a distinct utility derived from furthering the cause of the group in which an actor claims membership. Within our framework, therefore, a *Homo economicus* is transformed into a *Homo collectivus*, who seeks a balance between the conflicting demands of the individual self and the group. For the sake of simplicity, we hypothesize that private goods are produced by individual effort, whereas collective goods are produced either by joint effort or collective movements. We further assume that while public goods satisfy our group utility, individual utility is produced by the consumption of private goods.

The modified model of collective behavior postulates that an individual maximizes utility (U_i) by consuming optimum amounts of the two goods: Y_i, the private goods providing utility of the individual self and G_i, the collective goods providing utility of the group in which the actor has chosen to belong.

The actor maximizes her utility subject to the total availability of time or endowment (T). Thus, we may formally write:

$$U_i = U(Y_i, G_i) \tag{3}$$
$$\text{subject to } T = T_y + T_g$$

where U_i is assumed to be strictly quasi-concave; T_y is the amount of time an individual i decides to devote to the pursuit of private goods; and T_g is the amount of time spent on the production of public (or, alternately, group or collective) goods. The resulting Lagrangian function takes the familiar form:

$$L^* = U[Y_i(T_y) + G_i(T_g)] + \lambda(T - T_y - T_g) \tag{4}$$

The trade-off between goods producing individual utility and group utility implied by equation (4) is depicted in Figure 12.1.

In Figure 12.1, the vertical axis measures the amount of private goods that promote individual utility such as personal income, power, rectitude, and so forth accruing to the individual actor as a result of the employment of resources within his or her command. The horizontal axis measures the amount of public goods (e.g., end of discrimination, gaining of national independence, family security, and others) the actor can expect to obtain by contributing an additional unit of resource. The indifference curves measure an individual's relative preferences for the two goods. The budget line measures the constraint that an individual would face in producing the two utility-producing goods. Within Figure 12.1, a hypothetical individual attains

Figure 12.1   **Effects of Changes in the Political and Economic Environment**

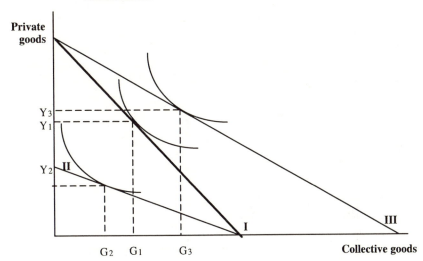

the point of equilibrium—the ideal mix between the pursuit of self-interest-producing goods and collective-utility producing goods—where Y_1 of the private goods and G_1 amount of collective goods are consumed.

In strict economic terms, the budget line can be interpreted as the ratio of the maximum amount of the two goods an individual can expect to produce by devoting the total available resources. These resources would include an individual's power, position, and social standing in the community. This budget constraint, however, is not fixed over time and can have shifts based on changed sociopolitical and economic conditions. Specifically, the conditions that might change the slope of this "budget line" depend on several factors:

Changes in Economic Opportunities. If economic opportunities deteriorate and high rates of unemployment plague the nation, the cost of diverting time from the pursuit of economic to collective goods would be relatively small. This situation is being depicted in Figure 12.1, where the budget line dips down to (II). As a result of this change in the relative price of the two goods—through the interaction of income and substitution effects—an actor adjusts his or her consumption pattern.

Changes in Political Opportunities. Changes in political opportunities can also cause changes in people's perception of their ability to achieve a proper mix of the two goods. For instance, if the central government weakens from war or some other natural or manmade catastrophe, the lessening of the government's coercive capabilities may cause a bandwagon effect. When the fear of retribution goes down, people feel free to express their disaffec-

Figure 12.2   **Self-Utility and Collective Utility: Effects of Leadership**

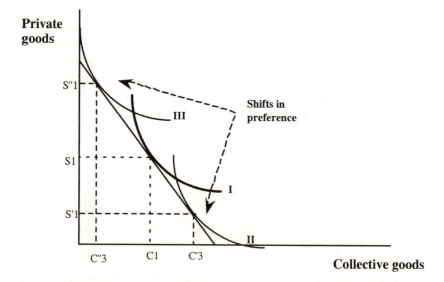

tion for an established political system. For instance, the virtual explosion of collective movements in the United States during the Vietnam War can be explained with the help of this scenario. Kuran (1995, 1998) has ably demonstrated this cascading effect in a series of books and articles. In Figure 12.1, this changed attitude causes the budget line (I) to shift to the right to (III). With many expecting to get a quick reward from collective action, an a priori fire of protest and rebellion is quickly started, often without much advanced notice.

Political opportunities can also be determined by the government's attitude toward repression of the views of its political opponents. For instance, if the government decides to crack down on dissidents, it can truly truncate the budget line and thereby cause the prospective participants to stay back, significantly reduce their involvement and drive a wedge between their public pronouncements and their private views.

Shift in Preference. Another important reason for the choice among people of a different mix of private and collective goods is the result of political entrepreneurs' influence on individual preferences. Figure 12.2 depicts the situation. Because collective identity is not constant and individuals may take on a number of collective identities, it is the political entrepreneurs of all sorts of ideologies who inspire their followers to sacrifice their private goods in favor of collective goods. As can be seen in Figure 12.2, inspiring leadership may cause the indifference map to shift to the right (II); people place more emphasis on the pursuit of collective goods by becoming political activist of all sorts, from freedom riders to urban guerrillas.

A shift in preference can also take place if the individual members feel a serious threat to their collective identity. A community can feel threatened as a result of some external actions (such as a war), an attack on a recognized symbol (such as flag burning), or the perception of a sudden change in social status hierarchy (immigration issue). In such cases, people may be willing to join the cause of the collective even at the detriment of their personal safety or extreme monetary loss. Throughout history, political entrepreneurs, from the Nazis in Germany to the Hutus in Rwanda, have manufactured the perceptions of a threat. For instance, in India, the fear of the Muslim minority resulted in the destruction of the Babri Mashjid Communal by the Hindus. This, in turn, was interpreted as a threat by the Muslims, causing widespread riots and communal mayhem (Gopal 1990).

Can Collective Identity Be Measured?

One of the arguments for not enlarging the fundamental behavioral assumption is the fear of engaging in tautology. In this section, I argue that the strength of a people's collective identity as an explanatory variable for collective action can be measured.

So far I have presented the case that to form groups is part and parcel of human nature. However, as soon as we form a group, we define who "we" are as a group as opposed to who "they" are as the outsiders. I have also shown how transient these feelings of "us" and "them" can be. How we feel today as a group may not hold the same feeling tomorrow. In fact, collective identity can and is manipulated by clever political operators and group leaders. That is the secret of their success as leaders. Whereas self-identity is invariant and omnipresent, collective identity is itinerant. However, the formation of collective identity follows a definite pattern. But before we go into the question of the formation of collective identity, let us examine the question of actually observing and empirically measuring its relative strength.

Because collective identity is part and parcel of human cognition, we can either conjecture its relative strength from the overall social condition at the macrolevel, or can directly measure it through survey instruments. There is, of course, no aggregate level data on collective identity. However, in his work, Ted Gurr attempted to estimate what he calls "group cohesion" for a large number of groups around the world (Gurr 1970). By our definition of collective identity, this group cohesion index comes extremely close to measuring the first half of collective identity, the "us" factor. However, as Gurr makes no attempt at creating an index for the intensity of perception toward the "out" group, his index only measures half the concept of collective identity.

Although there is no aggregate cross-country data on collective identity, it seems reasonable to assume that the intensity of collective identity within a nation will be greatly influenced by the depth of cleavages within a society. Kelman (1973) has pointed out that with increased levels of fragmentation, it is easier for groups to see each other as adversaries. This contributes to the overall hostility within a society. By extending Kelman's arguments, researchers have found strong empirical evidence suggesting that societies where income is concentrated in the hands of a few, and there is deep ethnolinguistic factionalism, the incidences of violent collective actions are high (Gupta 1990).

A psychological phenomenon such as the strength of collective identity can be directly measured through personal interviews. Gupta et al. (1997) wanted to examine the reasons why some seniors join the American Association of Retired Persons (AARP) (Gupta et al. 1997). The AARP is perhaps the most influential lobbying group in the United States, ever vigilant in protecting the interests of the senior citizens of the nation. Therefore, belonging to a political action group such as the AARP is also a form of collective action. As a further incentive for joining, the AARP also gives its members a number of discount coupons and a magazine, *Modern Maturity*, which provides information on voter education, health care and quality of life, workers' rights and retirement. Therefore, like most things in life, it is reasonable to assume that the senior citizens will be joining the AARP out of mixed motives of self-utility and collective identity.

For the Gupta et al. study, a stratified probability sample of over 600 senior citizens residing in the Youngstown, Ohio, area was interviewed by telephone in 1989. The sample was designed to represent the cross section of the noninstitutionalized elderly community of fifty-five years and older. In this extremely detailed survey, a large number of questions were asked respondents about their physical and emotional health, economic conditions, education and attitudes. They were also asked if they were members of AARP.

Gupta et al. (1997) hypothesized that a person's decision to join AARP would depend upon several factors: his or her assessment of personal and collective benefits of becoming a member, the cost of membership, and a set of exogenous factors based on cultural differences or some other aspect of individual "taste." Membership in AARP entitles people to get discount coupons, which include a wide variety of services (from traveling to health care) and goods of personal use. The study assumed that individuals' capability of getting benefits from AARP would depend upon their relative income capabilities and physical and mental health. Thus, if I do not have any discretionary money, it does not do me any good to have discount coupons for hotel accommodations in vacation retreats. Similarly, if I am of poor physical and psychological health, my ability to enjoy those private goods become severely restricted. By combining these three factors the investigators arrived at a person's ability to enjoy the private benefits of joining the AARP. They assumed that the greater a person's economic ability and health, the greater the incentive to join the organization.

The other motivation for joining the AARP is collective; the desire to improve the conditions of the senior citizens in the United States. Gupta et al. (1997) hypothesized that this desire is directly related to an individual's strength of collective identity. For collective identity, we constructed two separate composite measures of "us" and "them." If an individual pays close attention to the news about senior citizens, gets involved in activities designed specifically for the senior community, and is concerned about health and welfare of the elderly in general, he or she is assigned a high number for the "us" factor. The study measured the "them" aspect of collective identity by asking questions to ascertain whether the respondent views the younger generation in an adversarial context. That is, if an individual feels that the younger generation views the elderly in unfavorable light, and if television and films portray them negatively, then the subject gets a high index for "them."

The cost of joining the AARP is minimal ($5 per year at the time of the survey). Therefore, the investigators assumed that only those senior citizens who are below the official poverty mark would consider this to be a barrier for joining the organization.

Finally, the "taste" factor was measured by asking the subjects about their awareness and attitude toward complex issues of public policy and government in general. Those who showed little awareness of social and political issues scored low on "awareness." Similarly, those who felt that they could never trust the government or that they would not be able to influence public policy received high marks on the "cynicism" scale. Also, for unexplained cultural factors, the study included demographic variables, such as race, age, and gender.

When these four broad factors of individual interest, collective interest, cost of participation, and personal taste were included in a regression model, the investigators found that for the sample population, the strict economic argument of self-interest provides an inadequate explanation of membership in AARP. When all the four factors were introduced, the estimated results showed that people with a strong collective identity were significantly more inclined to join than were those with a weak identity. Interestingly, while factors of self-interest, collective identity, and cost (poverty level) turned out to be statistically significant, the factors of personal taste, other than race (whites are much more prone to join than are African-Americans), did not.

The model's ability to identify those who would join the collective action stood in contrast with its relatively low predictive capability to identify the nonjoiners. The estimated model had identified a much larger participation. However, 114 individuals, whom the model had predicted to be joiners, turned out to be nonjoiners. In fact, the model was able to recognize less than a third (30.4 percent) of a total population of 164 nonmembers. Gupta et al. (1997) called this cohort of 114 individuals the "true free-riders." This is because those individuals whom they had successfully identified as nonmembers had reasons (such as poverty, low collective identity) not to join. In contrast, the motives of those who should have joined but chose not to were particularly puzzling. Therefore, the investigators specifically looked at the two groups they had unsuccessfully identified as nonjoiners and the "true" free riders. The statistical analysis of the two groups found that the distinguishing features were the personal taste factors. Those senior citizens that did not take any interest in the overall political matters and were not aware of the issues facing the elderly in America and those who scored high marks on cynicism chose not to join.

A growing number of social-psychological studies are accumulating evidence pointing toward the importance of collective identity as a factor in the participatory decision in collective movements (Branscombe, Schmitt, and Harvey 1999; Simon, Pantaleo, and Mummendey 1995; Simon 1998; Kelly and Breinlinger 1996; Kawakami and Dion 1995; Kelly 1993). Simon et al. (1995), in an empirical work, combined collective identification with social rewards. In their study, through survey analyses the authors examined reasons why elders join the Gray Panther movement and homosexuals participate in the gay rights movement. The study finds three variables to be significantly correlated with participation in the Gray Panther movement. These are (in order of importance): "reward motive," "identification with the older people's movement," and "collective motive."[14] The *reward motive* measures expected personal gains, whereas the rest are measures of collective identity. However, in the case of the gay rights movement only two variables turn out to be statistically significant. They are (in order of importance): "identification with gay movement," and "collective motive." In other words, like Gupta et al., Simon et al. (1995) also find actors' collective identity to be a significant factor in the participatory decision of people to engage in collective actions. However, for Simon et al. (1995) the group motives were the only ones to explain the subject's decision to join a collective action.

These empirical findings, therefore, point to the fact that collective identity can be measured and that it plays a very important role in the decision of people to join a collective movement. In fact, in the literature on collective action, Mancur Olson's (1965, 2) often quoted remark stands out like the rock of Gibraltar: "Indeed, unless the number of individuals in a group is quite small, or unless there is coercion or some other special device to make individuals act in their common interest, *rational, self-interested individuals will not act to achieve their common group interests*" (emphasis is Olson's). In other words, if people get something for nothing, they will not volunteer to pay for it. Because reality clearly shows that people do participate even when there is little to be gained or they can get the same benefits without putting out the effort, I have argued that the explanation rests with the actor's collective identity. Thus, in contrast to Olson's blanket statement of inactivity by "rational" actors, Tajfel points out that participation in collective movements should be understood on the psychological level as "efforts by large numbers of people, *who define themselves and are defined by others as a group*, to solve collectively a problem they feel they have in common, and which is perceived to arise from their relations with other groups"(Tajfel 1981, 244, emphasis mine).

Conclusion

During the past four decades, the concept of collective identity has increasingly been the object of inquiry in many areas of academic disciplines. Although the notion of group identity was not unknown in academic circle, its inclusion as serious inquiry appropriately started with the social psychologists. Their experimental research clearly demonstrates the importance of collective identity in the human decision-making calculus.

Scholars from political science, sociology, and geography are attempting to include it within their paradigm (Iyenger 1993). However, economics, with its strict methodological tradition, has been slow to embrace social psychology. It is interesting that while many economists and public-choice social scientists have criticized the inability of economics to explain collective action (Ostrom 1998) few, until recently, have attempted to offer any concrete alternative for expanding economic methodology. With the possible exceptions of a few researchers, the expansion of multidisciplinary studies has been more or less a one way street as far as economics is concerned. For instance, Sen (1984) mentions identity and commitment as influencing an individual's goal achievement, but does not include it in the utility function. Similarly, Kuran (1995), while considering activities promoting ethnic identity, does not expand the traditional utility function to explicitly include collective identity as a separate argument. A few others (Margolis 1982; Landa 1994; Kevane 1994, Bowels and Gintis 1997; Akerlof and Kranton 2000) incorporate self-utility in their expanded objective functions. However, most of these studies define "identity" as "self-identity" and take these identities as given, similar to an exogenous taste factor. In this chapter, I have argued for a closer examination of an individual's collective identity by borrowing from social psychology without discarding the analytical elegance of economics.

Social psychology, especially its experimental branch, in turn typically takes a snapshot of group identity without viewing it within the dynamic context of a social being, motivated to a large extent by self-interest. Therefore, I argue that building a bridge between the disciplines of economics and social psychology may enrich both of them (Gupta 2001).

A new theory can be considered to be an improvement over an existing one if (1) it widens the domain of behavior that counts as action; (2) offers a more powerful theory that brings actions of various kinds under one theory; and (3) it provides a more accurate or precise set of predictions. I argue that this generalized framework, which explicitly includes collective identity as an essential component of individual utility functions, through further research may provide a new way of synthesizing the disciplines of economics and social psychology. This new approach may enable us not to disregard a wide-range of human behavior—the very foundation of our civil society—as "a-rational" or "irrational." Needless to say, a great deal of work—both empirical and conceptual—needs to be done to firmly establish an expanded framework within the academic mainstream.

Notes

1. Hirschman (1974, 9) correctly points out that "the preference for participation in public affairs over the 'idiocy' of private life is much more unstable, and subject to much wider fluctuations, than the preference for, say, apples over pears or for present over future consumption." Also see Rapoport and Bornstein (1989).

2. Mason and Krane (1989, 184) show a high degree of correlation between the number of youths in a locality with participation in the death squads. Because of high rate of population growth is strongly correlated with a higher proportion of young men and women, in my cross-national study, I found significant correlation between rate of growth of population (and consequently, a higher proportion of youth in the population) and political protest (Gupta 1990). Hobsbawm (1981, 31–33) reports that most "social bandits" come from the relatively young in the society.

3. See Popkin (1979) on peasants' natural aversion to risk taking. Also see Scott (1976). On the opportunity costs of participation in collective action, see Coleman (1990).

4. Lacouture (1968, 53). Because Karl Marx was keenly aware of the need for indoctrination of the masses to overcome their inhibition toward rebellion ("You have nothing but your chains to lose"), Lichbach (1995, 100) suggests that Marx, in fact, presupposed the problem of Rebel's dilemma. V. I. Lenin, while providing a road map to revolution, states that the revolutionary leadership will not come from the proletariat, but from a group of bourgeoisie (1902/1969, 40).

5. See, for instance, the Amnesty International Annual Report (2000) for punishment in China.

6. The argument goes as follows: As the cost of participation rises, the dissident groups find themselves in a resource crunch, which reduces their capability to engage in dissident activities. For a most recent argument along this line, see McAdam, McCarthy, and Zald (1996).

7. Ted R. Gurr (1970, 232) states "the most fundamental human response to the use of force is counterforce. Force threatens and angers men, especially if they believe it to be illicit or unjust. Threatened, they try to defend themselves; angered, they want to retaliate."

8. See John Dunn (1989). Also, Sidney Tarrow (1994) suggests that with more effective means of communication, movements would spread more rapidly.

9. Tarrow (1989, 93), for instance, mentions truck slowdown in the Italian border checkpoints as a successful means of protest.

10. Becker (1996, 1–29), in contrast, offers a slightly different solution to the free-rider problem. He argues that a bandwagon effect starts when an individual joins a collective action and finds that, because the others have joined in, his own costs have gone down and this will create a larger demand of participation.

11. The term "tragedies of commons" refers to the problem that common-pool resources, such as oceans, lakes, forests, irrigation systems, and grazing lands, can easily be overused or destroyed if property rights to these resources are not well defined (see Garrett Hardin 1968). Footnote quoted from Ostrom (1998, 1).

12. Social psychologists Daniel Kahneman and Amos Tversky (1984), in a long series of experiments, have demonstrated how we dispense with even the most fundamental precepts of economic rationality facing uncertain outcomes.

13. An incomplete list, for instance, would include Sweetser and Fauconnier (1996) in cognitive science; Entman (1993), Lakoff (1996), and Capella and Jamieson (1997) in communications studies; Emerson (1972) in psychology; McCaffery, Kahneman, and Spitzer, (1995) in law; Chong (1996) and Druckman (1999) in political science; Snow and Benford (1992) in mass movements; Gamson and Modigliani (1987) and Ekeh (1974) in sociology, and others.

14. Simon and his colleagues's (1995) definition of "reward" should be read as "net reward" for they consider both gains and losses. In estimating the "rewards" for joining a collective movement, the researchers considered an "expected-return model," where the perceived probability of success is multiplied by the expected reward. The rewards included the actor's improvement of one's own living conditions, social contacts with other older or gay people, and meaningful leisure time activity. They also considered the possibilities of two losses (health risks and loss of time). The identification with older/gay people measures the strength of psychological attachment to the community (similar to the "us" factor in Gupta et al. 1997). Collective motives included goals of the two movements.

References

Akerlof, George A., and Rachel E. Kranton. 2000. "Economics and Identity" *Quarterly Journal of Economics* 115: 715–754.
Anderson, Benedict. 1983. *Imagined Communities: Reflections on the Origins and Spread of Nationalism*. London: Verso.
Becker, Gary. 1965. *A Theory of Allocation of Time*. Chicago: University of Chicago Press.

————. 1976. *The Economic Approach to Human Behavior*. Chicago: University of Chicago Press.

————. 1981. *A Treatise on Family*. Cambridge, MA: Harvard University Press.

————. 1996. *Accounting for Taste*. Cambridge, MA: Harvard University Press.

Becker, Gary, and William M. Landes, eds. 1974. *Essays in the Economics of Crime and Punishment*. New York: National Bureau of Economic Research: Columbia University Press.

Bentham, Jeremy. 1970. *An Introduction to the Principles of Morals and Legislation.* [J.H. Burns and H.L.A. Hart, eds. Originally published in 1789.] London: Athlone Press.

Bowels, Samuel, and Herbert Gintis. 1997. "Optimal Parochialism: The Dynamics of Trust and Exclusion in Communities." Mimeograph, Amherst: University of Massachusetts.

Branscombe, N.R., M.T. Schmitt, and R.D. Harvey. 1999. "Perceiving Pervasive Discrimination Among African Americans: Implications for Group Identification and Well-being." *Journal of Personality and Social Psychology* 77: 135–149.

Brehm, John, and Scott Gates. 1997. *Working, Shirking, and Sabotage: Bureaucratic Response to a Democratic Public*. Ann Arbor: University of Michigan Press.

Capella, Joseph N., and Kathleen H. Jamieson. 1997. *Spiral of Cynicism: The Press and the Public Good*. New York: Oxford University Press.

Chamberlin, William. 1987. *The Russian Revolution, 1917–1918*. [Originally published in 1937]. Princeton, NJ: Princeton University Press.

Chong, Dennis. 1991. *Collective Action and the Civil Rights Movement*. Chicago: University of Chicago Press.

————. 1996. "Creating Common Frames of Reference on Political Issues." In Diana C. Mutz, Paul M. Sniderman, and Richard A. Brody, eds., *Political Persuasion and Attitude Change*, pp. 195–224. Ann Arbor: University of Michigan Press.

Coleman, James. 1990. *Foundations of Social Theory*. Cambridge, MA: Belknap.

Druckman, James N. 1999. "Do Party Cues Limit Framing Effects?" Paper presented at the Mental Models in Social Science Conference, University of California at San Diego, July 29–31.

Dunn, John. 1989. *Modern Revolutions: An Introduction to the Analysis of a Political Phenomenon*. Cambridge: Cambridge University Press.

Ekeh, Peter P. 1974. *Social Exchange Theory: The Two Traditions*. Cambridge, MA: Harvard University Press.

Emerson, Richard. 1972. "Exchange Theory, Part I: A Psychological Basis for Social Exchange." In Joseph Berger, Morris Zelditch, and Bo Anderson, eds., *Sociological Theories in Progress*, vol. 2, pp. 38–57. Boston: Houghton Mifflin.

Entman, Robert. 1993. "Framing: Toward Clarification of a Fractured Paradigm." *Journal of Communication* (43): 51–58.

Gamson, William A., and Andre Modigliani. 1987. "The Changing Culture of Affirmative Action." In Richard D. Braungart, ed., *Research in Political Sociology*, vol. 3, pp. 225–243. Greenwich, CT: JAI Press.

Gopal, Sarvepalli. 1990. *Anatomy of a Confrontation: The Babri Masjid–Ramjanmabhumi Issue*. New Delhi, India: Viking Press.

Gupta, Dipak K. 1990. *The Economics of Political Violence*. New York: Praeger.

Gupta, Dipak K., Harinder Singh, and Tom Sprague 1993. "Government Coercion of Dissidents: Deterrence or Provocation?" *Journal of Conflict Resolution* 37(2): 301–340.

Gupta, Dipak K., Richard Hofstetter, and Teri Buss. 1997. "Group Utility in the Micro-Motivation of Collective Action: The Case of Membership in the AARP." *Journal of Economic Behavior and Organization* 32: 301–320.

———. 2001. *Path to Collective Madness: A Study in Social Order and Political Pathology*. New York: Greenwood Press.

Gurr, Ted R. 1970. *Why Men Rebel*. New Haven, CT: Yale University Press.

Hardin, Garrett. 1968. "The Tragedy of the Commons." *Science* (December): 472–481.

Hardin, Russell. 1995. *One for All: The Logic of Group Conflict*. Princeton, NJ: Princeton University Press.

Heimer, Carol Anne. 1985. *Reactive Risk and Rational Action: Managing Moral Hazard in Insurance Contracts*. Berkeley: University of California Press.

Hirschman, Albert O. 1974. "Exit, Voice, and Loyalty: Further Reflections and a Survey of Recent Contributions." *Social Science Information* (February): 7–26.

Ho, T.J. 1982. *Measuring Health as a Component of Living Standards. Living Standard Measurement Study*. Working paper no. 15. Washington, DC: World Bank.

Hobsbawm, Eric. 1981. *Bandits*. New York: Pantheon.

Holstrom, Bengt. 1982. "Moral Hazard in Teams." *Bell Journal of Economics* 13 (Autumn): 324–340.

Iyenger, Shanto. 1993. "An Overview of the Field of Political Psychology." In Shanto Iyenger and William J. McHuire, eds., *Explorations in Political Psychology*., pp. 3–8. Durham, NC: Duke University Press.

Jenkins, Brian. 1982. "Statements About Terrorism." *Annals* 463 (September): 11–23.

Juergensmeyer, Mark. 1984. *Fighting with Gandhi*. San Francisco: Harper & Row.

Kahneman, Daniel. 1973. *Attention and Effort*. Englewoods Cliffs, NJ: Prentice-Hall.

Kahneman, Daniel, Paul Slovic, and Amos Tversky. 1982. *Judgment Under Uncertainty: Heuristics and Biases*. Cambridge: Cambridge University Press.

Kahneman, Daniel, and Amos Tversky. 1984. "Choice, Values, and Frames." *American Psychologist* 39: 341–350.

Kawakami, K., and K.L. Dion. 1995. "Social Identity and Affect as Determinants of Collective Action: Toward an Integration of Relative Deprivation and Social Psychology Theory." *Theory and Psychology* 5: 551–577.

Kelly, Caroline. 1993. "Group Identification, Intergroup Perceptions and Collective Action." In W. Stroebe and M. Hewstone, eds., *European Review of Social Psychology*, vol. 4, pp. 59–83. Chichester, UK: Wiley.

Kelly, Caroline, and Sara Breinlinger. 1996. *The Social Psychology of Collective Action: Identity, Injustice and Gender*. London: Taylor and Francis.

Kelman, Herbert. 1973. "Violence Without Moral Restraints." *Journal of Social Issues* 29: 29–61.

Kevane, Michael. 1994. "Can There Be an 'Identity Economics?' " Mimeograph. Boston: Harvard Academy for International and Area Studies.

Kuran, Timur. 1995. *Private Truths, Public Lies: Social Consequences of Preference Falsification*. Cambridge, MA: Harvard University Press.

———. 1998. "Ethnic Dissimilation and Its International Diffusion." In David A. Lake and Donald Rothchild, eds., *Ethnic Conflict: Fear, Duffusion, and Escalation*, pp. 35–60. Princeton, NJ: Princeton University Press.

Lacouture, Jean. 1968. *Ho Chi Minh: A Political Biography*. New York: Vantage.

Lakoff, George. 1996. *Moral Politics: What Conservatives Know That Liberals Don't*. Chicago: University of Chicago Press.

Landa, Janet T. 1994. *Trust, Ethnicity, and Identity: Beyond the New Institutional Economics of Trading Networks.* Ann Arbor: University of Michigan Press.

Lenin, V.I. 1969. *What Is to Be Done?* [Originally published in 1902.] New York: International Publishers.

Lichbach, Mark I. 1987. "Deterrence or Escalation? The Puzzle of Aggregate Studies of Repression and Dissent." *Journal of Conflict Resolution* 31 (June): 266–297.

———. 1995. *The Rebel's Dilemma.* Ann Arbor: University of Michigan Press.

———. 1997. "Contentious Maps of Contentious Politics." *Mobilization* 2(1): 95.

Margolis, Howard. 1982. *Selfishness, Altruism, and Rationality.* Cambridge: Cambridge University Press.

Mason, T. David, and Dale A. Krane. 1989. "The Political Economy of Death Squads: Toward a Theory of the Impact of State-Sanctioned Terror." *International Studies Quarterly* 33 (June): 175–198.

McAdam, Doug, John McCarthy, and Mayer Zald, eds. 1996. *Comparative Perspectives on Social Movements.* New York: Cambridge University Press.

McCaffery, Edward J., Daniel Kahneman, and Matthew L. Spitzer. 1995. "Framing the Jury: Cognitive Perspectives on Pain and Suffering Awards." *Virginia Law Review* 81: 1341–1420.

Milgram, Stanley. 1974. *Obedience to Authority: An Experimental View.* New York: Harper & Row,

Moore, Will. 1998. "Repression and Dissent: Substitution, Context, and Timing." *American Journal of Political Science* 42(3): 851–873.

Navarro, Marysa. 1989. "The Personal Is Political: Las Madres de Plaza de Mayo." In Susan Eckstein, ed., pp. 241–258. *Power and Popular Protest: Latin American Social Movements.* Berkeley: University of California Press.

Olson, Mancur. 1965. *The Logic of Collective Action: The Public Goods and the Theory of Groups.* Cambridge, MA: Harvard University Press.

Ostrom, Elinor. 1998. "A Behavioral Approach to Rational Choice Theory of Collective Action: Presidential Address, American Political Science Association, 1997." *American Political Science Review* 92: 1–22.

Popkin, Samuel. 1979. *The Rational Peasant.* Berkeley: University of California Press.

Popper, Karl R. 1968. *The Logic of Scientific Discovery.* New York: Harper & Row.

Rapoport, Amnon, and Gary Bornstein. 1989. "Solving Public Goods Problems in Competition Between Equal and Un-equal Size Groups." *Journal of Conflict Resolution* 33 (September): 460–479.

Rasler, Karen. 1996. "Concessions, Repressions, and Political Protest in Iranian Revolution." *American Sociological Review* 61: 132–152.

Reif, Linda. 1986. "Women in Latin American Guerrilla Movements." *Comparative Politics* 18 (January): 147–169.

Rud, George. 1964. *The Crowd in History.* London: Oxford University Press.

Satz, Debra, and John Ferejohn. 1994. "Rational Choice and Social Theory." *The Journal of Philosophy* 91(2): 71–87.

Schmid, Alex P., and Janny de Graaf. 1982. *Violence as Communication: Insurgent Terrorism and the Western News Media.* Beverly Hills, CA: Sage.

Scott, James C. 1976. *The Moral Economy of the Peasant: Rebellion and Subsistence in Southeast Asia.* New Haven, CT: Yale University Press.

Sen, Amartya K. 1984. *Collective Choice and Social Welfare.* [Originally published in 1979.] Amsterdam: North-Holland: Elsevier Science.

Sherif, M., and C. Hovland. 1961. *Social Judgment: Assimilation and Contrast Effects in Communication and Attitude Change*. New Haven, CT: Yale University Press.

Simon, B. 1998. "The Self in Minority-Majority Contexts." *European Review of Social Psychology* 9: 1–30.

Simon, B., G. Pantaleo, and A. Mummendey. 1995. "Individual Groups and Social Change: On the Relationship Between Individual and Collective Self-Interpretations and Collective Actions." In C. Sedikides, J. Schopler, and C.A. Insko, eds., *Intergroup Cognition and Intergroup Behavior*, pp. 257–282. Hillsdale, NJ: Erlbaum.

Snow, David A., and Robert D. Benford. 1992. "Master Frames and Cycles of Protest." In Aldon Morris and Carol McClurg Mueller, eds., *Frontiers in Social Movement Theories*, pp. 133–155. New Haven, CT: Yale University Press.

Sweetser, Eve, and Gilles Fauconnier. 1996. "Cognitive Links and Domains: Basic Aspects of Mental Space Theory." In Gilles Fauconnier and Eve Sweester, eds., *Spaces, Worlds, and Grammar*. Chicago: University of Chicago Press.

Tajfel, Henri. 1981. *Human Groups and Social Categories: Studies in Social Psychology*. Cambridge: Cambridge University Press.

Tajfel, Henri, ed. 1982. *Social Identity and Intergroup Relations*. Cambridge: Cambridge University Press.

Tajfel, Henri, and James C. Turner. 1986. "The Social Identity Theory of Intergroup Behavior." In Stephen Worchel et al., eds., *Psychology of Intergroup Relations*, pp. 7–24. Chicago: Nelson-Hall.

Tarrow, Sidney. 1989. *Democracy and Disorder: Protest and Politics in Italy 1965–1975*. Oxford: Clarendon Press.

———. 1994. *Power in Movement*. Cambridge: Cambridge University Press.

Volkan, Vamik D. 1990. "Psychoanalytic Aspects of Ethnic Conflict." In Joseph Montville, ed., *Conflict and Peacemaking in Multiethnic Societies*, pp. 81–92. Lexington, MA: D.C. Heath.

13

Concluding Comments

Shoshana Grossbard-Shechtman and
Christopher Clague

The chapters in this book are examples of the expansion of economics into other social sciences, and of the reorientation of economics that is partly the consequence of that expansion. As a result of this activity, borders between the social science tribes have shifted and have become more porous. It is now time to ask, What borders are still there? In other words, what is distinctive about the economics tribe? If there are such distinctions, are they in the best interest of economics and of social science?

Even though some of the specialization outlined in Table 1.1 still goes on, the subject matters covered by the various social sciences now overlap considerably. The overlap of economics with political science includes the study of politics, policy-making, voting, constitutions, and bureaucracy (i.e., a considerable portion of the entire territory traditionally covered by political science). As for sociology, it seems as if most of the traditional territory of sociology has recently become economists' foraging ground as well. Some subject matters that have traditionally been part of the territory of sociology have been addressed in this book: marriage and divorce, fertility, intrahousehold allocation, gender relationships, and religion. Other topics that in the past economists mostly left to other social sciences such as sociology and that they are now addressing include crime, discrimination, and education.

Convergence between the social sciences is also observed at the level of methodologies. Formal, mathematical models are now commonplace in political science and have started to appear in sociology (e.g., Harrison White 1988; James Coleman 1990). More sophistication in quantitative methods is being introduced by all the social sciences. So here, too, it is becoming increasingly difficult to distinguish economics from other social sciences. Does this convergence mean that economics and other social sciences are all blending into one melting pot? We can wonder whether Jack Hirshleifer (1976, 1) was right when he wrote:

> Economics and anthropology, and for that matter sociology and political science as well, are all—insofar as they are scientific—*ultimately the same science*. (emphasis in the original)

In our opinion, there remain substantial differences between economics and other social sciences. As we wrote in the introduction, two main criteria have been used to categorize the various social sciences: subject matter and methodology. Both of these criteria are now less applicable as criteria to subdivide social science. Even though methodological differences between the disciplines are diminishing in absolute terms, as the various social sciences communicate more with one another, these differences have gained in relative importance as subject matter has become an almost irrelevant criterion for marking borders between the disciplines. Indeed, the intellectual tool kits used by most economists continue to be quite distinct from those used by practitioners of other disciplines.

In broad terms, economists differ from political scientists and sociologists in two dimensions: the relative importance of formal theory in their research agenda, and in their theoretical conception of how society functions. With regard to the latter dimension, economists still tend to assume that people are self-interested and calculative, whereas sociologists and political scientists tend to emphasize social pressures and the constraints imposed by internalized group goals and personal identity. Practically all economists accept, implicitly or explicitly, the research strategy of methodological individualism; that is, social phenomena are to be explained, at the most basic level, in terms of the behavior of individuals. Many sociologists reject this principle, believing that society should be understood in terms of "structures of interaction" (see Geoffrey Ingham [1996] for a discussion). These differences in conceptions of society lead naturally to different types of explanation of the same phenomena; each discipline projects its theoretical predilections onto the observed facts and tries to come up with explanations. A potentially interesting competition is emerging from the relatively new field of "economic sociology," which offers a different view of the functioning of labor and product markets from that of economics. The networking theories developed by sociologists are now also becoming popular among economists (see, e.g., James Rauch 2001).

Political science and management science differ less from economics than sociology differs from economics: Political scientists and management analysts are often comfortable with models based on rational choice by individuals. There are plenty of practitioners in each of these disciplines whose assumptions about individual motivation are indistinguishable from those typically made by economists. Nevertheless, political scientists and management scientists are more inclined than are economists to stress the role of leadership, loyalty, and ideology (in organizations, or in politics).

Economists as Model Builders

The second dimension of difference between economics and the other social sciences is the relative importance attached to formal modeling. Formalization has contributed greatly to the advance of knowledge in the social sciences. Economics stands out as the discipline in which formal models are highly prized. As mentioned in the introduction to this book, the formalization of neoclassical economics in the first half of the twentieth century gave the discipline a power and precision that elevated it to the first rank among the social sciences. The advances in economics in the last fifty years would not have been possible had the ideas not been formulated in terms of models. Economists are fond of saying that a phenomenon has not been properly explained until the explanation has been formulated in an abstract model. "If you want your ideas to get the attention of the profession, construct a model." There are, to be sure, formal models in political science, management science, and sociology, but formal modeling does not command the degree of respect and attention in these disciplines as it does in economics.

In all the social sciences, including economics, considerable tension exists between the model builders and those who investigate the real world. Considering all the material in this book can help us gain a sense of both the benefits and the costs of model building. Formal models clarify our thinking and enable us to see relationships among the variables that we would not otherwise be able to understand. A number of chapters in this book pointed out these advantages of formal models in economics, including the chapters by Michael Gibbs and Alec Levenson, Clive Granger; Shoshana Grossbard-Shechtman; Laurence Iannaccone; and Richard Audas and John Treble.

On the other side, formal models are often so abstract that they neglect essential ingredients of the phenomenon under study. A number of chapters discussed some of the disadvantages of formal models in economics. See chapters by Christopher Clague; Clive Granger; and Vernon Ruttan. Clague and Ruttan emphasize how economic models typically overlook important variables, variables that are rooted in institutions. Granger points out how economists miss important facts and relationships that their data contain but they do not see it.

In recent years, the concern about excessive formalism in economics has led to a discussion about the training of graduate students. Widespread concern resulted in the formation of a commission on graduate education of the American Economic Association (Anne Krueger 1991; W. Lee Hansen 1991; Hirschel Kasper et al. 1991). The commission reported that many graduate students were disillusioned by the emphasis in graduate programs on solving technical puzzles and learning mathematical techniques, rather than learning to apply these techniques to real-world problems. Many professors also believed that graduate curricula should be altered to place more emphasis on substance rather than technique. This debate about the structure of the graduate curriculum clearly reflects an ongoing tension within the economics discipline with respect to the praise and rewards that should be accorded to technical sophistication as opposed to substantive insight (see also, for example, Deirdre McCloskey 1996).

Tensions over the relative importance of technique and formal modeling within the disciplines spill over to tensions across disciplines. When economists tackle phenomena that have been studied by other social sciences, they tend to employ the technical skills of their profession. These forays are typically criticized on grounds of excessive abstraction. Economists have been called "reductionists" by some anthropologists; for instance, see Grossbard-Shechtman 1993. If excessive technique is criticized within economics, it is hardly surprising that it should be criticized by other social scientists who have not been as thoroughly trained in the techniques, nor socialized as to their value.

Ultimately, the value of models lies in their explanatory power and in their practical value to policymakers and businesses. Practical constraints can help shake off excessive or deficient models.

Facing Reality

Is the United States an outlier in terms of excessive emphasis on formal models? Bruno Frey and Reiner Eichenberger (1993) observe that American economists tend to be more technique-oriented and less interested in substantive and institutional reality than do their European counterparts. They offer an interesting explanation of this phenomenon in the existence in America of a large national market for economics PhDs, in contrast to the much smaller local and regional markets for academics in Europe. In the latter region, knowledge of local institutions is valued in the market, and this encourages academics to contemplate government service to a greater degree than in the United States. (It would be interesting to see whether the same pressures for greater emphasis on technique exist for American political scientists and sociologists in comparison to their European counterparts.)

Traditionally, one of the functions of social science university departments has been to contribute to public discussion and resolution of societal problems. Professors comment publicly through newspapers and television; they sit on commissions, testify before legislatures, and take leaves to work in government agencies. When graduates of academic departments go to work in government, business, or international agencies, they can prove whether the skills they learned are useful.

Whether system dynamics or equilibrium models are the answer is ultimately a matter of practical results. Rational-choice models? If they work, economists should continue to use them. Is detailed knowledge of the real world essential? Then we need to study history and get more information on the institutions framing our lives.

The Future of Ivory Tower Economics

Those who criticize excessive formalism in social science often lament that seemingly one can get ahead in the academy without much knowledge of how society actually functions. As a result of the incentives toward formalism in academic research, these critics contend, the disciplines make less of a contribution toward resolving social ills than they otherwise would (e.g., Jonathan Cohn 1999). Practitioners who deal with real-world complexities of economic policy, international relations, campaign finance reform, day care policy, and business strategy often comment on the lack of relevance of the theoretical models to their work.

Formalism becomes excessive if it only works in ivory towers and cannot withstand practical tests. Scholars in management science and political science have tended to avoid such excessive formalism, importing from economics the models that work. Now some political scientists are beating economists at their own game (see chapter 5). Healthy competition between alternative views of how society functions is very desirable, and we are glad that economic models have to compete against models developed in other disciplines. Such competition could be healthy and productive, provided practioners from different disciplines can harmonize their language to the point where they can communicate effectively with one another.

The implication that we draw from these considerations is that the social sciences ought to and will continue to present a variety of methodological styles of research and public advocacy. There will continue to be room for models and for the kind of subject-matter expertise that cannot yet be usefully formalized. Also, developments in formal technique will permit the application of new techniques to subject matters that were not contemplated when the techniques were developed. In the last forty years, optimization techniques and market analyses that were originally developed in economics have been fruitfully applied to nonmarket behavior. In the last two decades, advances in our understanding of nonmarket interactions and human motivation have begun to enrich economic models of markets and organizations. Thus, economics has been both an exporter and an importer of theoretical ideas and techniques. We think this will continue.

References

Cohn, Jonathan. 1999. "Irrational Exuberance: When Did Political Science Forget About Politics?" *The New Republic* October 25: 25–31.

Coleman, James S. 1990. *Foundations of Social Theory.* Cambridge, MA: Harvard University Press.

Frey, Bruno, and Reiner Eichenberger. 1993. "American and European Economics and Economists." *Journal of Economic Perspectives* 7(4): 185–194.

Grossbard-Shechtman, Shoshana Amyra. 1993. *On the Economics of Marriage: A Theory of Marriage, Labor, and Divorce.* Boulder, CO, Westview Press.

Hansen, W. Lee. 1991. "The Education and Training of Economics Doctorates: Major Findings of the American Economic Association's Commission on Graduate Education in Economics." *Journal of Economic Literature* 39(3): 1054–1087.

Hirschleifer, Jack. 1976. "Further Comment on Grossbard's Economic Analysis of Polygyny in Maiduguri." Unpublished manuscript, Department of Economics, U.C.L.A.

Ingham, Geoffrey. 1996. "Some Recent Changes in the Relationship Between Economics and Sociology." *Cambridge Journal of Economics* 20: 243–275.

Kasper, Hirschel et al. 1991. "The Education of Economists: From Undergraduate to Graduate Study." *Journal of Economic Literature* 39(3): 1088–1109.

Krueger, Anne O. 1991. "Report of the Committee on Graduate Education in Economics." *Journal of Economic Literature* 29(3): 1035–1053.

McCloskey, Deirdre. 1996. *The Vices of Economists.* Amsterdam: Amsterdam University Press.

Rauch, James E. Forthcoming. "Business and Social Networks in International Trade." *Journal of Economic Literature.*

White, Harrison C. 1988. "Varieties of Markets." In Barry Wellman and Steven Berkowitz, eds., *Social Structures: A Network Approach,* pp. 226–240. New York: Cambridge University Press.

About the Editors and Contributors

Rick Audas holds a PhD in economics from the University of Wales, Bangor. He is an assistant professor in the Faculty of Administration and holds a Junior Research Chair at the Canadian Research Institute for Social Policy, both at the University of New Brunswick.

Serge Blondel received his PhD in economics from the University of Paris (Panthéon-Sorbonne). He teaches economics at the National Institute of Horticulture (Angers, France), and is a research fellow at TEAM (National Center for Scientific Research and University of Paris Pantheon-Sorbonne). His research focuses on the theory of choice under risk and experimental economics.

Christopher Clague received a PhD in economics from Harvard. After serving on the staff of the Council of Economic Advisers during 1967 and 1968, he joined the University of Maryland, where he worked until 1998. He is now professor emeritus from Maryland and lecturer at San Diego State University. He has published numerous articles in the fields of international economics and economic development. In recent years he has developed an interest in the application of the New Institutional Economics to less-developed and post-Socialist societies. In this connection he served from 1990 to 1997 as Director for Research at the Center for Institutional Reform and the Informal Sector (IRIS) in the Economics Department at the University of Maryland. He coedited *The Emergence of Market Economies in Eastern Europe* (1992) and edited *Institutions and Economic Development* (1997).

Michael Gibbs earned his PhD in economics from the University of Chicago. He teaches personnel/organizational economics at the Graduate School of Business of the University of Chicago, and has also taught at the Harvard Business School, University of Southern California, and University of Michigan. His research focuses on econometric analysis of firm-level personnel records to study internal labor markets, compensation, and organizational design.

Clive W.J. Granger holds a PhD in statistics from the University of Nottingham. He is professor of economics at the University of California, San Diego, where he holds the Chancellor's Associates Chair in Economics. In 1995 he was visiting fellow at All Souls College, Oxford, and in 1996 he held the position of visiting fellow commoner at Trinity College, Cambridge. He has been a Guggenheim fellow and is a fellow of the American Academy of Arts and Sciences, of the Econometric Society, and of the International Institute of Forecasters. His interests are largely in time series analysis, forecasting, applied econometrics, and finance, and he has roughly 200 publications or submitted papers, including ten books.

Shoshana Grossbard-Shechtman obtained her PhD in economics at the University of Chicago, where she studied with Professor Gary Becker, the recipient of the 1992 Nobel Prize in economics. She is professor of economics at San Diego State University and was a fellow at the Center for Advanced Studies in the Behavioral Sciences at Stanford during 1980 and 1981. Her specialty is household economics, with a special focus on marriage and labor supply. Her articles have appeared in economics, demography, sociology, and anthropology journals. Her book, *On the Economics of Marriage: A Theory of Marriage, Labor, and Divorce*, was published by Westview Press in 1993. *Marriage and the Economy, Theory and Evidence From Advanced Industrialized Societies*, a book she is editing for Cambridge University Press, is forthcoming. She edits a new economics journal, *Review of Economics of the Household* (the first issue will be published in 2003 by Kluwer) and is on the board of the *Journal of Socio-Economics* and the *Journal of Bio-Economics*.

Dipak K. Gupta obtained his PhD in economics from the University of Pittsburg. He is the Fred J. Hansen, professor of Peace Studies at San Diego State University (SDSU), where he is professor in the School of Public Administration and Urban Studies and Co-Director of the Institute for International Security and Conflict Resolution. His primary research interests involve the causes of ethnic violence, genocide and civil wars, as well as the impact of political instability on nations' economic growth. He is the author of five books, including *Path to Collective Madness* (Praeger, 2001) and *Analyzing Public Policy: Concepts, Tools, and Techniques* (Congressional Quarterly Press, 2001). Prof. Gupta has published over fifty articles in scholarly journals, research monographs, and newspapers. He is a regular contributor to the *San Diego Union Tribune*'s Opinion section.

David M. Heer received his PhD in sociology at Harvard. He is professor of Sociology Emeritus at the University of Southern California and Senior Fellow, Center for Comparative Immigration Studies, at the University of California, San Diego. He taught at the University of Southern California from 1972 to 2000 and was director of its Population Research Laboratory from 1995 to 2000. From 1964 to 1972, he was in the Department of Population Sciences at the Harvard University School of Public Health, from 1961 to 1964 at International Population and Urban Research at the University of California, Berkeley, and from 1957 to 1961 at the Population Division of the U.S. Bureau of the Census. He is the author of nine books, the most recent of which is *Immigration in America's Future: Social Science Findings and the Policy Debate* (Boulder, CO: Westview Press, 1996).

Jack Hirshleifer holds a PhD in economics from Harvard University and is a professor at UCLA. He is a fellow of the American Academy of Arts and Sciences, a Fellow of the Econometric Society, a distinguished fellow of the American Economic Association, and serves on the board of the *Journal of Bio-Economics*. He has been a vice-president of the American Economic Association, president of the Western Economic Association, and a member of the editorial boards of the *American Economic Review* and the *Journal of Economic Behavior and Organization*. His fields of specialization have included water supply and resource economics, investment and capital theory, applied theory of the firm, uncertainty and information, political economy, bioeconomics, and the economic theory of conflict. He has published seven books (the latest, *The Dark Side of the Force*, will be released by Cambridge University Press in 2001) and more than seventy articles in economics, political science, and biology journals.

Laurence R. Iannaccone received his doctorate in economics at the University of Chicago, where he studied with Professor Gary Becker. He is professor of economics at Santa Clara University and has worked at Stanford's Hoover Institution as a national fellow and a visiting scholar. He has written numerous articles on the economics of religion, a field he helped create. He has published his work in the *Journal of Political Economy*, the *Journal of Economic Literature*, the *American Journal of Sociology*, and other leading economics and sociology journals. His current research projects include a book on the economics of religion and a related volume of readings.

Alec Levenson received his PhD in economics from Princeton University. He is a research scientist at the Center for Effective Organizations in the Marshall School of Business at the University of Southern California, and an economist at the Milken Institute. His current research focuses on personnel and the economics of human resources. Topics include the role of temporary jobs in providing employment and training opportunities for entry-level workers; companies' rationale for implementing basic education programs in the workplace; return on investment for virtual teams; and factors impacting attraction, retention, and motivation of frontline employees.

Louis Lévy-Garboua received his PhD in economics from the University of Paris. He is professor of economics at the University of Paris (Panthéon-Sorbonne), research associate at TEAM (National Center for Scientific Research), and an associate fellow at CIRANO (Montreal). He held former positions at CREDOC (Center for Research on the Conditions of Life, Paris), and the universities of Brest and Paris-Nord. His work is about the application of economic theory to the problems commonly raised by psychologists and sociologists, including decision under risk and uncertainty, social preferences, family, education, and related topics. He has published *Economique de l'Education* (in collaboration with J.C. Eicher et al.) and edited *Sociological Economics* in 1979, and has published numerous articles in scholarly journals.

Shlomo Maital received his PhD from Princeton University. He immigrated to Israel with his wife, Sharone, in 1967. He is currently Sondheimer Professor of International Economics and Finance at the Technion-Israel Institute of Technology, and Academic Director of TIM-Technion Institute of Management. During 1987 and 1988, he served as Israel's Director of the National Planning Authority, Ministry of Economics. He has been a visiting professor at the MIT Sloan School of Management each summer since 1984. He is one of two founders of SABE, the Society for the Advancement of Behavioural Economics. His primary research interests include: management of new product development and innovation, and global macroeconomics. He is co-author (with Hariolf Grupp) of *Managing New Product Development & Innovation: A Microeconomic Toolbox* (Edward Elgar, 2001), and author of *Executive Economics: Ten Essential Tools for Managers* (Free Press, 1994).

Vernon W. Ruttan received his PhD in economics from the University of Chicago. He is regents professor emeritus in the Departments of Applied Economics and Economics at the University of Minnesota. He served as a staff member of the President's Council of Economic Advisers and as president of the Agricultural Development Council (1973–1978), and has been elected to membership in the National Academy of Sciences (1990). Prof. Ruttan is the author of numerous articles in the fields of agricultural economics, resource economics, economic development, and science and technology economics and policy. His articles have been published in leading journals in economics, agricultural science, and the social sciences. He is the author (with Yujiro Hayami) of *Agricultural Development: An International Perspective* (Johns Hopkins University Press, 1985) and *Technology, Growth and Development: An Induced Innovation Perspective* (Oxford University Press, 2001).

John Treble is a labor economist who holds a PhD from Northwestern University. He has held positions at Hull and Essex, and is now professor of economics at the University of Wales, Bangor, a fellow of the Institute for Labour Research at Essex, and a Visiting Professor at Paris II. He has held visiting appointments at Indiana, Northwestern, Munich, Australian National University, Arhus, and Amsterdam. His work has appeared in many leading journals, including *Labour Economics, The Journal of Economic History, The Economic Journal, Oxford Economic Papers,* and *Econometrica.*

Index